POP OUT

Michael Moon, and Eve Kosofsky Sedgwick

A series edited by Michèle Aina Barale, Jonathan Goldberg,

POP

Q   U   E   E   R

OUT

W A R H O L

EDITED BY JENNIFER DOYLE, JONATHAN FLATLEY, & JOSÉ ESTEBAN MUÑOZ

DUKE UNIVERSITY PRESS Durham and London 1996

© 1996 Duke University Press   All rights reserved
"I'll Be Your Mirror Stage: Andy Warhol
and the Cultural Imaginary," © 1996 David E. James
Printed in the United States of America on acid-free paper ∞
Typeset in Berkeley Medium by Keystone Typesetting, Inc.
Library of Congress Cataloging-in-Publication Data
appear on the last printed page of this book.

CONTENTS

ACKNOWLEDGMENTS

This book was put together with the energy and excitement generated by a conference we organized at Duke University in January 1993 called "Re-Reading Warhol: The Politics of Pop."

Our first thanks, then, go to the people who were instrumental in making that event happen, and especially to the people who participated in and attended the conference but did not contribute to this collection of essays. For their contributions to the conference, to its generative atmosphere, we send gratitude and admiration to Mark Francis of the Andy Warhol Museum; to Jane Gaines and the Program in Film and Video at Duke University; to Iris Tillman Hill and the Center for Documentary Studies; to Fredric Jameson and Duke University's Program in Literature; and to Carol Mavor, Cindy Patton, Sohnya Sayers, Kristine Stiles, Lynne Tillman, and Ellen Willis. Thank you also to Roy Grundmann, Tina Takemoto, and Christopher True for their valuable presence. Sandy Mills, Sandy Swanson, and Tom Whiteside deserve special acknowledgment for their tireless efforts helping us coordinate all the mechanical aspects of the conference.

We are especially grateful to the organizations—and the individuals behind those organizations—who contributed financial and material support for the conference: Kathy Silbiger of the Duke University Institute of the Arts and the Henry David Epstein Endowment, Michael Mezzatesta of the Duke University Museum of Art, and Ronald Feldman Fine Art.

For her support and advice we thank Callie Angel of the Warhol Film Project at the Whitney Museum of American Art and acknowledge her much-admired and appreciated work toward making the Factory films available to the public.

We could not have managed this project without the generous contributions of Eve Kosofsky Sedgwick (who came up with the title for this book) and Michael Moon (who helped shape this project from its most nascent stage) in the areas of brainstorming, crisis management, counseling, reading, editing, patience, and friendship. Jonathan Goldberg gave us encouragement at a moment when we really needed it. We are grateful most of all for our friends—Mandy Berry, Marcus Embry, Katie Kent, Mandy Merck, Janice Radway, Brian Selsky, and Gustavus Stadler—for the comfort, intelligence, humor, meals, and community they share with us.

Special thanks to Bertha Palanzuela for her help preparing the bibliography and index.

Finally, Ken Wissoker has been a great editor, and we feel lucky to have benefited from his kindness, patience, and experience.

POP OUT

JENNIFER DOYLE
JONATHAN FLATLEY
JOSÉ ESTEBAN MUÑOZ

Introduction

> "Pop Art took the inside and put it outside, took the outside and put it inside."
> —Andy Warhol, *POPism*[1]

Andy Warhol was queer in more ways than one. To begin with, he was a fabulous queen, a fan of prurience and pornography, and a great admirer of the male body. This queerness was "known," in one way or another, by the gay audiences who enjoyed his films, the police who censored them, the gallery owners who excluded his sketches of male nudes from exhibits, the artists who were made uncomfortable by his swishiness, not to mention the drag queens, hustlers, speed freaks, fag hags, and others who populated the Factory. Considering then, on the one hand, that many people knew enough about Warhol's sexuality to let it guide their response to and evaluation of him and his art and, on the other, that Warhol has become a central figure in work on postmodernism, the avant-garde, mass culture, film studies, high art/low art, and American art history,[2] we might expect that there *already* would be a rich body of criticism exploring, appreciating, celebrating, or at least mentioning the role of Warhol's queerness in the production and reception of his films and art.

However, with few exceptions,[3] most considerations of Warhol have "degayed" him.[4] Warhol's critics have usually aggressively elided issues around sexuality or relegated his queerness to the realm of the "biographical" or "private" to usher in his *oeuvre* to the world of high art. Or when they have alluded to Warhol's sexuality, usually without mentioning that he was *gay* (more often "asexual" or "voyeuristic"), it has only been in order to moralize about the "degraded" quality of Warhol's art, his career, and his friends. Despite the fact that many people "knew" that Warhol was gay, hardly anyone, at least in the world of criticism and theory, will speak of it. As Mandy Merck notes, "Out as Warhol may have been, gay as *My Hustler, Lonesome Cowboys, Blow Job* may seem, his assumption to the postmodern pantheon has been a surprisingly straight ascent, if only in its stern detachment from any form of commentary that could be construed as remotely sexy."[5]

In diverse fashion, the essays collected here call out and combat the degaying of Warhol. While they vary in methodological approach and disciplinary context, they all share the sense that to ignore Warhol's queerness is to miss what is most valuable, interesting, sexy, and political about his work. Disturbing the usually desexualized spaces of the academy, they bring their enthusiasm regarding Warhol's queerness to and from a wide range of disciplinary and critical contexts: art history, critical race theory, feminist theory, psychoanalysis, cinema studies, popular culture and television studies, social theory, literary theory, and work on postmodernism. Before discussing the essays specifically, we wish to characterize the gestures that have enacted the conspicuous critical silence around Warhol's sexuality by offering a couple of examples. It is a silence that, much more than a simple absence, has played an active role in creating the "commonsense" attitudes toward Warhol and his career which *Pop Out* seeks to challenge.

The academic disciplines, defining as they do what counts as scholarly work, have encouraged the process by which concerns around sexuality are perpetually deferred to some *other* body of knowledge, some *other* line of inquiry. As Foucault put it, "A proposition must fulfil some onerous and complex conditions before it can be admitted within a discipline,"[6] conditions that have played no small role in foreclosing the possibility of making any propositions about Warhol's queerness in relation to his rich body of cultural production. Often, some of Warhol's audiences, themes, figures, and indeed many of the works of art themselves are simply removed from the field of critical consideration.

Take, for example, one of the introductory essays to the MOMA Warhol catalogue, "Do It Yourself: Notes on Warhol's Techniques," by Marco Livingstone.[7] Livingstone writes about the shift in technique that later led to Warhol's signature use of the silkscreening process: "Although Warhol continued through the fifties to produce continuous line drawings with ball-point pen, for example in *his essentially private drawings of boys,* it was the blotted line technique that offered him the greatest scope for *his more public art* (64; emphases ours). Significant and typical, it is in passing that Livingstone describes and dismisses Warhol's sexy, homoerotic drawings of boys as "essentially private," cordoning off these drawings from Warhol's "more public art." Here, the public/private distinction works to underwrite Livingstone's formal distinction between continuous line drawings and blotted line technique. In describing them only as "drawings of boys," Livingstone conveniently relegates to the closet the eroticism of these drawings and their relation to Warhol's later work (such as the *Torso* series, the *Oxidation* paintings, or *Sex Parts*). The irony (and the insidiousness) of this is that it leaves the reader with the impression that Warhol was *himself* in the closet, when in fact these were among the *first* of his works of art that Warhol wished to have publicly exhibited. The drawings, which one of his biographers describes as "saying 'Gay is beautiful' a good dozen years or more before such a statement was acceptable,"[8] were, in fact, exhibited in 1956 at the Bodley Gallery. The next year, Warhol asked his friend Philip Pearlstein to submit some of them to the more exclusive Tanager Gallery. As Pearlstein remembers, "He submitted a group of boys kissing boys which the members of the gallery hated and refused to show."[9] Forgotten in Livingstone's account is not only Warhol's desire for visibility and publicity but also the homophobia with which he was confronted.

Our second example represents a more hostile variety of Warhol criticism. Conservative critic Robert Hughes's ability to allude to Warhol's sexuality without naming it in his conflicted attacks on the artist provides a stark example of the homophobic deployment of the open secret.[10] In the concluding remarks to his obituary of the artist in *Time* magazine, he makes the following comparison: "In a sense Warhol was to the art world what his buddy of the discos, Roy Cohn, was to law: Just as Cohn degraded the image of the legal profession while leaving no doubt about his own forensic brilliance, so Warhol released toxins of careerism, facetiousness and celebrity worship into the stream of American culture."[11] By comparing Warhol to Cohn, "his buddy of the discos," Hughes draws on the then current coverage surrounding the death of Roy Cohn and the rhetorics that were in circulation around his death—rhetoric around AIDS, the closet, and the closeted gay man who is homophobic—all of which facilitate Hughes's moralizing judgments of Warhol, without his having actually to mention Warhol's or Cohn's sexuality. By accessing the already existing open secret about Roy Cohn and his closetedness, Hughes places his commentary on Warhol's sexuality at a double remove, even as he elides the enormous differences between Warhol and Cohn.[12] The code words—"toxins," "careerism," "facetiousness," "celebrity worship"—that give Hughes the safe, unavowed subject position from which he can judge Warhol are the same ones that keep Warhol in the closet *and* punish him for having a public career shaped by his fagginess, his anti-homophobia, his campy relation toward the mass media, and his adoration of (certain) celebrities.

As if this were not bad enough already, the reference to Cohn also invokes the specter of the evil homosexual whose death from AIDS was an act of divine retribution. In its all too familiar rhetoric of toxicity and contamination, it "actively encourage(s) the forward slippage from corruption theories of homosexuality to contagion theories of AIDS."[13] In suggesting that Warhol's death constitutes no loss at all, Hughes's words resonate strongly with the public rhetoric on AIDS which "calmly and consistently entertains the possible prospect of the death of all western European and American gay men from AIDS . . . without the slightest flicker of concern, regret or grief."[14] In short, Hughes provides a textbook case of the complicated but willfull silences and poisonous rhetorics that provide considerable obstacles for anyone wishing to manage, let alone celebrate, a queer self and life.[15]

In drawing attention to the critical de-gaying of Warhol, we do not want, however, to underestimate the ways in which de-gaying and strategic silences may have been as useful to Warhol as a survival strategy in negotiating a homophobic culture as they were to critics such as Robert Hughes in enforcing one.[16] Warhol's relatively "straight assumption" to the art world pantheon, for example, also located him in a position of relative authority from which he could sponsor and nourish queer communities, projects, and energies. Thus, even given the mutually enabling relationships between Warhol and various gay communities and Warhol's devotion to making queer sex visible, public, and sexy, Warhol was never entirely "out" nor "in" the closet. In turns, he was both and neither, depending on context, exigency, and survival. In part, Warhol cannot be described as an "out" "gay" man because so much of how he managed his identity and his cultural contexts is rooted in the fifties, before Stonewall and before identity politics. But it was also one of Warhol's standard gestures in negotiating normative culture to take an apparent opposition and work both sides of it. He could be in turns shy and shameless, maximally public and defensively private, introverted and outrageously exhibitionist, childlike and sophisticated. The essays in *Pop Out* often explore how such gestures had the effect of transfiguring, exploding, or reworking the kinds of categories by which he might be policed or judged: inside/outside, gay/straight, work/sex, real/artifice, high art/low art, and many others.

Warhol was not always successful in combating or circumventing a homophobic culture, as his difficulty in addressing the AIDS crisis in his life and his work depressingly illustrates. Given Warhol's knack for publicity, his eye for disaster, his thematic preoccupation with mourning, and his skill at playing off of the logic of the mass media, one might have hoped that he would develop a canny or clever response to the "spectacle of AIDS." But aside from a singular, and perhaps incomplete, posthumous painting (*AIDS/Jeep/Bicycle*, discussed in Jonathan Flatley's essay), his work registers only a nonresponse to the pandemic. A review of Warhol's diaries from the early and mid-eighties shows a sad, ambivalent, and fearful relation to AIDS and persons with AIDS. We read about funerals attended and avoided, participation in AIDS benefits, and sadness about the absences of friends and lovers, and we see his fear of illness and ill people. Most infamous, Warhol snubbed Robert Mapplethorpe at a party apparently *because* he was sick. ("Bruno wanted to sit with Robert Mapplethorpe but I didn't want to. He's sick. I sat at another place.")[17] His phobia seems to have been as much about illness per se as about AIDS, a phobia deeply rooted, as Watney notes in his essay, in Warhol's class background and personal history. The following passage from the diary entry for August 30, 1986, adds to our understanding of his complicated and shame-filled response to the epidemic: "And after the play Martin met me backstage and there was a big chocolate leg there from Kron and everybody was eating it, and Martin was too. And it's so sad, he has sores all over his face, but it was kind of great to see Madonna eating the leg, too, and not caring that she might catch something. Martin would bite and then Madonna would bite. I like Martin, he's sweet." Although Warhol admires Madonna's unphobic reaction to Martin's illness, we also get a sense of his own anxiety around illness. The lack of a coherent response to AIDS on Warhol's part is a response that must be understood in its context, not overlooked or annulled. It testifies to the difficulties of assimilating the pandemic and its scope, especially at this moment in the eighties. It reminds us of the difficulty and necessity of developing counterdiscourses, practices, and publics—precisely what Warhol did not do in this case—where the official and unofficial discourses of the government and the mass media alike were hostile and homophobic.

The essays in *Pop Out* strive to situate Warhol in his specific contexts and to gesture toward a history of the different queer communities in which he participated. In reframing his work, these essays offer new perspectives on the political impulses in and around Pop's aesthetic strategies and on how Pop has been enabling to other queer projects and communities.

WARHOL'S QUEER CONTEXTS
■

In response to the de-gaying of Warhol that places whatever is queer outside the realm of critical consideration, *Pop Out* seeks to remember the homo-erotic subjects, the gay audiences, and the queer contexts that were crucial to the production and reception of Pop. This insistence on context displays not so much the desire to lay claim to a "gay aesthetic" in Warhol's name[18] or to define or explain what is inherently "gay" in Warhol's aesthetic practices. Rather, *Pop Out* aims to help understand the multiple relations between Warhol and the worlds that he transfigured and in which he found a home, to point toward the recovery of the histories of homophobia and resistances to it in the queer communities of the 1950s and 1960s.

Along these lines, Simon Watney starts off his contribution to this volume by recalling that "the first time I got busted was together with some two hundred people watching *Lonesome Cowboys* in its first week of screening in London in 1969" (p. 20). In "Cockteaser," Thomas Waugh reminds us just how important gay audiences and the conventions of gay male porn were as contexts for Warhol's films. Through his research in the gay press (to date a rarely used source for understanding Warhol's work), Waugh maps the reception of Warhol's films by a gay audience, while also demonstrating the importance of Warhol's films to the articulation of that audience as a community: "The late sixties . . . saw gay audiences beginning to be publicly constituted in theatrical venues for the first time . . . and expressing community through then experimental exhibition ideas like midnight showings" (pp. 68–69). Using these contexts as starting points for his inquiry, Waugh argues that many of Warhol's favorite filmic scenes—"endless scenes of grooming and bathing for example—Paul America drying every finger in *My Hustler,* Joe Spencer taking forever in the shower in *Bike Boy,* Eric Emerson helping Joe Dallesandro put meat on his buns or take the dandruff off his nipple in *Cowboys*" (p. 62) and so on—can be usefully understood in the context of the conventions of gay porn in the 1960s and the censorship laws to which they were forced to respond.

The refreshing ease with which Waugh accesses the sexiness of Warhol's films is a relief to the contortions we see in critical work on Warhol which is not engaged with the queer contexts of Pop and which can only digest Pop's "prurience" on an abstract level, if at all. In her essay, Mandy Merck describes how theories of postmodernism have set up Pop as a refusal of "any putative connection between its ostensible content and a social or symbolic context" (p. 228). The idea that Pop's emphasis on surface, its obsession with shoes and celebrity, and its challenge to processes of reading and interpretation might be crucially linked to a social or symbolic context, and a queer one at that, has been left untouched by most theories of postmodernism which, nonetheless, are endlessly fascinated by these elements of Warhol's work. Seeking to recover Pop's queer context and content, Merck recontextualizes Warhol's *Diamond Dust Shoes* in terms of his respect for the work it takes to be a drag queen, the labor involved in "being sexed," in learning to walk in high-heeled shoes or to produce a convincingly gendered "surface."

Jennifer Doyle is similarly interested in the ways that criticism has treated "sex" in Warhol's work. She examines the way a mobile "rhetoric of prostitution," which moralizes about *any* public display of a sexuality other than straight male ones, circulates in Warhol criticism to dismiss his art as only "business," his career as degraded, and his very subjectivity as fundamentally corrupted. In this tradition, a range of writers—contributing to everything from *Time* to the art journal *October*—use this rhetoric to gain a critical distance on Warhol and the highly volatile conjunctions of sex, art, and work to be found in his art. She writes, "The use of a rhetoric of prostitution and its stigma of outlaw sex to name the artistic practices of a famous (and famously) gay man more often than not functions to signal (but only through inference) Warhol's homosexuality while also displacing the discussion of sexuality in Warhol's work onto a feminized, particularly public and abjected figure" (p. 192). While prostitution does a lot of work for these critics—enabling them on one hand to announce that Warhol's work is all about sex and on the other to complain that it is about nothing at all—their work rarely if ever engages either the literal or metaphoric presence of hustling and prostitution in Warhol's *oeuvre*.

Another obstacle to serious consideration of the place of sex in Pop has been the paucity of attempts to link Pop and feminism as anything other than mortal enemies. The incessantly replayed scene of that battle is of course Valerie Solanas's attack on Warhol, which nearly ended his life. Marcie Frank considers the misappropriation of Valerie Solanas and her SCUM manifesto within cultural studies and feminist theory. In particular, Frank exposes feminist cultural studies pioneer Meaghan Morris's unacknowledged use of the SCUM manifesto to juice up the rhetoric of her arguments about the potential immediacy of theory to practice. Frank performs a reading and recovery of that remarkable, often-cited but infrequently engaged manifesto, which calls attention to the ways that Solanas explored and exploited gender terms. In considering Solanas's rhetoric, Frank concludes that "the repetition of the terms 'male' and 'female' in all possible combinations reinscribes the binary at the same time as it spins out endless possible recombinations that render almost incomprehensible any foundation for gender identity at all" (p. 216). The representation of Pop as antifeminist has by and large required the appropriation of Solanas's attack on Warhol as the translation of feminist theory into feminist practice. But, as Frank demonstrates, Solanas's SCUM manifesto articulated a pre–Judith Butler gender trouble that was powerfully in sync with the Warholian project in the ways that it scrambled all available gender codes. Frank's essay thus lets the reader not only think of Solanas and Pop as antagonists but also think of Solanas as part of Pop's context and of Pop and Warhol as a context for the manifesto.

By insisting on Pop's queer contexts and by exploring its relationship to, among other things, the "sexual revolution," it is worth emphasizing that the essays in this book are drawing attention to something that did not go unnoticed by Warhol's contemporaries: Take Philip Leider's February 1965 *Artforum* review of the Pop exhibit "Arena of Love": "If, on the one hand, all those lips, nipple-pinchings, harems and nudies are just a kick, the dead-pan comical subject matter of Pop, they hint, on the other hand at a sexuality that is more open, illicit, freer than, and consequently threatening to, bourgeois sexuality" (p. 27). Given the title of the exhibit, we can safely deduce that if Pop's relation to the sexual revolution was self-evident to those attending this exhibit, it was because Pop's relation to the sexual revolution was, on many levels, self-pronounced. Leider luxuriates in the obscenity and flirtatiousness of the works and gleefully identifies Warhol's filmic contributions as sustained attacks on the "heterosexual dollar" (a phrase he borrows from Allen Ginsberg's *Howl*). By reading Warhol's work as queer and antihomophobic and linking it to the projects of Ginsberg's Beat poetry, Warhol is placed in relation to a range of contexts that are too rarely explored.

The above-mentioned essays are not the only ones committed to the recovery of Pop's contexts. Warhol's homoerotic drawings, paintings, photographs, and films (Michael Moon and Jonathan Flatley), his campiness (Watney and Sasha Torres), his persistent battle with homophobia in the art world and elsewhere (Eve Kosofsky Sedgwick, José Esteban Muñoz, Flatley, and Watney) are the vantage points from which other contributors make arguments about Pop aesthetics, Pop's appropriations, how Warhol reflected on and influenced other contexts, and how other contexts were made queer by him.

POP AESTHETICS/POP IDENTITIES
■

If Monique Wittig's energetic critique of "the straight mind"[19] has been taken up to reveal the structuring effects of "heteronormativity"[20] in a number of social institutions and theoretical traditions, it has also suggested a more utopian question: What would or does a culture that is *not* imagined by the straight mind look like? Some of the essays in *Pop Out* understand the political and other energies behind Warhol's Pop aesthetic and his career as springing in part from Warhol's "practical social reflection"[21] on a whole range of social institutions and discourses—such as those around childhood, gender and sexuality, age, whiteness, the popular media, fame and publicity, authorship, and work. In doing this, many of the essays here share with Sedgwick the sense that "the subtitle of any truly queer (perhaps as opposed to gay?) politics will be the same as the one that Erving Goffman gave to his book *Stigma: Notes on the Management of Spoiled Identity*. But more than its management: its experimental, creative, performative force."[22]

Merck, for example, in underscoring the importance of drag as context and theme for Warhol, suggests the relevance of Warhol's Pop aesthetic to theories of gender. She argues that Warhol's aesthetics of simulation parallels Judith Butler's succinct and memorable formulation of the representational logic of sexuality: "Gay to straight is not as copy to original, but rather as copy is to copy." Similarly, in Warhol's statements such as "Having sex is hard work," "Being sexed is hard work," and "Love and sex are a business," Doyle sees condensed Warhol's career-long struggle to take advantage of incoherencies or contradictions in and around the definition of work in order to challenge limiting conceptions of authorship, art, and sex.

Or, take the way that Brian Selsky explores how the concept of genius has long served as a cover for identities—often Jewish or queer or both— that were otherwise unassimilable. Through a discussion of examples from George Eliot, Sigmund Freud, Gertrude Stein, and Warhol, Selsky identifies the attraction of the genius fantasy: if one can garner the mantle of genius, everything from one's hairstyle to one's sentence structure to one's object choices can be safely recuperated, if not celebrated. It is a rhetoric that may allow an artist or author to legitimize work that would otherwise be uncategorizable, perverse, too simple or too complex. He notes how faith in someone's genius is equally powerful for us as fans, critics, and readers because of the kinds of attention, idolization, and identification that it can enable.

Watney attends to the ways in which Warhol's aesthetic practices return to the strategies he developed for surviving his childhood, a childhood in which he faced a problem met by all queer kids: "How do you explain yourself to yourself, let alone to others, when you have absolutely no legitimate or legitimating model for your own most intensely personal feelings about other people and the world? You turn to those elements within what is culturally on offer and make them speak your queer feelings, as best you can" (p. 24). Thus Watney sees the roots of Warhol's Pop Art interest in mass media images such as celebrities, trademarks, and advertisements in Warhol's childhood experience forging a self from his investments in the mass culture available to him. Watney's is one of many essays in this volume (including those of Moon, Sedgwick, Flatley, and Muñoz) which explore or at least touch on the potentially puissant energies that charge reimaginings and articulations of a queer childhood.

In his essay, Moon turns to accounts of Warhol's childhood (not least Warhol's own) to "better understand the intersecting histories of gay or protogay identity and mass culture in the early to middle decades of this century" (p. 81). In unpacking these stories, he provides the basis for understanding Warhol's early Pop paintings of comic book characters (Dick Tracy, Popeye,

Superman, Nancy) as densely meaningful screen memories for some of the ways that Warhol creatively managed to survive his childhood through a series of (erotic) investments in an otherwise seemingly straight mass culture. His readings of these paintings thus recasts them as "representing not a total rupture with his flagrantly homoerotic art of the fifties but rather a continuation by other means of his fey but ferocious and, in some ways, ultimately successful war against the exclusion of swishiness and fagginess from the repertory of possible gestures that could be made and recognized in visual art" (p. 79). Moon draws out the promiscuous, even lubricious, energies within and around Warhol's paintings. In doing that, he, by example, refutes a criticism that would forget the importance of Warhol's homoerotic art in shaping his career, inviting us to make the most of its erotic and affective force.

Eve Sedgwick explores the ways that Warhol's shyness and shame embodied his exploration of what it might mean to produce a self as a "(white) queer in a queer-hating world" and a "white (queer) in a white-supremacist one" (p. 135). Drawing on the work of an important theorist of affect, Silvan Tomkins,[23] Sedgwick contends that the affect of shame, in Warhol and elsewhere, can be a "nexus of production . . . of meaning, of personal presence, of politics, of performative and critical efficacy" (p. 135). In this understanding, shame is self-constituting not as repression or prohibition might be but as a painful moment of interruption, when "the circuit of mirroring expressions between the child's face and the caregiver's recognized face . . . is broken. . . . When, for one of many reasons, it fails to be recognizable to, or recognizing of, the infant who has been, so to speak, 'giving face' based on a faith in the continuity of this circuit."[24] Through an examination of some of Warhol's long arias on his skin and its whiteness, Sedgwick demonstrates how Warhol cleaves to the scene of shame as a near inexhaustible source of transformational energy.

Along similar lines, Jonathan Flatley is interested in understanding the intense affective and political energies in and around Warhol's exploration of the "poetics of publicity." Flatley argues that many of Warhol's painterly interests and themes—from portraiture to pornography, celebrity, commodity fetishism, and mourning—can best be understood in terms of "prosopopoeia," the trope of giving or creating (poiea) a face or a person (prosopopon). As the medium of face intelligibility and recognition, prosopopoeia is the trope of fame and shame alike. And as the mechanism Warhol used to work with and around the logic of the mass public sphere from which he, as a swishy gay man, felt excluded, it is key to understanding how "Pop gave *him* a public" (p. 102). He is thus thinking about Warhol's Pop "way of seeing" as an inventive poetics that exposes the logic and attraction of publicity. And while these poetic strategies may have failed Warhol in the face of AIDS, his "insights into the logic of our public sphere" (p. 122) and Pop's "formal devices, the emphasis on faces, fame, recognizability, repetition, and reappropriation" (p. 123) have themselves been appropriated by AIDS activists such as ACT UP and Gran Fury as they "[take] the world of public images as their palette, [reappropriate] already recognizable images to mock or challenge them, and shamelessly [put] themselves in the public eye" (p. 123).

POP APPROPRIATED/POP'S CIRCULATION
■

A group of essays address our culture's persistent fascination with Pop, proposing, in David James's words, to "work outward" from Warhol, to consider his "existence as [a] myth and . . . the forms he has taken in the cultural imaginary" (p. 35). These essays are concerned with the theorization and recovery of the queer energies around, within, and masked by the appropriation and circulation of Pop both as a signifier and as an aesthetic strategy and with examining how Pop aesthetics have been used for the negotiating of queer selves, scenes, and relationships.

In James's estimate, Warhol's presence in the cultural imaginary is always a "projection of fantasy and desire . . . unusual, indeed remarkable, for its extensiveness, for its occurrence on all cultural levels and for the variety of Warhols it projects" (p. 32). His essay follows his earlier writing on Warhol, which, while investigating how he engaged advertisement and production in his work, insisted on the necessity of foregrounding our investments in Warhol as his fans and as his critics. The focus here is a close reading of two elegies, Lou Reed and John Cale's *Songs for 'Drella* and Jonas Mekas's *Scenes from the Life of Andy Warhol*. He explores how they incorporate their own investments in Warhol into their representations of him and how, as memorials, they, in a sense, pay their respects to Warhol by leaving open the mirroring circuits of memory, elegy, and fan culture.

In her essay on the *Batman* TV series, Sasha Torres argues that discussions of camp in the sixties and in more recent TV theory have been unable to account for the queer energies surrounding and animating both camp and Pop. Challenging the argument that camp provided an "elitist solution" to Pop's challenge to "the traditional panoply of tastemaking powers" (p. 242), Torres asserts that "Pop and camp bear multiple relations to each other in the public discourse of the period . . . any account of camp's 'management' of Pop is insufficient to describe the richness and multiplicity of these relations" (p. 244). In other words, there is a lot more going on in camp than a play on elitism and taste. Even as it may have helped de-gay *Batman* and Pop, camp also provided cover for queer identifications. The ways in which the *Batman* series sustained queer content and yet succeeded within a homophobic public sphere, in part enabled by the success of Pop and the emergence of camp as a category of taste, both testify to the rich queerness of Pop's circulation and recall Warhol's own tactics for surviving and succeeding.

Ironically, Warhol's influence and image continue to circulate in Hollywood cinema, a place Warhol himself never made it, though he tried. For example, characters in film and television are regularly brought to ruin at those wild Factory parties (think of *Midnight Cowboy*). Oliver Stone's 1991 filmic biography *The Doors* used Warhol to metonymically signify Jim Morrison's (played by Val Kilmer) degradation. Significantly, it is at the Factory that Morrison has his only encounter with homoerotic desire; he and a queer admirer exchange cruisy glances. As the other band members exit, they tug on Morrison's sleeve, suggesting he leave with them because "these people are vampires." Morrison stays, however, to meet Andy. Crispin Glover's Warhol is only on the screen for a few moments, but that scene is sufficiently hyperbolic to define the macho, drug-induced spirituality of the Doors in contrast to the perverse and sinister Factory.

Society portraits evocative of Warhol's style are ubiquitous in film and television as the immediately recognizable trophies of vanity, fame, social climbing, and decadence. They establish the narcissism and social position of, for example, Kelly in *Beverly Hills 90210* and Whitley in *A Different World*. In the film *Beaches*, they are prominently displayed over the mantle of CiCi's (played by Bette Midler) fireplace as a somewhat campy announcement of her "arrival" in showbiz. In these instances, the society portrait undermines the character it represents by suggesting that she, too, is all surface and no substance. A more densely charged and hostile appearance of Warhol's work occurs in the display of a poster for a Los Angeles exhibit of the *Torso* series in the climax of the film *American Gigolo*. The following description, taken from a positive review of the series, celebrates the series as astonishingly sexy: "It is not only in the pose (a [man's] ass, sphincter muscles very tight, supported by muscular legs straddling an awkward distance) but in the relation of one panel to the next and through manipulation of color and paint texture that there emerges a visual energy potent enough to mimic the rhythms of orgasm."[25] What might look like a very sexy work of art to some audiences hangs in *American Gigolo,* however, as a marker of toxicity, betrayal, and abjection. The owner of the posters is Leon, a black gay pimp who has framed the film's hero (Richard Gere's Julian Kay) for murder. Against the lush yet seedy background of Leon's apartment, in which hangs a row of these images, Julian Kay, a "straight," white, "class-act" gigolo pieces together the blackmail, murder, and hustling that constitute Leon's betrayal. As the markers of Leon's sensibility, the posters facilitate the condensation of sinister greed, perversion, and betrayal onto the gay and black body of Leon, who, in the ensuing struggle, falls off a balcony and dies. The Warhol images help to set in motion the representational logic of the scene, which in dramatizing the abjection of Leon does racist and homophobic work at the same time.

José Muñoz suggests that similar tactics might be used to resist both homophobia and white supremacy. In an essay on the power of cross-identifications between Warhol and Jean-Michel Basquiat, artists who do no match along the lines of race, sexuality, class, or generation. Muñoz describes the similar lines of disidentification which exist within the survival strategies of queer kids and racial minorities. Disidentification, in Muñoz's reading, is the process not only of cracking open the code of normative texts but also of using this code as the raw material for representing a disempowered politics or positionality that has been rendered unthinkable by dominant culture. Muñoz makes the case that Warhol's Pop practice disidentifies from mainstream (straight) normative culture and that Basquiat in turn disidentifies with the queer artist and the Pop Art project, in a way appropriating the very process of disidentification. Specifically, he focuses on how Basquiat reappropriates images from the mass media—comic book heroes, sports figures, and trademarks—to refigure and explode dominant culture's reductive ways of representing the minority subject.

Although the tragically short career of Jean-Michel Basquiat may provide one of the richest examples of Warhol's queer tutelage, a number of places in contemporary culture show us what Watney describes as the "metonymous shade of Andy Warhol."[26] Warhol helped increase the repertory of moves admissible in the art world to include the recycling and remaking of mass culture images, swishiness and homoeroticism, the interrogation of the distinctions made between high art and popular culture, and the use of the public sphere as a medium—gestures that are crucial to a wide range of cultural productions.

We can see the shades of Warhol, for example, in U.S. Latino visual artist Felix Gonzales-Torres's interests in mourning, commodities, publicity, and sexuality. His *Untitled* (1991) addresses the work of mourning by putting a very private and intimate image—the photo of a bed with empty pillows— onto the most public, even commercial, of venues, a billboard. This reversal of spaces can also be seen in his installation piece *Untitled* (Go-Go Boy on a Platform), in which a queer Latino dances and disrobes on the art house pedestal of a SoHo gallery. We might also turn to a filmmaker such as Gus Van Sant, perhaps the most famous gay North American filmmaker since Warhol, and a celebrity such as Keanu Reeves, whose fame and large queer following have only grown despite the accusations of "bad acting" leveled against him. Warhol's theory of acting works as a rebuttal to various misinformed critics of Reeves's work, helping us see a bit of Warhol in Reeves's stilted and casual delivery as well as his charmingly spastic body movements. Says Warhol, "I can only understand really amateur performers or really bad performers, because whatever they do never really comes off, so therefore it can't be phony."[27] The idea is that the performance that avows its performanceness acknowledges the difficulty of fitting into roles, finding identities, and managing a self, especially a self vulnerable to the effects of stigma.[28] This is a gesture that, along with Reeves's superstaresque good looks, make him unsurprisingly attractive to queer audiences.

Other examples of Warhol's legacy could include such figures as Barbara Kruger, whose career (begun in advertisement) has strong parallels with Warhol's own and whose sardonic work is as engaged with consumer culture as Warhol's ever was; Keith Haring, whose public-minded graffiti art is both politically engaged and interested in representing queer acts and desires; and Gran Fury, whose cultural activism for ACT UP intervenes in the public sphere by taking as its palette already recognizable public images such as dollar bills, the faces of public figures, and trademarks.[29]

Part of the unique appropriability of Pop—for the artist, activist, actor, and fan alike—has to do with the way that Warhol persistently confused the category of authorship. Warhol's legacy is not one of "influence" in the sense of a progenitor or father figure to whom homage must be paid; remarkably little "anxiety of influence" is to be seen in the shades of Warhol in contemporary culture. As David James has suggested, Warhol is less an author so much as a producer, an enabler, a stage setter.[30] Warhol was always (and famously) excited by the thought of mixing up his authorship with other voices and ideas from "outside," by the hope that audiences would be aroused by his films and paintings, that others would appropriate his gestures. It is our hope that *Pop Out* recovers and helps make accessible Warhol's incredible skill for doing something so basic and fundamental as taking interest in the world by producing sites of identification where there seemed to be none, by turning the serious and straight into camp, by finding queer sexiness in a queer-hating world. In promoting mottoes like "If everybody's not a beauty, then nobody is," Warhol encouraged us all to take interest, find glamour, and be aroused when and where we could, since, in his words, "the Pop idea was, after all, that anybody could do anything."

NOTES

■

1   Andy Warhol and Pat Hackett, *POPism: The Warhol Sixties* (New York: Harcourt Brace Jovanovich, 1980), p. 3.

2   There are too many examples to list them all here. We refer you to the exhaustive bibliography of the MOMA catalogue *Andy Warhol: A Retrospective,* ed. Kynaston McShine, with essays by Kynaston McShine, Robert Rosenblum, Benjamin H. D. Buchloh, and Marco Livingstone (New York: Museum of Modern Art, 1989). A few books that make use of Warhol as a prominent example in a broad theoretical argument include Peter Burger, *Theory of the Avant-Garde* (Minneapolis: University of Minnesota Press, 1984); Jean Baudrillard, *Simulations* (New York: Semiotext(e), 1983); Fredric Jameson, *Postmodernism, Or, The Cultural Logic of Late Capitalism* (Durham, N.C.: Duke University Press, 1991); W. F. Haug, *Critique of Commodity Aesthetics,* trans. Robert Bock (Minneapolis: University of Minnesota Press, 1986); and Andreas Huyssen, *After the Great Divide: Modernism, Mass Culture, Postmodernism* (Bloomington: Indiana University Press, 1986). See also *The Work of Andy Warhol,* ed. Gary Garrels (Seattle: Bay Press, 1989).

3   In film criticism, one finds a few considerations of the place of sexuality in Warhol. See, for example, Stephen Koch, *Stargazer* (New York: Praeger Publishers, 1973); Parker Tyler's collected essays in *Screening the Sexes* (New York: Grove, 1969); Richard Dyer, *Now You See It* (London: Routledge, 1990); and the chapter on Warhol's films in Steven Shaviro, *The Cinematic Body* (Minneapolis: University of Minnesota Press, 1993). See also Simon Watney, "The Warhol Effect," in *The Work of Andy Warhol,* ed. Gary Garrels (Seattle: Bay Press,

1989); Michael Moon, "Outlaw Sex and the 'Search for America': Representing Male Prostitution and Perverse Desire in Sixties Film (*My Hustler* and *Midnight Cowboy*)," *Quarterly Review of Film and Video* 15, no. 1 (1993): 27–40; and David James, "Andy Warhol: The Producer as Author," in his *Allegories of Cinema* (Princeton: Princeton University Press, 1989).

4   We owe this formulation to Simon Watney. During the course of the conference, "Rereading Warhol: The Politics of Pop," where versions of these essays were presented, Watney made the suggestion that what many of the essays shared was a concern with the "degaying" of Warhol. In making this observation, Watney was drawing on Cindy Patton's use of the term to discuss the discourse around AIDS in *Inventing AIDS* (New York: Routledge, 1990). Patton writes: "People who were not gay recognized the importance of making people aware that there was risk through behaviors engaged in by people who did not identify as gay. The gay community helped degay AIDS in order to stem the tide of increased discrimination and violence resulting from the perception that all gay people (including lesbians) had AIDS. AIDS organizations also helped degay AIDS by asserting that their group served anyone with AIDS and were not 'gay' political or social organizations" (117–118). See also note 18 below.

5   Merck, "Figuring Out Andy Warhol," below, p. 225.

6   Michel Foucault, "The Discourse on Language," in *The Archaeology of Knowledge,* trans. A. M. Sheridan Smith (New York: Pantheon, 1972), p. 224.

7   Marco Livingstone, "Do It Yourself: Notes on Warhol's Techniques," in *Andy Warhol,* ed. McShine. Page references hereafter will be given in text.

8   Fredrick Lawrence Guiles, *Loner at the Ball* (London: Black Swan, 1990), p. 123.

9   Quoted by David Bourdon, *Warhol* (New York: Harry N. Abrams, 1989), p. 51.

10 The term "open secret" has become a productive analytic tool in recent years in part because of the work of D. A. Miller. In Miller's formulation, the social function of secrecy is not "to conceal knowledge, so much as to conceal the knowledge of the knowledge." *The Novel and the Police* (Berkeley: University of California Press, 1988), p. 206. In this vein: "Secrecy would then be the subjective practice in which the oppositions of private/public, inside/outside, subject/object are established, and the sanctity of their first term kept inviolate. And the phenomenon of the 'open secret' does not, as one might think, bring about the collapse of these binarisms and their ideological effects, but rather attests to their fantasmatic recovery" (207). Because the speech acts that make up coming out are dependent for their effort on their audience, contexts, and publics, they are both strangely specific and unpredictable: one can never tell in advance whether the response to gay self-disclosure will be silent nonrecognition, homophobic exclusion, or transformational revelation.

11 Robert Hughes, "A Caterer of Repetition and Glut: Andy Warhol, 1928–1987," *Time,* March 9, 1987, p. 90.

12 See Eve Kosofsky Sedgwick's discussion of the "poisonous coverage of the recent death of the poisonous Roy Cohn" in *Epistemology of the Closet* (Berkeley: University of California Press, 1990), pp. 242–244.

13 Simon Watney, "The Spectacle of AIDS," in *AIDS: Cultural Analysis, Cultural Activism,* ed. Douglas Crimp (Cambridge: MIT Press, 1988), p. 77.

14   Ibid., p. 85.

15   Robert Hughes's most well-known writing on Warhol, "The Rise of Andy Warhol" (*New York Review of Books,* February 18, 1982), has had a pervasive influence on commonsense views of Warhol. This influence was underscored for us when, as we were writing this introduction, a columnist for a local weekly, Hal Crowther, felt compelled to paraphrase Hughes's argument in order to moralize about the opening of the Warhol museum in Pittsburgh.

16   A similar point has been made by Cindy Patton regarding the efforts in the mid-1980s to disassociate homosexuality from AIDS, efforts that had both homophobic and antihomophobic motivations and effects. De-gaying here takes the form of a strong impulse to universalize AIDS: to separate out the epidemic from the minoritizing discourse of homosexuality so that it could be recognized as a "public health" issue and not exclusively a "gay" issue, so that transmission of the virus could be understood as a matter of "acts" and not "identities" (only good epidemiological common sense) and because this was the only way that research, prevention, and treatment programs could be recognized by the government as worthy of funding. In addition, there was motivation to de-gay AIDS to disable the homophobic narrative that links together and confuses the rhetoric of disease and contagion around AIDS with the pathologization of homosexuality. Unfortunately, public health concerns around AIDS were put in terms of the "general public" or "general population," to the *exclusion* of gay men. Most infamous, a Reagan aide explained that the reason that the president had not so much as mentioned the word AIDS publicly until 1985 was because "it hadn't spread into the general population yet." In this formulation, "general population" serves as a euphemism for "heterosexual" and is deployed, as Simon Watney has shown, to enforce a particular vision of "family values." The gay population, which has been hardest hit, is caught in a double bind where first one discourse then another serves to exclude, malign, or erase the presence of gay men. The minoritizing narrative (only gays have AIDS, so it need not be addressed as a public health threat) excludes on the basis of difference, the universalizing one (it's a question not of identity but of "risky" behavior, so we don't need to address our efforts toward gay men but can ignore them) simply forgets that there is any difference at all.

  See the entry on "general population" in Jan Zita Grover, "Keywords," in *AIDS: Cultural Analysis, Cultural Activism,* ed. Douglas Crimp (Cambridge: MIT Press, 1988), pp. 23–24. Also on the "general public," see Watney, "The Spectacle of AIDS," in *AIDS, ed. Crimp, and Watney, Policing Desire* (Minneapolis: University of Minnesota Press, 1987), esp. pp. 83–84.

17   Andy Warhol, *The Andy Warhol Diaries,* ed. Pat Hackett (New York: Warner Books, 1989), entry for Friday, January 16, 1987. Interestingly, about a month later, Warhol saw Mapplethorpe again, and as he was looking and feeling better, Warhol sat and talked with him (February 10, 1987): "Robert Mapplethorpe was there. He looked more healthy than I've even seen him, he had color in his face. I think they're trying out a new drug on him, I hope he makes it. And we talked about people from the seventies. I asked him about his old girlfriend Patti Smith and he said he'd just shot her and I said why didn't he give the pictures to *Interview,* and he said *Vogue* already had them."

18   David Anfam, for example, in his review article "Handy Andy," *Art History* 14, no. 2 (June

1991): 270–273, touches on this issue, noting Wendy Steiner's remark that "it is tempting to see everything about him as part of a gay aesthetic." Anfam is one of few critics who has noted the lack of any writing that addresses the relationship between sexuality and Warhol's art, criticizing this implicit "modernist precept" against the "biographical" and calling for "an art history sensitive to the formation of sexual difference at a social level in addition to the modernist and post-modern aesthetic currents which Warhol channeled" (273).

19   Monique Wittig, "The Straight Mind," in *"The Straight Mind" and Other Essays* (Boston: Beacon, 1992), pp. 21–32.

20   See the essay by Andrew Parker, "Unthinking Sex: Marx, Engels, and the Scene of Writing," pp. 19–41, for a discussion of heteronormativity in Marx, Engels, and the Marxist critical tradition, in *Fear of a Queer Planet: Queer Politics and Social Theory,* ed. Michael Warner (Minneapolis: University of Minnesota Press, 1993).

21   A suggestive phrase taken from Michael Warner's introduction to *Fear of a Queer Planet.*

22   "Queer Performativity: Henry James's *The Art of the Novel,*" *GLQ,* 1, no. 1: 1–16.

23   See Silvan Tomkins, *The Negative Affects* (New York: Springer, 1963; vol. 2 of *Affect, Imagery, Consciousness,* 4 vols., 1962–1991).

24   Sedgwick, "Queer Performativity," p. 5.

25   David Rubin, "Andy Warhol," review of *Torso* series, *Arts Magazine,* December 1978.

26   Simon Watney, "In Purgatory: The Work of Felix Gonzalez-Torres," *Parkett* 39 (1994): 44.

27   Andy Warhol, *The Philosophy of Andy Warhol* (New York: Harcourt Brace Jovanovich, 1975), p. 82. Steven Shaviro glosses Warhol's theory the following way: " 'Good' or 'professional' performance (whether in life or on the stage) is the calculated attempt to project a consistent and substantial self, one identical to itself at every moment. Bad or amateurish performance subverts this art of projection, reminding us," as Warhol says, that "no person is ever completely right for any part, because a part is a role, is never real." Or as David Bowie puts it, "Dress my friend up just for show, see them as they really are." Shaviro, *Cinematic Body,* p. 219. The rest of this passage from the *Philosophy* reads: "So if you can't get someone who's perfectly right, it's more satisfying to get someone who is perfectly wrong. Then you know you've really got something" (83).

28   See for example Dennis Cooper's interview with Reeves in (where else) *Interview* in which Cooper defends Reeves's acting as "punk" acting, which has clear similarities to Warhol's idea. He says, "I've always thought there was something very punk about your acting, not only your erratic energy but the way you seem incapable of conveying dishonesty, no matter who you're playing. Which I guess is why you have this punk cult following."

29   For documentation of the graphic work of Gran Fury and other graphics groups associated with ACT UP, see Douglas Crimp and Adam Rolston, *AIDS Demo Graphics* (Seattle: Bay Press, 1990).

30   See James, "Andy Warhol: The Producer as Author."

SIMON WATNEY
Queer Andy

"He thought he was grotesque"—Carl Willers[1]

The first time I got busted was together with some two hundred people watching *Lonesome Cowboys* in its first week of screening in London in 1969. Serious structuralist film critics undoubtedly attended too, but by and large it was a very queer audience indeed, as were the audiences for all Warhol's film screenings in London in the seventies—and to this day. To this teenager, two years before the first meetings of the U.K. Gay Liberation Front at the London School of Economics, Warhol positively reeked of a seductive American queer culture at its most exaltedly blatant. Yet as soon as one turned to Warhol criticism, one was confronted by a virtual cliff-face of denial and displacement, one consistently directing attention away from any question of subject matter in his films toward primarily if not exclusively technical questions—the speed of film stock he used, details about projection speeds, and so on. Butch, "masculine" things like that. Of the people and issues in these films one learned only that they were deliberately "bland," empty of significance, banal, mere coat hangers for formal filmic experimentation. There is certainly still a powerful and influential critical view that the value of Warhol's films and the rest of his nonfilmic work lies in their concern with such lofty abstractions as time, death, process, and so forth. But never sex, let alone queer sex. Certainly the local police from Tottenham Court Road took a line much closer to that of the audience. They hardly stopped the screening on aesthetic grounds, for crimes against the conventions of the Hollywood Western. On the contrary, they understood only too well that Warhol had made a "dirty" film, a film that encouraged the Western to speak its unconscious, which is, of course, always sexual and usually perverse.

Early Warhol art criticism in Britain followed a similar tendency to the early Warhol film criticism. For example, writing in the catalogue of the highly successful 1971 Warhol exhibition at the Tate Gallery in London, curator Richard Morphet argued that Warhol's choice of subject matter was "relatively passive" and that what matters most in his work is the extent to which it addresses the "painting process."[2] Indeed, trying to relate Warhol's paintings to such contemporaries as Ellsworth Kelly and Frank Stella, Morphet found it "paradoxical that an art so concerned with process should need to involve figurative images."[3] Thus, he concluded, "the flagrant reproduction of banal images in a painting was a means of ridding the process of openly expressive intent in order to give a new directness of effect to the act of making a mark on a canvas."[4] Warhol was therefore seen essentially as an "abstract" artist, and one wonders what he must have felt, being informed by powerful European critics, that the only thing shared by Marilyn Monroe, Elizabeth Taylor, Elvis Presley, and Jackie Onassis was their "banality." Here one senses the sheer force of obliterative homophobia at work in contemporary Pop Art criticism and throughout sixties Anglo-American high culture.

In the course of the seventies, European critics became far more interested in the *Flower* pictures and the *Disasters,* which they could safely regard as Goyaesque. Hence the incomparably strange critical incarnation of Andy Warhol as a warrior of the class struggle in the interpretive work of many critics. To imagine that one might find some hidden subtext of revolutionary socialism in the work of Andy Warhol must have struck many other gay men like myself as particularly absurd and fanciful. And, ultimately, insulting, insofar as it sustained a continued refusal to engage with the most glaringly obvious motif in Warhol's career—his homosexuality.

Before the emergence of Gay Liberation in the United Kingdom in 1971, Warhol was one of only a handful of cultural exemplars who represented a public face of queerness. He was transparently queer, especially to a generation that in Manchester or Malmo or Manhattan had grown up weeping to *Now Voyager* on Sunday afternoon TV matinees or who rushed home from school to hear Dionne Warwick's latest record on the radio. All of us doing more or less the same thing, in total isolation from one another, doing our best to make sense of our queer feelings in a world that relentlessly denied our existence or dismissed us as monsters. In this respect, Warhol is second to none in the pantheon of twentieth-century American queer heroes. It is important to remember that in 1969, very few people in Britain or elsewhere in Europe were familiar with the names of Johns or Rauschenberg. Yet *everyone* knew about Andy Warhol. Hence the typically vicious and vengeful homophobia of the U.K. press in its reporting of his death.[5]

Above all else, Warhol was camp. From Susan Sontag to Andrew Ross, critics have tended to regard camp as if it were an entirely voluntary stance, a conscious cultural posture. But this seems to me largely to miss the point about queer experience, especially in childhood. As for countless others, Andy's campness was a fundamental survival strategy. But it was no more a matter of conscious volition than his queerness. This comes out very clearly indeed from Victor Bockris's invaluable biography, which begins with a very terrible story of a Pittsburgh child, a little boy who desperately wanted to be a little girl, terrorized by his father and brother, dominated later by his peasant mother, who effectively lived an authentic medieval life in late-twentieth-century Manhattan. Such contradictions were constitutive of Andy Warhol, as he came to eclipse Andrew Warhola. There is a whole, much-needed book to be written on the subject of the relations between Andy and Andrew.

This serves only to reinforce the point on which psychoanalytic criticism will insist—that even at the best of times, childhood is a very dangerous place, whatever else it may also be. Yet Warhol also exemplifies the type of the precociously talented, intuitive artist whose gifts were identified in earliest childhood. Modernist art criticism has great difficulty thinking about artists' childhoods. Early-twentieth-century critics such as Kandinsky and Roger Fry retained a late Victorian notion of childhood vision as an essentially abstract, undifferentiated form of seeing, untainted, as it were, by adult experience. Yet this hardly begins to account for those many artists who, like Warhol, were evidently "artists" almost before they were out of diapers. The biographical literature is saturated with images of little Andrew cutting photographs out of magazines, drawing, and painting. He chose his mother's clothes from an early age, and so on. Such repeated anecdotes call attention to our inability to articulate together questions of precocious artistic talent— and precocious queerness.

Little, queer, mommy's boy Andrew was predictably teased, bullied, hurt, and humiliated, but this does not in or of itself explain the imaginative passion with which he began to invent his own America, out of the elements that came most immediately to hand, from the radio, comics, Saturday morning children's cinema, and so on. Just as he invented Andy. Indeed, it is worth noting that Warhol learned to speak English only comparatively late in his childhood, and he learned it from the lips of Shirley Temple and the Shadow.

For Warhol was a child of the thirties. He was born in 1928. By the age of nineteen he had learned to paint his fingernails different colors, at the same time that he was learning the commercial department store display trade. In other words, alongside the famously shy, stumbling Andrew Warhola there coexisted a fantastically confident, courageous, and outrageous Andy Warhol. Such deeply constitutive contradictions are not simply voluntary, in any very useful sense. As we know from Bockris and elsewhere, he used to choose shoes from different pairs for his feet when he was young. He was a born stylist and, moreover, a stylist who knew that "style" is not a superficial issue but a way of surviving, a strategy for remaking public America in the likeness of his own private "America," which derived from sources as diverse yet queerly related as Truman Capote's novel *Other Voices, Other Rooms,* Walt Disney, Marilyn, and so on. The Carnegie Institute lifted him bodily out of the Middle Ages that his family inhabited, in one great jump, associated with his artistic talent. I am personally less interested in the element of fetishism in Warhol's life and work than in this curious, quintessentially queer combination of intense shyness and dandyism, both of which equally inform his dazzling fantasy of stardom. He was never in the least intellectual, which is, perhaps, one of his saving graces. Yet many critics continue to emphasize the supposed "influence" of the Bauhaus on his student work and God knows what else from within the canon of high modernism. This is surely but rather spectacularly to miss the point that he went to college with students who unlike him didn't have to earn every dollar they spent. He was a student who had to work just to be at college in the first place. A very real class issue is at stake here, the issue of the working-class queer aesthete.

It is therefore important to be able to locate Warhol within the historical context of the history of homophobia and its resistances. He grew up and flourished during the forties and fifties, and if he felt helpless, he was clever enough to realize that helplessness can be an effectively manipulative design for living. Warhol was endlessly sensitive to the maternal pull of American culture, with its countless cultural images of strong, confident, and articulate women. This is one of the reasons for his queer popularity in Europe, representing a warm, emotional America to our experience of cold, dry irony. Warhol was never an ironist.[6] So, if we look at Warhol's career from beginning to end, we find a fantasmatic of considerable complexity and consistency. Of course, process was important to Warhol. He didn't need to question the "materiality" of popular culture or of any system of representations, because there was never any question for him of their absolute material reality. For Warhol, the question of Disney cartoons was not posed in terms of arcane theory; on the contrary, he took it for granted that cartoon characters people the world as substantively as anyone else. For him, TV and cinema were basic, constitutive parts of the social world, not mere "reflections," and in his work he explores this insight as shrewdly and sensitively as any other artist one might care to name.

In this sense, Warhol's work leads directly into the concerns of the late eighties and nineties with interventionary work at the level of mass media representations and the institutions that define and regulate them. For in Warhol one always has the strong sense of the interface between the psychic and the social at work in our variously excited or indifferent responses to the great, iconic "types" of twentieth-century American culture, from Mickey Mouse to Madonna. This cannot be explained by means of a traditional, class-based analysis that seeks to reduce all meanings in relation to supposedly "primary" economic determining factors, however important these were in his childhood. Warhol became an exemplary fifties queer, a pilgrim in New York, drawn to glamour and secrets. He was, as we know, profoundly unhappy about his own appearance, and the sheer extent of work that he put into his own looks and his body takes us back to the damage involved in growing up in the fifties, which Gore Vidal once memorably described as the worst decade in the history of the world. Not for nothing did Warhol joke as a child that he came from another planet. It was a joke and not a joke. Such fantasies speak almost too accurately (and painfully) of the experience of queer childhood, before the acquisition of an affirming identity grounded in homosexual desire. For this is exactly how queer children feel, as if we come from another planet—Planet Queer. How do you explain about yourself to yourself, let alone to others, when you have absolutely no legitimate or legitimating model for your own most intensely personal feelings about other people and the world? You turn to those elements within what is culturally on offer and make them speak your queer feelings, as best you can.

To say as a child that you come from another planet is to speak from the narrative of comics and science fiction movies, which do indeed describe people who are very pale and fair, who come from elsewhere, disguised as earthlings. That strikes me as a not entirely inaccurate description of how queer Andrew felt. Thus when other fifties homosexuals such as Frank O'Hara and Truman Capote gave him the cold shoulder because, in their times, he was too "swishy," too much of a window dresser, something very profound was at stake. They had accepted a deal that was not available to Warhol. They had, if you will, dehomosexualized themselves, especially in their *social* role as artists or critics. Take Warhol's relations with Leo Castelli. Warhol was the one great homosexual artist in New York who refused to dehomosexualize himself, and he was the one artist whom Castelli didn't recognize or take on until much later in the day.

Warhol himself was symptomatically terrified of money. This in turn is not unconnected to his notorious greed. The paradox hinges on the relation between feeling you don't deserve to be paid, the experience of hoarding money under the bed because banks are unknown and threatening and dangerous institutions, and an overwhelming ambition that requires considerable financial outlay. An ambition that was nothing less than to recreate the entire social world "in little," to construct a safe space in which everyone and everything is queer. According to Bockris, his mother "made him feel insignificant, made him feel that he was the ugliest creature God put on this earth."[7] This repeated emphasis on the scenario of a mother telling her child how ugly he is runs very much against the grain of most people's idea of "good enough" mothering. Indeed, his entire relationship with his mother was shot through with a somewhat grim passive-aggressive intensity, on both sides. Warhol was provocatively passive and always able to initiate the most intense rivalries between his acolytes, lovers, friends, and family. Everyone had to compete for his attention. One reads endlessly of his having been uptight, stressed out, speechless, mute with anger, and so on, as if he had learned early on that words were useless, that it simply wasn't worth talking about things, that language itself was not to be trusted. For both Andrew and Andy, images were quite literally his principal means of direct communication. He thought in images. This is, after all, what it means to be the type of instinctive artist of which Warhol is such a clear example.

Such extreme dualisms run right through Warhol's life: generosity and extreme meanness, strength and frailty, masculinity and femininity, hair and baldness, adult and child, loyalty and betrayal. Such self-contradictory tropes are wholly characteristic of Warhol, from whatever angle one regards him. Henry Geldzahler has argued he was a voyeur/sadist who needed exhibitionists/masochists around him to fulfill both parts of his identity but that there were always more people around than he could use up in any one situation. I suspect this is a very shrewd comment from someone very close to Warhol over a considerable period of time. It is somehow related to the image of Andy intently watching his lovers sleeping.

In one of the wisest texts of early-twentieth-century art history, Ernst Kris and Otto Kurz looked in detail at stories and anecdotes associated with the discovery of precocious or otherwise unexpected artistic talent.[8] In this study of "fixed biographical themes" in the biographies of artists, the anecdote is regarded as the "primitive cell" of biography.[9] They isolate two types of such narratives: one attempts to explain adult achievement by reference to significant events in childhood, whereas the other regards childhood talent not in terms of causality but "premonitory signs."[10] This latter view is probably more ancient, though the two are by no means mutually exclusive of each other. Certainly the Warhol biography as it emerges in composite combines elements of both narratives. It was pure chance he grew up in the Pittsburgh of the Mellons and the Carnegies. At the same time, his talent was "discovered" almost as soon as he entered college.

As Kris and Kurz pointed out in 1934, "The flotsam of ancient conceptions of the artist carried forward on biographical waves entirely corresponds to the attitude with which we still approach the artist."[11] Thus Warhol's career at first sight falls entirely within the biographical trope of the young child prodigy "triumphing over obstacles put in the way of his chosen profession, often by those nearest to him."[12] In modern art criticism, however, homosexuality (and, for that matter, femaleness) are usually regarded as if they were intrinsic "obstacles" in themselves rather than sites of intense vulnerability to masculinizing and dehomosexualizing myths of creativity and creative worth. This explains much of the homophobic displacement that is typical of most Warhol criticism, a "disturbance of vision," however, that ultimately serves only to draw our attention back to what it was from which academic Warhol criticism averts its gaze.

It is therefore worth pointing out that homophobia may also be periodized by levels of intensity, narrative emphases, objects, aims, and so on. This is where Warhol's age becomes such an important issue. For example, it is very dubious to describe Warhol as an "out" gay man or to describe him at all as a gay man in the pre-Stonewall period. Warhol grew up in a series of urban homosexual "milieus" that had no concept whatsoever of how homosexuality might be articulated politically. Warhol was a "homosexual," constituted by induced social and cultural shame, personal shame. Yet shame has its own intense psychic validity, forever gauging the gulf between self and other, providing both confidence and doubt about the world. Hence, perhaps, some of the contradictions that Warhol enacted, as it were, in his own appearance and his attitudes to his own and other people's bodies, were forever polarized between idealization and contempt.

For example, he was terrified of illness, having grown up in a class and time period when to be ill and poor was to risk death. All the way through his diaries one comes across this terror projected out onto the world, as he cuts or otherwise avoids people who were sick. Yet Warhol's most explicit *Skull* pictures are perhaps the least interesting area of his work in this context, precisely because they are so literal. They evidently attract those who wish to establish connections of supposed "influence" from, say, Picasso's celebrated still lifes with skulls from the 1940s. Yet the skull beneath the skin was an everyday perception for the Warholas. Besides, all painters are aware of the skin/skeleton relation between paint and surface or canvas and stretcher. For Warhol, this awareness was especially highly developed. For how long can an artist's work survive her? The writer's words may be translated, they may go onto disk, into third editions. But a painting is ever only a painting. It is highly vulnerable and may easily be damaged or destroyed. This is doubtless one reason why paintings are so frequently the subject of physical violence.

It is not in the least surprising that Warhol has been posthumously taken to task as a result of his rejection of old friends with AIDS, such as Robert Mapplethorpe. Yet it hardly helps to judge overly a man who was evidently himself helpless in the face of his own profound projective anxieties about illness, pain, and dying. It should never be assumed that the experience of physical suffering leads automatically to a subsequent identification with others in similar pain after one has oneself recovered. On the contrary, pain may simply provoke a barrier to identification with what is in effect too painful to think about. Thus, for example, it is not very helpful to argue of the later work that Warhol failed to deal with AIDS, because he was never in any sense a didactic artist, and it is frankly misleading to think of him as someone who supposedly should or should not have "dealt" with anything.

It is therefore yet another Warholian paradox that Warhol's work has inspired and informed AIDS activist culture interventions such as the work of Gran Fury, as well as artists such as Robert Gober, whose work constitutes a form of cultural poetics of the epidemic. Thus, for example, Warhol's cow wallpapers, and others, present a form of interior decoration that in many respects provided the model for the cultural activist strategy of, as it were, wallpapering the streets. The graphic directness and simplicity of Warhol's screen prints is felt throughout the cultural activist movement associated with the great days of ACT UP in the late eighties.[13] At the same time, the scale of the image in Warhol's wallpapers (which is one way of thinking about much of his output) puts us back into perceptual alignment with the viewing position of a child, looking at the (to her) vast repeats in any wallpaper. Or consider the pinups tacked to any child's bedroom wall. It is this sense of the specific *scale* of childhood vision that Robert Gober in particular has explored in much of his work, thus leading us back into his queer childhood and its relations to queer adult life—and death.

Thus we may return to the impact of comics and cartoons in Warhol's taste and imagination and the deeper analogy between the Factory and the Disney studios. For surely Warhol's *Superstars* have at least as much in common with the shape-shifting, larger-than-life characters of American cartoons as they have with the actual flesh-and-blood products of the Hollywood star system in its heyday. Warhol's *Superstars* also speak something retrospectively of the pathos that lies in their heroic attempts to emulate the strangely polymorphous, perverse condition of the American cartoon universe. Indeed, it is from Warhol's profound immersion in American popular culture and the fantasy world he constructed to shield himself from the realities of a brutal society that we may begin to separate out the various strands of pleasure and reverie that constitute the overall Warhol phantasm. Hence the significance of Keith Haring's celebrated image of *Andy Mouse*, identifying something fundamental in Warhol's position behind the characters and scenarios he mobilized in his work. The Warhol/Haring couplet is similar to many others in Warhol's career, including, of course, his close collaborative work with Jean-Michel Basquiat, couplets that represent the types of reinvented parenting that he fostered throughout his working life, often cruelly mothering his extended queer family.

From precisely this perspective we return to the question of Warhol's profound anxieties about his own appearance and his intense sense of being ugly, which it is difficult not to regard as a more or less violent displacement from a deeper sense of childhood shame. He seems to have lived with his mother in Manhattan to guarantee the undermining of any sexual self-confidence he might achieve, just as throughout his adult life he played his immediate friends and colleagues against one another as he had learned to play members of his family against one another when he was a child. Warhol's sense of his ugliness is also closely connected to the intensity of his fandom, his craving for the contingency of the rich, the famous, and the beautiful, a habit that in Rainer Maria Rilke's image from the *Duino Elegies* "liked him and stayed." Yet the true fan's identification with the adored star is always ambivalent. Does one seek to have the star for oneself, or does one wish to *be* the star? Much of Warhol's career revolves around this persistent, unanswerable question. Does the star confer beauty on her acolytes, or does she merely reinforce their inferior status?

By the time of his death, Warhol owned several hundred hairpieces for his own use. The complexity of his attitudes to his own appearance tells us much about the anxious mobility of his imaginary identifications with others, fantasized looking at him and judging him harshly:

> I decided to go grey so nobody would know how old I was and I thought I would look younger to them than how old they thought I was. I would gain a lot by going grey: (1) I would have old problems, which were easier to take than young problems, (2) everyone would be impressed by how young I looked, and (3) I would be relieved of the responsibility of acting young—I could occasionally lapse into eccentricity or senility and no one would think anything of it because of my grey hair. When you've got grey hair, every move you make seems "young" and "spry," instead of just being normally active. It's like you're getting a new talent.[14]

Perhaps one reason why Warhol has been so comparatively neglected by gay cultural critics is the extent to which his work frankly and painfully enacts scenarios of homosexual shame which were largely incompatible with the aesthetic of normative "positive images" that so dominated lesbian and gay Anglophone culture in the seventies and early eighties. He was too tortured and "nelly," too *embarrassing*. In the necessary struggle for political rights, the entire question of the psychic constitution of identity in intensely homophobic societies was left to behaviorists, New Agers, and a largely depoliticized psychotherapy movement. Warhol's project takes us, however, directly into the intensely private, guarded world of queer childhood, playing indoors when the frightening older boys are outside doing incomprehensible and terrifying things with footballs, cars, and girls.

Cans of soup are only "banal" to those who didn't have to grow up on canned food. In Warhol's case, these same cans had been magically transformed into flowers by his mother's shears, to raise cash to buy little Andrew a projector to screen Orphan Annie films at home. We might compare them to one of those still lifes by Caravaggio, in which a bowl of fruit stands right on the edge of a table, near to toppling off, while on closer consideration the leaves are seen to be rotting and the fruit is going off. Recognizing the tenacious heroism of Queer Andy, we can release him from the theoretical embrace of all those who have mistakenly required him to be a didactic moralist and belatedly begin to get to grips with the queer poetics that lie at the heart of his greatness as an artist.

NOTES

1   Carl Willers, quoted in Victor Bockris, *The Life and Death of Andy Warhol* (London: Penguin Books, 1989), p. 119.

2   Richard Morphet, "Andy Warhol," in *Warhol* (London: Tate Gallery, 1971), p. 13.

3   Ibid., p. 24.

4   Ibid.

5   See Simon Watney, "The Warhol Effect," in *The Work of Andy Warhol*, ed. Gary Garrels (Seattle: Bay Press, 1989), pp. 115–124.

6   Ibid.

7   Bockris, *Warhol*, p. 122.

8   Ernst Kris and Otto Kurz, *Legend, Myth, and Magic in the Image of the Artist* (1934; reprint, New Haven: Yale University Press, 1979).

9   Ibid., p. 4.

10 Ibid., p. 13.

11 Ibid., p. 31.

12 Ibid., p. 30.

13 See Douglas Crimp and Adam Rolston, *AIDS Demo Graphics* (Seattle: Bay Press, 1990); see also Simon Watney, "Read My Lips: AIDS, Art, and Activism," in *Read My Lips: New York AIDS Polemics* (Glasgow: Tramway Gallery, 1992), n.p.

14 Bockris, *Warhol,* p. 120.

DAVID E. JAMES

I'll Be Your Mirror Stage:
Andy Warhol in the Cultural Imaginary

"he became his admirers, . . ."—W. H. Auden, "In Memory of W. B. Yeats"[1]

In Jonas Mekas's documentary of his presentation of the 1964 Independent Film Award to Andy Warhol, he gives the filmmaker a basket of fruit and vegetables. Warhol distributes them—apples, bananas, mushrooms, and carrots—among Baby Jane Holzer, Gerard Malanga, Ivy Nicholson, and the others in his entourage who surround him in a tableau racked vertically through the frame—a composition that recalls Méliès rather than the Lumières, the "primitive" filmmakers of whom Warhol was supposed to be a recapitulation.[2] To the sound of early Supremes' records, they all begin to eat, but very, very slowly! The whole film was overcranked so as to simulate in screening the scandalous temporal attenuation of *Sleep, Eat, Empire,* and the other works here being honored, though the net effect of Mekas's film—"wholly pastoral and unneurotic in feeling," in the words of one of its few commentators—is quite different from that of Warhol's own.[3] After some time, Warhol exits the frame, leaving a vacant space around which his entourage continue to sway from side to side like retarded fish in an underwater ballet. But then, just as he reenters, the end flares claim him and burn the entire scene into a blank ethereality that is held for several minutes until "Run, Run, Run" finally plays out.

Thirty years on, the film appears an augury of Warhol's life and death as well as our dance around the vacancy he left. We conjure his return but are able to raise only a ghost, which disappears almost as soon as we glimpse it. Gestures simultaneously of homage and mourning, our attempts recall the

Figure 1. *Blitz* cover,
September (1989).

peculiar thematics of his own elegiac invocations of dead stars such as Marilyn and his picturing of Jackie's bereavement, as these have been poignantly
summarized by Thomas Crowe: "How does one handle the fact of celebrity
death? . . . How does one come to terms with the sense of loss, the absence of
a richly imagined presence that was never really there?"[4]

Like our engagement with other dead celebrities, our postmortem commentary on Warhol is the occasion for the projection of fantasy and desire, of
other connections we might have made in our own lives, other roles we
might have played; but it is unusual, indeed remarkable, for its extensiveness, for its occurrence on all cultural levels and for the variety of Warhols it
projects. Mass culture's references to him are ubiquitous: the Warhol cameo
in Oliver Stone's film *The Doors* is a recent instance, along with a rumored
Hollywood biopic, and the more or less casual asides about him and his
works that have become part of popular lore.[5] A highbrow invocation is
enacted in the many academic conferences about him that have been held
since his death. And something in between is instanced in the edition of
Blitz, an English Pop magazine, published on the occasion of his London

retrospective (see figure 1).[6] It is, in fact, insightful and quite scholarly, and even as it both mocks and exploits him, its cover announces a summary desire. These all, in their different but overlapping ways, illustrate the personal and social investment and restructuring by which we accommodate items in industrial culture into our lives. But Warhol's ongoing ability to sustain this unprecedentedly diverse and multilocational fan culture reflects, of course, his singularity among the other Pop artists: they all appropriated industrial technologies in their representations of the icons of industrial culture, but he alone became such an icon. As Keith Haring remarked, in reference to his own *Andy Mouse* prints, "[Warhol] was part of American culture, like Mickey Mouse was."[7] Becoming what he beheld, Warhol became synonymous with his era because his deconstruction of the self-definition of art against commerce—more vivid, more prescient, and more thorough than anyone else's—occurred in both his work and his life.[8] Given the permeation of his activities by his desire for wealth and fame, any consideration of the iconography or formal properties of his prints or films that excludes their function for his own career in and as publicity must risk missing what is most essential to them: their role in his self-creation, self-promotion, and self-examination. All the works, from the soup cans and the *Marilyn* series to the *Ads* and the *Myths,* are allegorical self-portraits that narrate the conditions of his life as a media icon, the very life they brought into being.

The circulation of the thematics of the art through the praxis of his life, through the dissemination of his celebrity in the mass media, and through the popular production and consumption of him as a star has provided the terms for endless, irresolvable arguments about the critical component in the entire field. Questions concerning the status of his art—whether it is, via some distancing effect, "about" advertising and industrial culture or whether in it the avant-garde's critique of bourgeois society has so collapsed that the art is essentially of the same order as advertising—are inseparable from questions about his personality; about his ambition, venality, and exploitation of celebrity; or, alternatively, about his innocence, loneliness, and Catholic devotion. Parallel conundrums pivoted on the possibility or impossibility of authenticity and integrity subtend the contexts in which he appears: the psychological one of his personal subjectivity, the social one of his biography, the aesthetic one of his work, and the political one of the historical meaning of Warholization. But because (and to invoke a structuralist vocabulary still appropriate here) the binaries shift in their interarticulation through the

different levels of the total field, the myth of Warhol sustains endless recon-
figurations. The floating signification of the life tells the same stories as the
art—or, more precise, leaves the same questions open.

My sense—and at this point it is only an intuitive one—is that if any way
exists of bringing some kind of productive focus or direction into this hermeneutic excess, queer theory will supply it, and it will do so not by resolv-
ing the aporiae I have tried to sketch and especially not by proposing a break
between the problematics of an early and a late Warhol but by a metacom-
mentary that will take the irreducible contradictions in Warhol's multiple
aspirations as themselves the data of study. In this, questions of Warhol's
sexuality will have a double leverage. On the one hand, full recognition of
the gay component in his work will force a reconceptualization of the oeuvre
as a whole: the meaning of the work of the 1960s and the terms of the all but
ubiquitous valorization of it and the concomitant denigration of the work of
the 1970s and 1980s will have to be reassessed when the *Myths* and the *Ads,*
the *Oxidation Painting* and the *Torso* series, for example, find their proper
place in the canon. On the other hand, understanding of the various seman-
tic displacements, slidings, and recodings that both characterize Warhol as a
queer artist and allowed the gay component in his work to be ignored in his
assimilation to many ideologies of American culture may also provide for a
more general political hermeneutic. In the *Myths* series, for example, a decoding in gay terms is compelling in itself, but it also has implications that
lead beyond specifically sexual issues. Recognition that Howdy Doody, Superman, the Witch, the Star, and the others model a range of gay subjectivities linking the first (a photographed double image of Warhol himself in
which his pasty face is turned just so in order to produce a straight-nosed,
firm-jawed shadow) to the last (a hollow-eyed and visibly anxious Uncle
Sam) also provides for a more general reading of the relation between individual subjectivity and social vocabularies for it, between private identity
and its public, even national, forms. Neither mindlessly celebrating industrial culture nor reductively indicting it, this series interrogates it, recognizing the diversity of subject positions within it and the flexibility of personal
self-fashionings within them that it allows.

As himself such a media image, Warhol is available for a similar plurality
of uses; we all choose among his various roles and invest ourselves in those
which we find most useful. Here, instead of moving centripetally to examine
the structures in Warhol's art and the events in his life that facilitate this

projection, I will work outward to some of its more significant instances, considering Warhol's own existence as myth and some of the forms he has taken in the cultural imaginary—where the issue of his sexuality has been mostly repressed.

REPRESENTING WARHOL

■

By way of approach, we may consider the catalogue of the 1989 MOMA retrospective, which is anomalous in that it supplements the reproductions, scholarly essays, and other paraphernalia of its genre with a thirty-page "Collective Portrait of Andy Warhol" by nearly eighty other artists and friends. Most of these are verbal portraits, and most are as confectionery as Warhol's society portraits of the seventies. But a number are visual—paintings or photographs—and in some instances keenly expressive. For example, Richard Avedon's 1969 photograph *Andy Warhol, Artist, New York City* and Alice Neel's 1970 oil *Andy Warhol* (see figure 2) document the effects of Valerie Solanas's assassination attempt. Neel's piece, painted when she herself was seventy years old, emphasizes Warhol's frailness, with his corsetry, spreading hips, and sagging breasts resembling those of an old woman. But in the Avedon, framed by the suggestively drawn-aside leather jacket and underpants, the torso is flat, the hands seem strong, and the same wounds look like decorative or even erotic scarification; the photo might well be an advertisement for a tattoo-and-piercing nightclub. In other instances, the artist's own fantasy self-projection causes any but the broadest biographical detail to be jettisoned. In Julian Schnabel's *Portrait of Andy Warhol* (1982) and Jean-Michel Basquiat's *Dos Cabezas* (1982), all that remain of the ostensible subject are caricature motifs, trademarks like the wig, which invoke Warhol, but only to record his assimilation to the signature style and thematic interests of the portraitist, however articulate within those interests the image may nevertheless be.[9]

These "art," for want of a better word, representations are paralleled by a similar use of Warhol's image in other cultural spheres. In a frame from a 1973 *Mad* movie satire (see figure 3) and ten years later in an ad from *Vogue* (see figure 4), his appearance is remarkably constant, but the two narrate his cultural role quite differently. In the former, as a point of stable verisimilitude but also the origin of a maelstrom of cubist psychedelia, he is framed by the

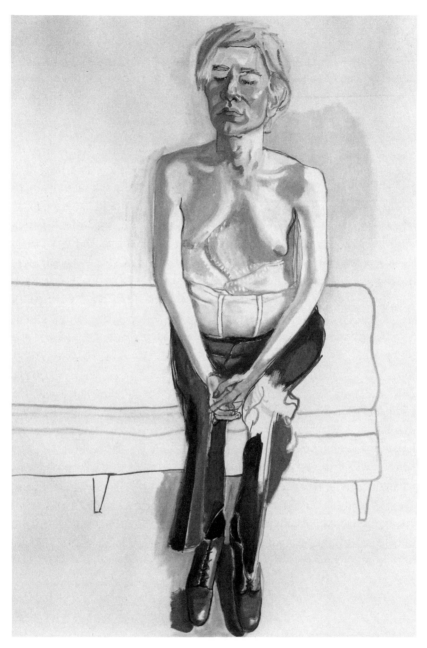

Figure 2. Alice Neel, *Andy Warhol* (1970).

two levels of mutually antagonistic readings of his significance: *Midnight Cowboy's* parody of his entourage, and then *Mad's* own parody of this as *Midnight Wowboy*. In the second, the countercultural location and the comic affection that sustains this itinerary have been replaced by the exclusive hyperspace of Dior advertising and an appropriate, indeed inevitable, cynical condescension. Now, as white and blank as the canvas on which he will represent whoever buys him, he is a commodity addressed by other commodities in a world consisting entirely of commodities.[10] These and the many other uses of Warhol's image attest to its power but also to its flexibility.[11] An icon of immediate cultural currency, it works as a summary statement of the meaning of his own work and so as a particular take on postmodernism; but within those general parameters, it is endlessly variable.

In what follows, I want to explore two more extended portraits of Warhol: the Lou Reed and John Cale collaboration *Songs for 'Drella*, and Jonas Mekas's film *Scenes from the Life of Andy Warhol*. Both are works by major artists whose careers were closely entwined with Warhol's. Both were made shortly after Warhol's death, and while both confront the public myth with more personally informed recollections, they capitalize on the media interest in him at that time. In this, they recapitulate Warhol's own strategy of exploiting the fame of his subjects as vehicles for his own career; and, perhaps as a consequence, both fall off from their authors' characteristic achievements in ways that relate directly to their encounter with the weight and diversity of the thematics of Warhol. In considering these portraits, I will be concerned with such questions as: What terms do they propose as the myth of Warhol's life? What is the relation of their aesthetics to Warhol's own—do they, for example, refer to it, even if (as in the case of *Award Presentation*) the simulation of Warhol's technique produces a quite different effect? And what is the position of the Warhol elegy in the artist's oeuvre in general—what insights or expressive possibilities did it occasion, or what limits did it present?

SONGS FOR 'DRELLA: A FICTION[12]

■

The initial relationship between Warhol and Lou Reed[13] seems to have been one of mutual exploitation. In the summer of 1965, Reed, John Cale, and Sterling Morrison, who, with the addition of Maureen Tucker, would eventually form the Velvet Underground, had been introduced by their then drummer, Angus Maclise, to the Expanded Cinema events organized by Jonas Mekas at the Cinematheque, and they played at various screenings of underground films.[14] Warhol was himself beginning to experiment with multimedia events in the ensemble eventually called the "Exploding Plastic Inevitable," and though the Velvets' abrasiveness and contempt for their audience were quite unlike the tenor of the pop records he played when initially marketing himself as a Pop artist, he took them into the Factory entourage. Foisting an ex-model, Nico, on them as a singer, he projected his movies over their performance as the centerpiece of the E.P.I., designing the cover of the first album, *The Velvet Underground and Nico,* with its peelable banana (a reference to his film *Eat*) and stamping it with his own name. More important, he provided publicity and a powerful umbrella under which the Velvets were able to assert themselves in the recording studio. Thus, though he made no musical contribution apart from approving everything the Velvets did,[15] he was credited as the "producer" of the album. As I have argued elsewhere, the role of producer is not peripheral to Warhol's creativity so much as a critical and summary form of it;[16] but in this case it was short-

Figure 3. Mad Magazine, *Midnight Wowboy* (1973).

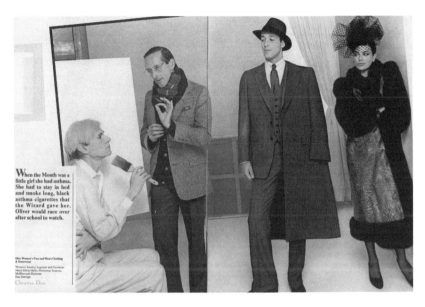

Figure 4. Vogue, advertisement for Christian Dior (1983).

lived. When (in the words of 'Drella, though seconded in other accounts) he admonished Reed with the options of continuing to "play museums like some dilettante" or "expanding [his] parameters" (presumably in the direction of greater public accessibility), Reed fired him, terminating both their personal and professional associations.

More substantial connections that could accommodate Reed's claim that Warhol had told him that he (Reed) "was to be to music what [Warhol himself] was to the visual arts" are suggested by parallels in certain of their aesthetic strategies.[17] First, the characters who inhabit Reed's lyrics resemble the bohemian types who form the cast of the movies of Warhol's second (and, arguably, finest) period, the sound films of 1965 that culminate in *The Chelsea Girls;* and in a number of cases—"All Tomorrow's Parties," "Chelsea Girls," "Candy Says," and "Walk on the Wild Side," for example—they are literally the same people. In making these portraits, both artists refuse moral censure, instead presenting their subjects with a cinema verité deadpan that nevertheless accommodates varying degrees of sympathetic identification. And, second, the Velvet's invocation of but self-distancing from middle-of-the-road pop music resembles Warhol's denaturing quotation of the icons of industrial culture. The group's best commentator, Ellen Willis, was the first to demonstrate this parallel with Warhol, elaborating it through a distinction between "art rock" and the Velvets' exemplary and seminal "rock-and-roll art."[18] Some form of reference but also superiority to generic rock and roll was typically invoked in the largely positive reception that greeted 'Drella (though what was recognized was more "art rock" than "rock-and-roll art"). But the first parallel, the celebration of the bohemian demimonde, is the more relevant to the ambitions of 'Drella's narrative of Warhol's life and to its limitations.

Songs for 'Drella is a cycle of fifteen songs, mostly told in Warhol's voice. The first half traces his decision to leave Pittsburgh, his attempts to make friends in New York, and the early stages of his career. His industriousness, his discovery of the power of repetition in the reproduction of mass culture images, and other aspects of his aesthetic are described, with the films—the social world of the early ones and later the attempts to woo Hollywood— receiving more attention than the advertising and the painting. At the peak of his creativity, when he is making the Brillo boxes and the early movies, Warhol discovers the Velvet Underground and projects his movies on their performances because "they have a style that grates and I have art to make." The narrative thrust of the songs generally predominates over thematic tex- turing, but halfway through, a new dimension of ambiguity appears. On "Slip Away (A Warning)," Reed has Warhol fancy that if, as he has been advised, he abandons the Factory's open-door policy, not only will "all the crazy people" slip away but so will all his ideas and he himself—as if (as *Award Presentation* indicated) once he quits his entourage, he won't be able to return.

"Slip Away" ends with Warhol refusing to exclude the "crazy people." To do so, he argues, would both jeopardize his creativity and be "an infamy," and Reed's abrupt vocalization ratifies his refusal. But as the narrative unfolds further, Warhol's friendships and creativity, which before had sustained each other, both fail. First, in "It Wasn't Me," Warhol is faced with accusations that his toleration of the self-destructive behavior of some of his associates made him responsible for their deaths, and then in the next song, "I Believe," one of them almost murders him. Introduced in the performance and video ver- sions by slides of Warhol's electric chair prints, here Reed ceases to speak in Warhol's voice and assumes his own in an attack on Valerie Solanas ("From inside her idiot madness spoke / And Andy fell onto the floor") that culminates in his desire that she should be executed, including his brutal claim that he would have "pulled the switch on her" himself, before it modulates into his own regret for not visiting Warhol in hospital. The last few songs are about betrayal of friendship: in "A Dream," which contains several references to his diaries,[19] Warhol complains of being ignored and abandoned by his old friends, especially by Reed; and in the last song, "Hello It's Me," Reed tries to make amends and bids him farewell.

In general, both musically and lyrically, 'Drella is relatively flat and one-dimensional—though you could equally well say sparse and restrained—only occasionally illuminated by the flash of an image ("My hair's silver like a Tiffany watch," from "Open House") or the grain of Reed's voice or Cale's instrumentation. Rarely heard are echoes of either the multivoiced abrasiveness of the Velvets or the melodic inventiveness and lyricism with which it was leavened. Of course, artists age and change, and it would be absurd to evaluate the work simply in terms of its resemblance to "Heroin" or "Sunday Morning." But in one respect, comparison to the Velvets and Reed's solo work of the seventies is appropriate.

The Velvets' songs were distinguished by the tensions among their various forms of textual and textural depth and multidimensionality. At once pop and anti-pop, capable simultaneously of the loveliest melodies and extreme atonal drone, with Reed's vocals oscillating between speaking and singing, between poetry and music, their formal vanguardism corresponded to a moral vanguardism, a celebration of otherwise anathematized people, practices, and ways of life. The drug songs, for example, or the songs about transvestism or sadomasochism, were so powerful because Reed introduced otherwise unspeakable pleasures into the impoverished discourse of pop lyrics, because the expanded expressive vocabulary of the music was able to communicate some of the nuances of the subjectivities associated with them, and also because he refused to reduce them to an overtly moralized one-dimensionality. As with the scandal over Warhol's serigraphs—movie star photos as art—in "Heroin," sin and salvation were the same; as with the scandal over the early movies, in "Venus in Furs" and "Walk on the Wild Side," people who couldn't even get into other pop lyrics were made welcome.

Such an appreciation of the flowers of evil, very common in modernist high culture, is especially ambivalent when it is commodified, as it was when the prospects of success in the record industry replaced the aggressively anti-industrial stance of the Velvet's performances.[20] But despite these inescapable contradictions, the Velvets' recordings remain a source, probably more important than any other in rock and roll, of real musical and moral expansiveness. In 'Drella's return to that milieu, in the individual songs but also in the narrative as a whole, the depth and richness are mostly lost. By effectively identifying the murder attempt with Warhol's actual death, Reed is able to disregard the events of the twenty years between them, the transformation of his social milieu and the corresponding changes in his art practice. These omissions allow him to center the narrative tensions of Warhol's life on his relations with the Factory entourage and so to propose a black-and-white differentiation between an honorable and faithful Warhol and the undeserving and ungrateful canaille, including both Reed himself, whose neglect occasions Warhol's anguish, and Solanas, whose degeneracy causes his death.

The strategic oversimplification of this hagiography does not totally exclude the dialectical depth of the earlier music. It can be glimpsed, for example, in "Slip Away"—for the first time in the cycle, Reed employs his skill in shifting the resonance of a refrain by differently contextualizing it in successive stanzas. In "Slip Away" the phrase itself slips through a register of different implications, so that mention of the departure of the Factory habitúes, the departure of Warhol's creativity, his leaving the factory, and even his leaving this life, each echoes the implications of all the others. Even if you can't hear the echoes of one of Reed's most poignant songs, "Street Hassle," which employs the same refrain and in which love and death are similarly juxtaposed, "Slip Away" (and the structurally similar "Nobody but You") still accepts moral ambiguity, accepts the interdependence of creativity and danger, in a way which recalls Reed's best and most characteristic writing but which is anomalous in 'Drella.

The reading of Warhol's life and death was, of course, in competition with the myriad other contemporary versions; in interviews Reed cited the "little tinkertoy society plaything" he imputed to Ultra Violet's book[21] and also to Warhol's own diaries, whose gossipy image he attributed to Pat Hackett's editorializing.[22] But 'Drella's attempted refutation of these and the sanitized Warhol it promotes at the expense of the social underground Reed had celebrated in his Velvets songs also correspond to emerging one-dimensionality in his own vision and career. Indeed, the critically acclaimed New York, the album before 'Drella and named by Rolling Stone as one of the twenty best albums of the eighties, contains in embryonic form the same polarity. The last song on the album, "Dime Store Mystery," dedicated to "Andy-honey," associates Warhol with Christ, envisioning his death as a "Last Temptation," while outside, the city screams and shrieks. The previous songs on the album detail the city's travails—ten-year-old cop-killers, drug dealers, AIDS victims, polluters, racists, and so on, ad infinitum—in a vitriolic outrage that, although punctuated by moments of macabre grotesqueness, is generally a one-dimensional rant. Of course, the social meaning of drugs had changed in the intervening twenty years, and AIDS had totally transformed gay culture. Still, Reed's social vision can no longer recognize the contradictory energies of city life or celebrate its forbidden pleasures—let alone sympathize with the urban poor—and so sustain the poised irony, the "negative capability" of his early work. On the other hand, as if he had worked through his alienation, on *Magic and Loss* (the album after *'Drella*), he regained the dialectical vision and musical sophistication of his greatest songs. Again the album was a requiem for dead friends, but this time it triumphed because Reed was able to identify with them, even with the disease that killed them, and with the measure of victory they gain over it.

SCENES FROM THE LIFE OF ANDY WARHOL
■

Jonas Mekas was an early, strong, and loyal champion of Warhol's filmmaking,[23] and the aggressive amateurishness and cinema verité component in Warhol's early films, as well as his obsessive photography of his everyday life, undoubtedly influenced Mekas's own diary filmmaking, which crystallized as his mature mode with *Walden* in 1968. Assembling footage shot between 1965 and 1982, most of which had already been used in previous diary films, *Scenes from the Life of Andy Warhol* was completed in June 1990 and shown at the New York Film Festival that year. It was the first of Mekas's films to be so honored, a fact that undoubtedly reflects its use of Warhol's name, which in turn reflects the potential for greater public interest in his work allowed by Mekas's shift from autobiography to biography.[24] But in this case a number of factors cloud the distinction between the two modes, generating tensions that destabilize the film, in some ways adding to its interest and in others crucially fracturing it. First, the similarities between Warhol's life and Mekas's—both were essentially working-class immigrants from preindustrial Eastern Europe seeking to make their lives as artists in postmodern America—facilitated Mekas's practice of defining himself through his imaging of other people to make his biography of Warhol an extremely proximate scenario for his own autobiography. Second, the material conditions of photography, which typically traces the co-presence of subject and object, make Mekas's footage of Warhol or anyone else equally germane to his own autobiography and to his biography of them. Because the two modes so closely inform each other, in *Andy Warhol* qualities relating to the biography tend to spill over into the activity of the biographer and vice versa. *Andy Warhol* is organized in three main phases, the first of which, the mid-1960s New York scenes, begins with Warhol's appearance at the annual banquet of the New York Society for Clinical Psychiatry (the first time he appeared with the Velvets).[25] It continues with the Exploding Plastic Inevitable at the Dom, Warhol's 1971 Whitney show, and other New York events, involving culturati such as Allen Ginsberg, Ed Sanders, Barbara Rubin, and George Macunias. The second phase, an extended section, dominates the film, showing summer scenes at and around Warhol's house at Montauk, Long Island, when it was rented by Lee Radziwill. These scenes feature visits by Warhol and Mekas (who for a time had been employed to teach filmmaking to one of the Kennedy children) and, at great length, the Radziwill sisters and various Kennedy offspring. They are pictured at home and on the beach, often engaged in games of one kind or another, and often photographing each other with both still and movie cameras. In the final phase, Mekas returns to the city and Warhol's studio portrait work, ending with a reprise of and lament for the Montauk scenes. At this point, the virtually continuous soundtrack of the Velvet Underground, recorded live at the Dom, gives way to choral singing from Warhol's funeral service. Typically, Warhol is only peripherally glimpsed in the footage of the 1960s, and although he does appear in more extended shots in the Montauk scenes, he is hardly as prominent as the Radziwill sisters and their children. The net amount of Warhol footage is thus quite small, and while some of the material possesses historical and tabloid kinds of interest, the overall account of Warhol's life is skeletal and schematic.

Like Reed, Mekas proposes a myth of Warhol's life and an integral role for himself at its apogee, but he situates that myth very differently. For Reed, it begins as Warhol leaves Pittsburgh, finds its fulfillment and tragic climax in the artwork and underground society of the original Factory in the sixties, and fades away thereafter. For Mekas, it begins in the late sixties, and while the musical soundtrack continues to invoke this period, the visuals synecdochically condense the era of Warhol's great film work and both this and the later phase of his art practice, leaving them essentially as frames for the Montauk summers of content with the American aristocracy and its scions. The period of this social elevation appears as the high point of Warhol's life and of Mekas's. As an elegy, the film mourns Mekas's loss of Warhol, but it figures that loss as their common loss of (in the words of a late intertitle) "The Summers of Montauk [which] Were Full of Happiness and Sun," summers exemplified in the person of Lee Radziwill, to whom the film is dedicated. The differences between Reed's myth and Mekas's reflect historical fact—Reed's separation from Warhol in the seventies and Mekas's limited association with him—and also presumably the material fact of the footage Mekas happened to have shot and preserved. But Mekas's vision of Warhol's life and his own role in it is responsive, not so much to the raw biographical material as to the structure and motifs of Mekas's previous autobiographical films.

In the great diary films that followed *Walden,* the master myth of loss that informs all Mekas's works had been successively deployed in the various instances of his Lithuanian homeland, of his mother, and of various friends. When they were found, compensations always centered on the community of close friends and the practice of filmmaking, with the summary figure for them, filmically written, being the rediscovery of both biological family and rural homeland in the community of underground filmmakers in urban Manhattan. These compensations were justified by Mekas's own practice as a filmmaker: by his signature shooting style of somatically attuned single-framing, by the intricate editing of sound and image, by the formal rigor and sophistication of the films themselves, and by his negotiation of a domestic film practice into an anti-industrial, oppositional public sphere.[26] The originary and summary figure is Mekas's discovery/recognition of his own film work and the community of filmmakers in his visit to the Brakhages that is the crisis of *Walden.*

The elements of the master myth—the same seasonal cycles and city-country oppositions, and the same centrality of the filmmaking community—are present in *Andy Warhol,* and sometimes they register real tensions; a late interlude at the Union Square farmers' market, for example, is rewritten as Lithuania in the same way that Mekas generally succeeds in rewriting Manhattan as his homeland. But by and large they appear in a simplified, attenuated form, casually subsumed in the apotheosis of the Montauk celebrities. The ease with which Mekas finds himself at home with Warhol and the Radziwill/Kennedys reveals none of the struggles, biographical and filmic alike, that give the moments of redemption in the earlier films their immense resonance. Here, redemption is marbled with wish fulfillment, and its implications in terms of Warhol's relation to Mekas as a friend and filmmaker are cavalierly overlooked.[27] The fantasy projection involved in Mekas's inscription of himself in this circle—itself a parody of the role of the Brakhages in *Walden*—is carried even further in the Montauk home movies, not in the representation of Mekas's friendship with the Radziwills per se but in the form of its narrative inscription: Warhol and Mekas together take the place of the missing patriarchs to complement the Radziwill sisters as stand-in fathers to the Kennedy boys. In the coda, Mekas even goes so far as to rhyme Lee Radziwill with the lonely figure of Hollis Melton, his own wife and subsequently mother of their two children, yet a person who is almost entirely excluded from his autobiographical films.

Again these self-projections both reflect and interrupt the trajectory of the oeuvre as a whole, specifically with respect to the editing of a thematized narrative from the raw footage and to the initial shooting style. Mekas's immediately previous major work, *He Stands in a Desert Counting the Seconds of His Life,* had begun the separation of public from private, the refusal of which had made the previous diaries so powerful a critique of the reification of modern life.[28] And in it an unbalancing fascination with the really rich and famous became apparent in an obsessive return to extended shots of the figure of John Lennon. But *Scenes* takes both propensities to new extremes. Much of it (including the footage of Warhol's 1971 Whitney show and of his studio portraiture, a good deal of the Montauk scenes and the Union Square sequence mentioned above) is drawn from *He Stands,* with the exclusion of the remainder, especially of the scenes of other underground artists and of Mekas's own family, effectively supplanting the earlier film's contemplation of Mekas's life across the various social groupings within the New York avant-garde as a whole by the exclusive focus on the Warhol/Radziwill microcosm. And while his signature camera style informs and energizes the New York sequences, when he is photographing the Montauk aristocrats, he photographs them in long takes. This is the same way that they, in their interpolated shots of him, photograph him—the way only rich people can afford to shoot film! At these moments, the intensity of his characteristic mode of perception is sacrificed for an extended, flaccid gaze that, in the context of his work as a whole, is as profligate in its expenditure of film stock and empty of visual incident as *Empire*—a film that only Warhol, of all the underground filmmakers, could have made because only he could afford to do so.

At issue here is not Mekas's personal desire to place himself at the apogee of American society in real life but rather that fantasy's interruption of an aesthetic predicated on quite opposite principles. For Warhol, such social aspirations were the logical extension of his art, its raison d'être. But Mekas's whole career has been premised on a radically democratic cinema as the means to populist social renewal. His has been one of the handful of definitive instances of an *arte povera,* an "imperfect cinema" where financial privation, which made every foot of stock a crisis, has been turned to community empowerment, where the mundane has been turned into an explosive visual adventure. Here, the social aspirations and aesthetic strategies associated with Warhol have occupied Mekas's film about him; the discourse of the object has colonized the discourse of the subject.

Warhol claimed to be a mirror, as did the Velvets after him, "Reflect[ing] who you are / In case you don't know" ("I'll Be Your Mirror"). But as we know, the mirror stage always also entails misrecognition, an idealization of an image superior to the self's own experience of disunity and incompletion. Likewise, in these two cases, the discovery of a self-image in the portrait, of an autobiography inhabiting the biography, also involved an unconscious projection—of guilt in the one case and desire in the other. It is a mechanism that all of us who find ourselves in Warhol do well to respect.

NOTES

My thanks to Briana Cassidy, Callie Angell, and Paul Arthur for assistance in the preparation of this essay.

1   *W. H. Auden: Collected Poems,* ed. Edward Mendelson (New York: Random, 1976).

2   *Award Presentation to Andy Warhol* (Jonas Mekas, 1964) was photographed by Jonas Mekas and Gregory Markopoulos. The citation of the award in *Film Culture* proposed that Warhol was "taking cinema back to its origins, to the days of Lumière, for a rejuvenation and a cleansing." "Sixth Independent Film Award," *Film Culture* (1964): 33, 1.

3   James Stoller, cited in *Film-Makers' Cooperative Catalogue No. 7* (New York: Film-Makers' Cooperative, 1989), p. 361.

4   Thomas Crowe, "Saturday Disasters: Trace and Reference in Early Warhol," *Art in America* (May, 1987): 133.

5   See, for example, this from a formula detective novel: as the heroine is processed into jail, she notes: "We waited while the cameras inspected us. I've seen the big console where the MCR operator sits, surrounded by black-and-white monitors showing the equivalent of twelve totally boring Andy Warhol movies simultaneously." In Sue Grafton, *"H" Is for Homicide* (New York: Fawcett Crest, 1992), p. 105.

6   *Blitz,* September 1989. The essays inside give informed accounts of Warhol's life and work and include several sidebars useful for Warhol tourists, for example, a map of Manhattan marking sites important to him.

7   Bruce D. Kurtz, *Haring, Warhol, Disney* (Munich: Prestel Verlag, 1992), p. 149.

8   The interpenetration of the artwork and the personality of the artist is figured in Warhol's ongoing negotiation with his own image in the self-portraits he made throughout his life. These are unusual in the genre in consistently showing him not at work or in the company of his models but always alone in a photo-derived head shot in which he stares directly into the camera. Apart from the implication of gayness in the sixties and an increasingly articulate and fearful morbidity after the mid-seventies, nothing anchors or explains the subjectivity; he simply encounters his own gaze in an endless catoptric circularity—the kind of emptiness that would move him, however wrongly, to claim, "I don't think I have an image, favorable or unfavorable." Kynaston McShine, ed., *Andy Warhol: A Retrospective* (New York: Museum of Modern Art, 1989), p. 466.

9   A similar instance is Keith Haring's *Andy Mouse* prints (1986), which have been specifically recognized as "idealized self-portraits." In Kurtz, *Haring, Warhol, Disney,* p. 149.

10 My attention was drawn to this by Thomas Lawson's discussion of it in "Collective Portrait," in *Andy Warhol,* ed. McShine, p. 450.

11 I have listed his appearances in advertisements in "The Unsecret Life: A Warhol Advertisement," *October* 56 (Spring 1991): 23–24. In a bizarre culmination of this utility, in 1988 it was reported that Lewis Allen, a Broadway producer, was constructing a computerized Warhol robot that "could have a highly lucrative career as a commercial spokesman." In Meg Cox, "Warhol Is Dead, but He Still Puts on a Profitable Show," *Wall Street Journal,* April 18, 1988, pp. 1 and 15.

12 Commissioned jointly by Arts at St. Ann's (church) and the Brooklyn Academy of Music (BAM), *Songs for 'Drella* was performed on January 8, 1989, at the former and for five nights at the latter beginning November 29, 1989. Initially a mixed-media presentation accompanied by Jerome Stein's slide projections primarily of Warhol's silkscreens, it was released as a record in 1990 and as a video of the BAM performance. Either an abbreviation for Cinderella or a combination of it and Dracula, "Drella" was a nickname for Warhol.

13 In what follows, I largely omit John Cale's role. The songs are credited to Reed and Cale jointly, though Cale has indicated that Reed "did most of the work." My omission of reference to Cale's work outside his collaborations with Reed should not be taken as a denigration of his importance in the Velvet Underground. Indeed, the tension between the conservatory-trained and Fluxus-influenced Cale and the streetwise, possibly more

Pop oriented Reed is key to the high-art/low-art dialectics the Velvets so powerfully mobilized.

14 Mary Harron, "The Lost History of the Velvet Underground," *New Musical Express* (London) (25 April 1981): 27–30, 53. Jonas Mekas, *Movie Journal: The Rise of the New American Cinema, 1959–1971* (New York: Collier, 1972).

15 Bill Flanagan, "White Light White Heat: Lou Reed and John Cale Remember Andy Warhol," *Musician* 126 (April 1989): 74–80.

16 David E. James, *Allegories of Cinema: American Film in the Sixties* (Princeton: Princeton University Press, 1989).

17 Dave Thompson, *Beyond the Velvet Underground* (London: Omnibus Press, 1989).

18 Ellen Willis distinguishes between "art rock," which she correctly disparages as a failed attempt, beginning in the mid-sixties, to " 'improve' rock-and-roll by making it palatable to the upper middle class" with greater lyrical or musical sophistication, and "rock-and-roll art," which used "the basic formal canons of rock-and-roll as material (much as pop artists used mass art in general) . . . refining, elaborating, playing off that material." Willis attributes the point of origin in the Velvets version of the latter to Lou Reed, who "made a fateful connection between two seemingly disparate ideas—the rock-and-roller as self-conscious aesthete and the rock-and-roller as self-conscious punk." Willis, *Beginning to See the Light* (Hanover, N.H.: Wesleyan University Press, 1992), pp. 111–112.

19 Andy Warhol, *The Andy Warhol Diaries*, ed. Pat Hackett (New York: Warner Books, 1989).

20 Hence Lester Bangs's distinction between the Velvets and Reed's subsequent parody of their achievements: "Lou Reed is the guy that gave dignity and poetry and rock'n'roll to smack, speed, homosexuality, sadomasochism, murder, misogyny, stumblebum passivity, and suicide, and then proceeded to belie all his achievements and return to the mire by turning the whole thing into a monumental bad joke." *Psychotic Reactions and Carburetor Dung* (New York: Vintage, 1988), pp. 170–171.

21 Flanagan, "White Light White Heat," p. 77.

22 In the last song, "Hello It's Me," he asserts, "Your Diaries are not a worthy epitaph."

23 Even before it was complete, Mekas celebrated *Sleep* in his *Village Voice* column, "Movie Journal" as a "simple movie that will push Andy Warhol . . . further than we were before" (in Mekas, *Movie Journal,* p. 97) and saluted subsequent works; for example, he ranked *Chelsea Girls* with *Birth of a Nation* and the works of James Joyce. His "Notes after Reseeing the Movies of Andy Warhol" (in John Coplans, ed., *Andy Warhol* [New York: New York Graphic Society, n.d.] was one of the first extended considerations of Warhol's work. Mekas also photographed *Empire*.

24 Its subtitle, *Anthropological Sketches,* does suggest a break with Mekas's films since *Walden* (1968), almost all of which were part of a series collectively designated *Diaries, Notes, and Sketches.* But it was followed in 1991 by *Scenes from the Life of George Maciunas,* a consideration of which is necessary to any fully adequate discussion of *Andy Warhol* and especially to the inscribed autobiographical element. Again the subject is a working-class immigrant from Europe, whose art involves the possibility of a contemporary reenactment of dada, though in quite different terms. Maciunas developed an essentially absurdist/conceptual

aesthetic akin to Warhol's in several ways, but he deployed it against, not on behalf of, consumer society. *George Maciunas* and *Andy Warhol* together thus represent a schematic allegorization of the tensions in Mekas's own life between the approach to and avoidance of success in the terms of capitalist America.

25   The combined assault of the Velvet Underground and Warhol's films routed most of the guests; the event, including Mekas's filming of it, is described in David Bourdon's *Warhol* (New York: Harry N. Abrams, 1989), p. 221.

26   Paul Arthur's account of the political dimension of Mekas's vision of *communitas* is definitive; see his "Routines of Emancipation: Alternative Cinema in the Ideology and Politics of the Sixties," in *To Free the Cinema: Jonas Mekas and the New York Underground,* ed. David E. James (Princeton: Princeton University Press, 1992).

27   Warhol's reciprocation of Mekas's support and friendship had been very erratic. He withdrew all his films from the Film-Makers' Cooperative when they became financially viable, for example; he gave no public support to the alternative institutions to which Mekas devoted his life; and in his diaries, the only times he mentions Mekas is to ridicule him. His attitude toward Mekas in the 1970s and 1980s probably reflects his discomfort with his own early films and his refusal to circulate them. One of the most puzzling entries in the diaries, dated 13 September 1984, reads: "Cabbed to 52nd and Lex to meet Jonas Mekas and Timmy Forbes at Nippon (cab $6). They're trying to raise money for the Filmmaker's Co-op. I asked Jonas if he'd seen any movies lately and he said no, that he was just trying to raise money. And really (*laughs*) he *never* saw movies. He never did." See Warhol, *Diaries,* pp. 598–599. Ironically, the next day's entry records Reed's snubbing of Warhol to which 'Drella's "A Dream" refers.

28   The cast list concludes "friends, such as John Lennon, Jackie Onassis, Lee Radziwill, John Kennedy Jr. & Caroline, Tina and Anthony Radziwill, Peter Beard, Andy Warhol, Richard Foreman, P. Adams Sitney, Yoko Ono, Raimund Abraham, Herman Nitsch, Allen Ginsberg, George Maciunas," cited in *Film-Makers' Cooperative Catalogue,* p. 366.

THOMAS WAUGH
Cockteaser

During this period [1969] I took thousands of Polaroids of genitals. Whenever somebody came up to the Factory, no matter how straight looking he was, I'd ask him to take his pants off so I could photograph his cock and balls. It was surprising who'd let me and who wouldn't.

Personally, I loved porno and I bought lots of it all the time—the real dirty, exciting stuff. All you had to do was figure out what turned you on, and then just buy the dirty magazines and movie prints that are right for you, the way you'd go for the right pills or the right cans of food. (I was so avid for porno that on my first time out of the house after the shooting I went straight to 42nd Street and checked out the peep shows with Vera Cruise and restocked on dirty magazines.)—Andy Warhol, POPism[1]

INTRODUCTION
■

My title is inspired by an offscreen line from the 1964 Warhol film *Harlot,* "There's a cockteaser around here."[2] This felicitously ambiguous line sums up for me a number of important areas of inquiry concerning Warhol the filmmaker: his elaboration of eroticism as a primary discourse of his films, his situation within American gay male culture as it lurched toward Stonewall, and his relation to the gay audience of the 1960s.[3] Of course, my title also both describes and pays homage to Warhol's bluntly descriptive, scabrous, and efficient film titles like *Kiss, Eat, Blow Job, Couch, Harlot, Fuck, Flesh, Trash,* and *Heat.* Like a true pornographer, Warhol coined titles that served to lure prospective audiences with a promise, or more nearly a *tease.*

Since Warhol's 1987 death, we have left behind the formalist disavowals of the primacy of sexual representation in the Warhol oeuvre. Critics of the modernist, postmodernist, or heterosexist persuasion routinely failed to mention that the male sleeper in *Sleep* (1963) is nude, and somehow forgot that *Haircut* (1963) and *Horse* (1965) include a slow male striptease and a cowboy strip poker game, respectively. This kind of criticism no longer occupies the whole stage.[4] The post-1987 literature has begun a frank, intelligent, and materialist questioning of Warhol's sexual address in his films and of his relation to erotic and specifically homoerotic mythologies of his day.[5]

I attempt to extend this work by two means. In the first part of this essay, I discuss the Warhol films in the context of a continuum of the gay-male imaginary, a long tradition of narrative fiction principally within the art cinema. In the second part, I reconstruct and reclaim Warhol's gay audience of the 1960s. I will refer primarily to the later narrative works that began with *My Hustler* (1965), though the patterns seem to be borne out as well by the earlier homoerotic works the more they become accessible.

THE QUEEN AND THE HUSTLER
■

De was such good friends with both Jasper and Bob that I figured he could probably tell me something I'd been wanting to know for a long time: why didn't they like me? Every time I saw them, they cut me dead. So when the waiter brought the brandy, I finally popped the question, and De said, "Okay, Andy, if you really want to hear it straight, I'll lay it out for you. You're too swish, and that upsets them." . . .

Finally I just said something stupid: "I know plenty of painters who are more swish than me." And De said, "Yes, Andy, there are others who are more swish—and less talented—and still others who are less swish and just as talented, but the major painters try to look straight; you play up the swish—it's like an armor with you."

. . . As for the "swish" thing, I'd always had a lot of fun with that—just watching the expressions on people's faces. You'd have to have seen the way all the Abstract Expressionist painters carried themselves and the kinds of images they cultivated, to understand how shocked people were to see a painter coming on swish. I certainly wasn't a butch kind of guy by nature, but I must admit, I went out of my way to play up the other extreme. —Andy Warhol, *POPism*[6]

In this section, I will discuss Warhol's films as they engage a gay-male imaginary. In particular, I am interested in the ways that Warhol revises the queen-hustler paradigm as it is outlined by Richard Dyer, who has shown how these two strange bedfellows emerged as primary icons of Euro-American gay-male culture in the 1960s.[7] This pair of opposites dominated both the fiction writing and the underground cinema of that transitional decade, from John Rechy to Jack Smith, with Warhol being one of many artists, high and low, engaged in this iconography. I have argued elsewhere that the dualism of queen and hustler is in fact simply an incarnation of a fundamental subject-object split that extends through the entire corpus of gay cinematic narrative from 1916 to the present.[8] Same-sex love does not preclude dynamics of difference from determining the gay male cinematic sensibility. Far from it: we love the Other with a tenacity matched only within the protocols of heterosexuality.[9]

With Warhol, as with most other pre-Stonewall filmmakers, the queen type is the gay subject par excellence, as if mirroring Andy himself, presiding swishingly over the Factory in that controlling den-mother role inherited from earlier urban gay subcultures ("swish" being a word that was part of Warhol's own image of himself and one that recurs with regularity in the Warhol literature). In general, the Warhol queen must be read to encompass not only the drag queens and transsexuals among the Factory superstars, from Mario Montez to Holly Woodlawn, but also the swishy gay men from Taylor Mead to *My Hustler's* Ed Hood.

The queen category must also usually include, if a brief digression is to be allowed, the biological heterosexual women in the corpus—or as Valerie Solanas put it, Warhol's "female females."[10] I have yet to be convinced how any of them, with the possible exception of Edie Sedgwick, Viva, and a few of the *Chelsea* girls in their particularly vaginal roles,[11] are constructed dramat-ically as autonomous women characters. On the whole, Warhol women are conceived and operate with a specific gay male orality, competing with the biological men, both transpeople and swishes, for the hustler, the butch/trade objects of their desire. So much for the cinema verité glasses through which some sixties onlookers saw the Warhol menagerie. My critical reading of fictional females as subjects of gay male desire may well echo earlier homophobic unmaskings of the heroines of Tennessee Williams, Edward Albee, and George Cukor.[12] Yet a simple recognition of the fundamentally misogynist setting in which Viva (*Cowboys*), Jane Forth (*Trash*), and Terri the GoGo Dancer (*Flesh*) were induced to improvise rape and seduction fantasies and other hysterical histrionics need not have a homophobic color in itself. I think this recognition is what Parker Tyler, Warhol the filmmaker's most reliable contemporary gay critic, was getting at when he dismissed Viva as a parody of a heterosexual woman;[13] it is also, I think, the problem Bryan Bruce and Gloria Berlin are trying to solve in exploring the nasty "fag hag" category.[14] Audience dynamics around women characters are also murky: to what extent does the historic gay audience pattern of intense identification with screen women, whether tinsel goddesses or Warhol superstars, undercut gender entirely as a useful category in thinking about audiences and their reception of film? Warhol's women, and in particular their jokey articulation of rape in *Cowboys, Flesh,* and *Trash* (not to mention similar aspects of Jack Smith's *Flaming Creatures*), need delicate handling. Because gender is such an unstable category in the films, it seems more productive to read Warhol's females as "queens" rather than as "women"; the recognition of this gender instability should be a starting point for sifting through two tricky issues at once—the misogynous elements in the films *and* the homophobia in the traditional critical equation of gay culture with misogyny. Aside from these provisional conclusions, Warhol's women are a topic for extended further study.

If the queen is effeminate, intense, decked out, oral, desirous, and, to use Tyler's 1960s word, "offbeat," the hustler—or "trade"—is butch, laid-back, stripped bare, taciturn, ambivalent, and "straight." The queen looks, the trade is looked at;[15] she verbalizes and he is spoken to or about. The trade's iconographical manifestations include a few subtypes, from the biker, the muscleboy, the gigolo, and the cowboy to the surfer (*Lonesome Cowboys*), but the variations are in the getup, not in substance or style. As Dyer explains, the trade is as preoccupied with the trappings of masculinity as the queen is with those of femininity, and for both it is this involvement in the paradoxes of surface and authenticity that makes them ideal Warhol icons. Together, the queen and the trade echo the other subject-object pairings of the gay narrative tradition: the dandy and ephebe, the bourgeois and prole, the mentor and protégé, the artist and model, the "dirty old john" and the adolescent, the European and the "Oriental," and so on.

It is not simply the parallel emergence of queen and trade but their dialogue, interaction, and confrontation that constitute the key dynamic of the 1960s. They interact literally within the texts of the films, where the queen incessantly looks at, speaks to, and touches the trade, who grudgingly, unresponsively assents. Queen and trade interact contextually as well, namely, on the screen of the embryonic gay exhibition spaces of the late sixties, where, as we shall see momentarily, short films of camp queen performance customarily ran alongside trade-flavored beefcake. Queen and trade encounter each other also in the gay urban geography of that period, where the tenderloin of the sex and drugs market overlapped with an increasingly self-confident gay ghetto with its own emergent repertory of new types (the most prophetic and visible new type being the clone consumer). It is ironic that during a decade then drawing to a close, when the organized gay movement was notable for its agenda of narrow neckties and discreet respectability, the two marginal and disreputable types of queen and trade were so conspicuously present and interacting within gay culture.

Interacting yes, fucking no. The queen or gay subject almost never, in Warhol or in any other gay narrative, consummates his desire as he would within the master narrative of the hetero-patriarchal cinema, at the wheel of the conjugal drive. Queen and trade remain separate, never coming together; the cocksucker stays perpetually offscreen in *Blow Job* and everywhere else, and the duality of subject and object is entrenched (see figure 1). In this, Warhol matches the pattern on other layers of the cultural hierarchy. Remember, for example, Dick Fontaine, the irrepressible Los Angeles beefcake entrepreneur, who in the late sixties attempted to move his mail-order movie business onto the new public gay screens, unleashed Glory Holedon and other queenly subjects into his narrative universe of trade bodybuilders. Glory and the other queens drool a kind of lust that makes New Yorkers like Mario Montez and Francis Francine seem cerebral and sophisticated. Seeing Warhol side by side with such work confirms his place within a 1960s continuum of gay imagery that had at its base a structure of familiar dualities, not only queen and trade, but also mind and body, voice and image.

This last duality of voice and image, the separation of soundtrack from picture, is especially symptomatic. The voice of the gay subject commonly plays off or over the image of the trade on the screen; it is technically detached, seldom emanating from within the same cinematic space as the body of the trade. The offscreen voices of Warhol's *Beauty # 2* and *Harlot* have frequently been discussed; they resurface even in *Cowboys'* strangely wild soundtrack (for example, Taylor Mead's voice points out "look at him" over surfer Tom Hompertz's close-up as the eponymous cowboys arrive in town),

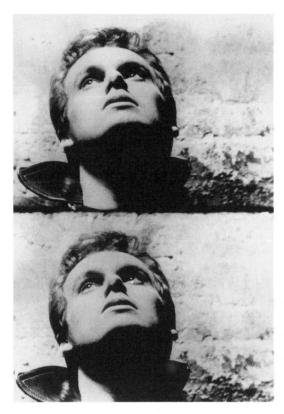

Figure 1. "The duality of subject and object, look but don't fuck." Frame sequence from *Blow Job* (1964).

but they are most striking in *My Hustler*'s first half. From his Fire Island deck, an offscreen Ed Hood, hustler service customer, watches Paul America, his blonde trade employee, frolic onscreen with the speaker's female rival:

> Oh my God, they're going off together. Oh hell, what is that witch doing? . . . Aren't they happy splashing around in the sea. You see it's all so sexless with women. Fantastic. She's got her three-inch claws hooked into him.
>
> . . . [to another rival, the Sugar Plum Fairy] What do you think about his body, for example? Would you like to see what's in that bathing suit? . . . Yes, he's very well hung. Sometimes, the big butch ones aren't— they're very deceptive. . . .[16]

Compare Dick Fontaine's similar use of offscreen voice in a characteristic film. In *Hot Harem,* Glory Holedon comments offscreen on her role as a

Baghdad queen raiding the palace stud harem and taking a Mario Montez–style banana break:

> Oh she's started this banana now. Watch. She just loves to stick round things down her throat.
>
> Didn't I tell you? She swallows seeds and all, too. She says that tastes so good, I'll have another bite of it. . . .
>
> . . . Oh look at her! I knew she was around somewhere. She's got those lips going. Whenever she sees a man. Oh isn't she trashy. Watch her snatch this one right away from her husband. She knows a pretty one when she sees it.

Voice-image separation extends as well, of course, to the post-Stonewall canon of homoerotic narrative cinema—from Curt McDowell's *Loads* to *The Law of Desire, Caravaggio, Looking for Langston,* and several of Gus Van Sant's works, not to mention everything by 1980s Manhattan cable porncaster Rick X and his L.A. video counterpart "Old Reliable." The popularity of this technique, I would argue, reflects more than its logistic and economic suitability for artisanal and underfinanced industrial cinema. The voice-off or voice-over, emitting from the body of author-subject as he/she retreats once more behind the camera or mixing console, may articulate a level of retroactive self-reflexivity or simply a sportcasting-style simultaneity, descriptive or directive, diegetic or extra-diegetic. This dynamic is at the center of the erotic give-and-take, the tease of the viewer's response by the controlling yet unpossessing author. The apocalyptic moment in the history of the device comes when the forever offscreen Rick X bangs his microphone against his unzipped scrotum, replicating the frenzy of unconsummated desire for both gay subject and gay spectator. Image-sound separation thus cements the irreconcilability of subject and object, exacerbates the tension of the teasing relationship of look-but-don't-touch, touch-but-don't-possess, appear-but-don't-speak, speak-but-don't-appear, and so forth.

From the structure of sound to that of narrative closure, gay narratives for the most part posit separation, loss, displacement, endless deferral, and open endings. *Lonesome Cowboys* and *My Hustler* deserve a special look in this regard, for they are at once the two most conventionally structured films in the Warhol corpus and offer the most struggle with the patterns of image-sound and subject-object separation. In the former, the climactic fuck scene between Viva and Tom Hompertz, deliriously prurient and distended, is a case in point. Somehow managing to get the nonverbal Tom's pants off through a paraphrase of the Sermon on the Mount, the run-on heroine sings a Latin benediction and declares ominously that she is ready to die after such great sex. When she asks Tom for the same union in death that they have barely had in sex, there is no response. But the scene's brilliant play with the pattern of deferred desire unfolds alongside other more conciliatory narrative moments where the cowboys flirtatiously dance together (Dallesandro actually does a swish chorus kick and tenderly touches another man's chest) and Eric Emerson's semi-butch cowboy entices surfer Tom off to California. With their aura of active trade desire and romantic closure, no matter how tongue-in-cheek, the last scenes unsettle if not overturn the pattern of subject-object split.

My Hustler gives a more focused yet still subtle attack on the duality of queen and trade. There is a critical moment when the older hustler, the Sugar Plum Fairy, asserts his desire for Paul America and the latter seems to reciprocate—at least according to some sustainable readings of the film, including Parker Tyler's. The pattern is problematized at that moment, as much through nonverbal communication as through the men's verbal sparring (for example, what R. Bruce Brasell calls Paul's "ecstasy" as his partner rubs his nipples). Henceforth, the constellation of look, tease, and consummation enters what I would call a post-Stonewall regime of flux. Tyler instinctively recognized that something important and much more "palatable" was going on with this twist in *My Hustler,* rechristening it *The Hustler Hustled,* reading a gay conjugal closure into the apparently open ending and seeing it as a corrective to the image of impotence attached to the hustler in the "Morrissey" films (*Flesh* and *Cowboys* were actually released about the same time, hard on the heels of *Hustler*'s commercial run on 42nd Street).[17] Tyler may have been influenced by ambiguous *Blow Job*–style "orgy footage" that was apparently added to the end of *Hustler* for the theatrical run, but his point stands. He certainly is right about Morrissey, who not only injected the marker of impotence and a questionable moralism into the Joe trilogy but also restored the inseparability of subject and object, queen and trade, as a basic dramatic and moral principle.

Warhol then must be situated within a continuum inaugurated in the teens and twenties by Mauritz Stiller and Jean Cocteau, a trajectory of fluctuating relations between gay (or protogay) subject and object.[18] It is a continuum in which Warhol, as Stephen Tropiano puts it, "blaze[s] the trail for John Waters, Rainer Fassbinder and Pedro Almodóvar,"[19] post-Stonewall filmmakers who permanently reverse and transform the subject-object inertia of earlier generations of gay narrative. I have already hinted that Warhol also blazed the trail for more disreputable artists than even John Waters, not only Rick X ("How to Seduce a Preppie") but also the pioneer journalist-editor Boyd McDonald (*Straight to Hell*), both arbiters of a rich New York–based folk porno countertradition of the 1970s, 1980s, and 1990s, whose erotics of documentary minutiae have much in common with Warhol's cinema verité voyeurism of the 1960s. It is within this framework of border crossing between art and sleaze that I would like to probe Warhol's dialogue with his gay male audience of the 1960s.

FULL HONORS FOR MALE NUDITY

◼

My first experience with public sex was in an Air Force base library. I was 12 years old at the time. I had finished reading the L.A. Free Press, which was quite a liberal publication for an A.F. library. I noticed that while reading the review of Warhol's "Lonesome Cowboys" that my groin was cramped, warm, and slightly damp. I remembered the description of the piss scene in the film, and after reading it I had to relieve the hardness in my pants. So I went to the head and sat on the toilet planning to jerk off.—Anonymous first-person account, *Straight to Hell*[20]

In this section I explore Warhol's relationship to his gay male audiences. First, I discuss the ways that censorship and film industry pressures shaped the *form* of Warhol's cockteaser-like address to his gay male audiences. And, second, by drawing on a number of sources—from mainstream and gay media reviews to film criticism to advertising and anecdotal recollections—I undertake to advance the historical work of reconstructing Warhol's gay male audience.

But, first, my p.c. students would insist that I disclose how my spectatorship is constituted, and accordingly I must declare that—white, yuppie, intellectual baby boomer that I am—I am turned on. Joe's flesh and Andy's cowboys premiered on the screen in the same 1968 that I premiered, serene as Viva, amid an alien YMCA room. My erotic sensibility is stamped by the erotic tease of the eve-of-Stonewall gay mags that Joe and Louis are reading in *Flesh* (I never saw the movie equivalents at the time but might as well have and I

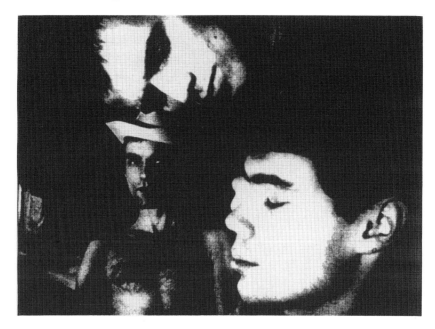

Figure 2. "Sexually and aesthetically, the hottest film ever made."
Frame enlargement from *Haircut (No. 1)* (1967).

now tumesce as if in a time warp at the sight of those hippie cowboys wrestling in their long johns). Around Warhol, the master of *ars erotica,* a certain amount of denial still exists: I understand how a nongay critic like Peter Gidal found *Lonesome Cowboys* "not erotic,"[21] but it is beyond my comprehension how Mark Finch could see the film as a limp refusal to be porn and the exquisitely tortuous opening scene as neither simulated sex nor parody thereof, all visual and empirical evidence to the contrary.[22] Even Dyer seems to give short shrift to the erotic rhetorics of Warhol's work. Different strokes, of course, but the infinite variability and relativity of gay male erotic response does not let us off the hook. The eroticism of the films as experienced by Warhol's audience must be addressed head on; the turn-ons and the tease must be reclaimed as an integral and valid dynamic of our cultural and political history.

Tropiano is one critic to evoke Warhol the cockteaser, referring to "the thrill without the danger, the excitation without the release," the "[titillation of] the spectator with the possibility and threat of explicit homoerotic activity but . . . the position of merely teasing the viewer without any real fulfillment of those expectations."[23] Echoing this, Gary Indiana argues that "Warhol's films are gloriously erotic [but] sexual pleasure is immanent, a possibility."[24] Bruce Brasell calls the filmmaker's sexual address "tantalizing." Focusing on the key work *My Hustler,* he argues that the spectator is not only aroused by the film but symbolically solicited as well: "In the second half of the film, we are positioned as participants in a cruise—as Joe cruises Paul, he also begins to cruise me/you/us. He eyes us through the bathroom mirror, inviting us to eye him back. To continue to look at him on the screen is thus to become implicated in the process of cruising." Amy Taubin is one of the few heterosexual women to touch on this aspect of Warhol's films—indeed on *any* aspect. Her original reaction to *Haircut* (1963) had been "that sexually and aesthetically, it was the hottest film ever made" (see figure 2). Twenty-seven years later, her response is similar, intensified this time by an analytic perspective:

> The slow motion [shots of the eponymous haircut] creates a feeling of languour and also of anticipation and anxiety stretched to the breaking point.
> The action can be read as foreplay or as a metaphor for a more explicit s&m exchange. The focus of attention is the bottom, the man whose hair is being cut. Immobile, he submits to the gaze of the camera and to the attentions of the top—haircutter—who, despite his peripheral position on the screen, has total control of pace, duration, and incident. Wielding a potentially lethal instrument, he has life-and-death power.
> What *Haircut* taught me is that viewer identification is less a matter of gender than of sexuality, of psychosexual fantasies that cross gender lines and are about the deployment of power rather than the specifics of genitalia.[25]

Together, these four critics, by focusing on the erotic effect of anticipation and power both within and around the films, sum up a formative stage in the evolution of erotic culture in the West. The tease, an erotic enunciation orchestrated like a tantalizing power game, was still the characteristic erotic rhetoric of sixties public culture, the sexual revolution notwithstanding. Warhol viewers of the 1990s must not forget that long before our sense of subversive anticipation and play was dulled by the overkill of *Deep Throat* and *Boys in the Sand,* not to mention the instant-access uniformity of 1980s video porn, the promise of gratification was routinely deferred and rarely

Figure 3. "Taking forever in the shower." Frame enlargement of the shower scene in *Bike Boy* (1967).

fulfilled. Warhol's endless scenes of grooming and bathing for example—Paul America drying every finger in *My Hustler,* Joe Spencer taking forever in the shower in *Bike Boy* (see figure 3), Eric Emerson helping Joe Dallesandro put meat on his buns or take the dandruff off his nipple in *Cowboys,* Tom Hompertz drying his chest for three hours in the same film (actually two minutes), Louis Waldron helping Joe with the zits on his back in *Flesh*—were permutations of standard conventions in the gay erotic cinema of the day. The pretense that an erotic image had to be art or exercise instruction was yet a painful recent memory, and a gay porno consumer's first impulse was still to declare he was a bodybuilder or art student (with the law usually but not always pretending to believe both). Here surely is where Warhol and his generation borrowed their love of the interactive put-on, their pleasure in the games of open secrets and winking covers, in the spectatorial process that Brasell equates to cruising (see figure 4).

Warhol's other experiments with minimal structure, duration, and "metagenre" were anticipated in the work of such exemplary postmodernists as, once again, Bob Mizer and Dick Fontaine, the L.A. mail-order physique moguls (see figure 5).[26] In their five- and ten-minute physique loops of posing, wrestling, and rudimentary narratives (1950 to 1970), proto-Warholian strategies are simply the commercial exigencies of artisanal cinema. Letting a reel of film run out while the trade model desperately continues his smile, his pose, or his mock-casual sunbathing was the simplest way to produce the standard mail-order product. In fact, the physique artisans went through the same staggered reinvention of the "primitive" cinema as did Warhol: the first

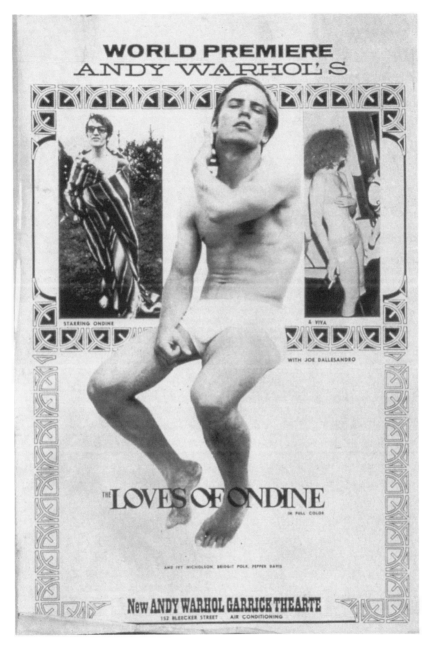

Figure 4. "Addressing the gay audience." Andy Warhol, *The Loves of Ondine*, poster for Greenwich Village premiere (1967). Courtesy the Andy Warhol Film Project, Whitney Museum of American Art.

Figure 5. "Queens and Beefcake" (*left*) and "Glory Holedon" in frame from video transfer of Dick Fontaine's *Hot Harem* (c. 1964).

static confirmations of the properties of medium led to almost accidental discoveries of the erotics of the look and the fascination of documentary grain, then to ontological explorations of the frame, narrative, offscreen sound, sync sound, and, above all, the phenomenon of the star. Alibi of art or alibi of athletics, high-culture Pop minimalism or low-culture physique minimalism, 57th Street put-on or 42nd Street turn on—the voyeurs, the investors, the critics, and the censors were equally satisfied.

In short, the structures and conditions of Warhol's erotic tease were all inextricably shaped by contextual factors. Gidal, James, and others may insist that Warhol's relation to porn is as a mediator and deconstructor, as a "metagenre" practitioner,[27] and Mark Finch may well declare that *Cowboys* bears no comparison with late-sixties, soft-core porn,[28] but porn, pure and simple, is exactly the contextual framework that is indispensable for under-

standing the films. Was Warhol familiar with his kindred spirits in the world
of physique soft-core porn? How else to interpret Little Dallesandro's great
wrestling scene *The Loves of Ondine* (see figure 6) where his steel interthigh
headlock on the eponymous star ensures the only moment of silence in all of
Ondine's performances (this may have been Dallesandro's inaugural role for
Warhol, but Little Joe had been posing for Mizer's Athletic Model Guild and
for another physique giant, Bruce of Los Angeles, for some time). Connois-
seur also of the hetero "beaver" films of the late sixties, Warhol struck one
interviewer as a "listless conversationalist" who became "animated" only
when the "beavers" came up.[29] Parker Tyler's contemporary discussions are
similarly animated by familiarity with "beavers," "meta-beavers," "nudie posing," and other features of the exhibition and censorship landscape of the
late sixties. The FBI wasn't off in seeing Warhol as a fellow traveler with
the fast-buck operators of the interwoven distribution circuits around art/
foreign cinema, indie-sexploitation cinema, and the underground.[30] All were
equally engaged in the put-ons, games, and teases imposed by the legal and
commercial dynamics of an era when censorship was dissipating and the
genre conventions of porn and everything else were in total flux. To his late-

Figure 6. Ondine and Joe Dallesandro wrestling in *The Loves of Ondine* (1968).

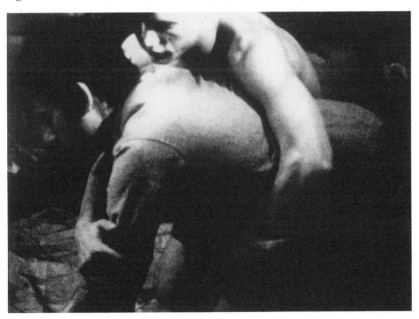

sixties gay constituency, Warhol was an artist brilliantly manipulating the art market and the film industry to produce sexy funny movies, teasing the legal and cultural establishment as skillfully as he was teasing his horny, voyeuristic fans.

With regard to the volatile censorship atmosphere I have described, one film title on everyone's lips was *I Am Curious (Yellow)*. The landmark Swedish art film showing incidental limp penises and simulated hetero intercourse was banned in 1967 and 1968 but finally released by the Supreme Court for an anticlimactic run in the spring of 1969. The new critic at the *New York Times*, Vincent Canby, provided blurbs for Warhol features that may well be apocryphal but made the connection: *Flesh* offered "as much genitalia and sexual union as *I Am Curious*," whereas *Cowboys* ads more vaguely proclaimed "just about as much as *I Am Curious*."[31] Like *Curious*, most of the milestone films of the sixties were straight, but two major court decisions affecting beefcake physique magazines cleared the air considerably. The first came down in 1962 and concerned male nudity, the era's essential iconographic marker of danger and liberation, for which the matter-of-fact Warhol was the art world's fearless and undisputed champion. Later, in 1967, the stake was frank homoerotic address and the legitimacy of the homosexual audience.[32] As each successive threshold passed—explicit homosexual reference, nudity, genital nudity, simulated sex, erections, and finally hard-core penetration—Warhol and company leapt aboard, commenting on, ironically playing with, and eagerly exploiting each newly permissible zone of imagery.[33] At the same time, injudicious legal complications were scrupulously avoided: art world lion Warhol had more lawyers and fewer principles than Jonas Mekas and the other hetero-righteous, poverty-stricken exhibitors who had faced the cops martyrlike in mid-decade around the films of Jack Smith, Jean Genet, and Kenneth Anger.[34]

Small wonder that gay audiences obsessively fastened on each infraction of the current standard of permissibility as if waiting for a holy relic to be undraped. The fuck scenes of *Cowboys*, for example, for all their aura of supposedly random framelines and lustfully clumsy zooms into one crevice or another, fastidiously maintain the standard decorum of 1967, eschewing the slightest glimpse of pubic hair, let alone a cock. The only exception was a fleeting long-shot peek at Waldron's penis in a nonerotic early morning scene that culminated in the rearview urination scene of which the mere mention drove twelve-year-old future deviates to acts of depravity. Forced into genital hide-and-seek—literally cockteasing—by the conjunction of censorship and industry caution, artists and audiences alike took on the challenge like a game, pushing the boundaries, subverting the rules, joining in the game, even celebrating the limits. A film society audience at Columbia, exposed to *Blow Job,* reportedly sang in unison "We Shall Never Come!"[35] the way an earlier generation would have responded by chanting "Take it off!" at a burlesque show (burlesque is incidentally a cultural phenomenon similar to sixties soft-core porn in its total centering on the borderlines of the permissible). Dick Fontaine's stringless spring-mounted posing pouches (for which he has gone down in history as the inventor) and Warhol's playfully ugly black G-strings in *Nude Restaurant* were explicit homage to the silliness of the soft-core teases of 1967.

It is clear that Warhol had a gay critical constituency, judging from contemporary commentary by writers as diverse as Parker Tyler, Frank O'Hara, Tony Rayns, the budding gay teenager David Ehrenstein, and the still "heterosexual" Richard Goldstein, as well as by the Factory's queer intellectual performers Gregory Battcock, Henry Geldzahler, and Ed Hood.[36] In what sense did Warhol also have a gay audience? About this Morrissey was quite explicit:

> Most of our audiences are in New York City, LA and San Francisco; most of the audiences are degenerates, looking for sex and filth. We have a small audience of people who like films, and who go to see them as films, and then some people looking for art films go to see them. Actually the audience has grown bigger and bigger, and I think we're hitting a popular audience. Degenerates are not such a great audience, but they're a step up from the art crowd; we would always rather play a sexploitation theatre than an art theatre.[37]

The cultural geography of the screens that ran Warhol products after the *Chelsea Girls* sleeper success make their degenerate appeal absolutely clear: *Girls'* seven-month run on the Lower East Side; the Times Square run of the sexploitation cycle inaugurated by *My Hustler*'s sensational stint at the soft-core house, the Hudson, in the summer of 1967 (*The Loves of Ondine; Bike Boy; I, a Man; Nude Restaurant*); the seven-month run of *Flesh* in Andy's own West Village theater starting in 1968; the special *Cowboys* placement on both coasts in theaters that were well on their way to becoming gay male houses—the 55th Street Playhouse in Manhattan and the Cinema Theatre in L.A.[38] As one of the *Hustler* ads proclaimed, it was not your Aunt Fanny who was filling up the theaters.[39]

The embryonic gay media of the day confirm the impression that an audience of gay men was the decisive factor in Warhol's commercial success. *Drum* (Philadelphia), the most intelligent, sexy, and principled popular gay magazine of mid-decade, kept readers up to date on the latest censorship of *The Chelsea Girls,* denounced a Chicago critic who called it "3½ hours of homosexual sewage disposal" and gleefully predicted that *My Hustler's* commercial success was a "harbinger of things to come."[40] At the upstart L.A. community magazine *The Advocate,* critics raved at each new Factory release. *Flesh* was "a perfect film," and Joe's memorable line was well worth quoting: "What's straight? Nobody's straight! All you're doing is letting somebody suck your peter." The second stringer's review of *Bike Boy* was lukewarm but ensured the usual mobs at the theater with its conscientious consumer info: "You might like a few scenes: Joe Spencer taking an endless shower (and showing nothing); a bathing suit shopping spree in a gay shop (again cutting at the right moment); and a nude scene with Viva Superstar in which you do finally get a glimpse of Joe's (and Andy's) pride and joy!" For *Lonesome Cowboys,* the *Advocate* reviewer again gave his readers a fastidious accounting of the film's nudity and erotic quotient, exuding a general critical fervor worth quoting at length: "The mindblower of the year. . . . *Hair* on the hoof! *Space Odyssey* of the mind! *Nude Restaurant* a la ranchero. . . ." "Humor as great as this can be achieved only through the improvisations of this wild group of freaked-out, spaced-out, yet highly perceptive personalities. . . ." "[Waldron's] is the only frontal exposure and he comes off very well." "Honors for male nudity go to Tom's well developed, yet slim physique. He has two mother-naked sex scenes with Viva!, the second one is a masterpiece of a kind."[41]

As for both the crypto-gay New York entertainment monthly *After Dark* and the closety London film monthly *Films and Filming,* Andy could do no wrong, and Little Joe was coverboy extraordinaire.[42] The only dissenter in the gay media constellation was the stuffy movement-based *Tangents* (Los Angeles), whose reviewer had sniffed that *Blow Job* was "anti-art and anti-everything" and never returned to the subject of the most visible gay filmmaker of the decade.[43]

The late sixties, then, saw gay audiences beginning to be publicly constituted in theatrical venues for the first time, not necessarily in 42nd Street

Figure 7. "Beefcake and the Avant-garde." Advertisement for Los Angeles's Park Cinema's "First Gay Film Festival," The *Los Angeles Advocate*, July 1968.

ambiences either, and expressing community through then experimental exhibition ideas such as midnight showings. At least in the three major coastal cities that Morrissey correctly pointed to as the crucibles of postwar degenerate culture, exhibitors were beginning to recognize what the mail-order moviemakers had known for more than fifteen years—that a gay audience was both identifiable and profitable. The Park, one of L.A.'s several gay cinemas in the years on either side of Stonewall, initiated the most ambitious gay programming (see figure 7). There Warhol and other gay underground works lined up alongside an interesting range of mostly artisanal material: physique loops by the likes of Mizer and Fontaine; camp parodies of canonical "gay" movies such as *What Really Happened to Baby Jane* by the legendary grassroots hobby group "The Gay Girls Riding Club" (GGRC); combinations of camp and beef along the lines of the Fontaine potboiler referred to above, *Hot Harem*; amateur attempts at "serious" themes discovered in the two annual amateur film contests held at the theater (both sellout successes); and finally, 35 mm program toppers to complement the 16 mm fare, such as special-interest Hollywood classics (*Some Like It Hot*),

European art features offering gay themes or men in underwear, and the occasional MGM musical! Needless to say, the programs were exported wholesale to San Francisco and Manhattan.

Letters from *Advocate* readers occasionally griped about the steep five-dollar admission, the technical quality of some offerings, and the odor of exploitation, but the crowds apparently liked what they saw. In an audience survey at the Park, [44] the respondents, mostly men in their thirties, loved the queenly spoofs from the GGRC and praised the underground movies that dealt more or less directly with trade themes, such as *Bike Boy* and *My Hustler.* In general this eager audience requested stronger plots, better quality, more wit and style, and protection from censorship (there is nothing new under the sun). The respondents' negative judgments were also interesting: "Underground" movies that consisted of "far out crap" were a definite no, and physique loops showing too much "posing, self-conscious posturing, exercising, and weight lifting" had their death knell sounded (sending Bob Mizer back to the mail-order business he knew). Finally, the survey shows a certain sophistication about the tease of sexploitation exhibition practice and a willingness to play along under certain conditions: "While many cry that nudity alone was not enough, they qualify this view with 'If it isn't good, it damn well better be 100% nude.'" Respondents were more cautious about one sexploitation practice that the *Advocate* writer referred to as the shotgun approach: "Films that mix both nude men and nude women (other than in necessary plot situations) are obviously made by straights who think that if they fire a blast from a shotgun, they're bound to hit everyone." The manifesto "No Nude Women!" in this context reflected less a phobic response to "the lack" than a collective refusal to have a distinct collective identity denied ever again.

Looking back at the Warhol films of the sexploitation period, one recognizes that the Factory was particularly adept at the shotgun approach. Of the 1967 sexploitation run, all the films except *Hustler* situated male nudity in the context of at least a fifty-fifty balance of homo and hetero material, and even *Hustler* had a hetero bikini sequence for good measure. *Cowboys, Flesh,* and *Trash* were fastidiously fifty-fifty (see figure 8). Of the latter, *After Dark* warned of a "plethora of nude females on view" despite the "basically homosexual" "overall aura."[45] Morrissey was once more candid about box office strategy: "All Joe's encounters are neatly balanced for sex preferences,"[46] and "Andy makes the kind of movies he likes to make, and the sex was added

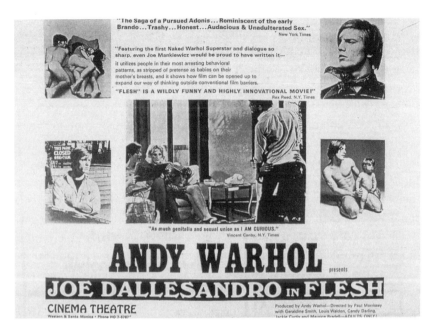

Figure 8. Advertisement for *Flesh* at Los Angeles's gay moviehouse, "Cinema Theatre," The *Los Angeles Advocate*, August 1969.

later, because without it people wouldn't sit through them. . . . Now we're making films for the public. *Chelsea Girls* had the obligatory homosexuality in a psychedelic context."[47] The Factory's distributors were of like mind: *Cowboys* was handled by Sherpix, but this "art house" distributor's other major product of the year 1967 was on the other side of the divide, a straight exploitation title *Censorship in Denmark,* which happily led to charges and a windfall of publicity.

The burgeoning homo marketplace affected more than Warhol and the sexploitationists. The lineups for *Chelsea Girls* and *My Hustler* drew the attention of *Variety* and in turn of Hollywood's sleeping giants, thus sparking the second queer cycle in Tinseltown's postcode history. The first (mini-)cycle, dancing on the fresh grave of the code, had featured Shirley MacLaine, Capucine, and Don Murray as dead queers; the second was much more substantial, killing off Sandy Dennis, Rod Steiger, Marlon Brando, Dustin Hoffman, and Cliff Gorman. Indeed, *Variety* pronounced in March 1969 that themes dealing with sexual deviation were now box office, listing seventeen deviate films already made or definitely set, with three more in the possible category.[48] (In one symptomatic coincidence of queer film history, the sunny *Cowboys* premiered at the same San Francisco Film Festival as the most gloomy of the 1968–69 queer cycle, Steiger's unsuccessful vehicle, *The Sergeant.*)

Gay expectations of Hollywood were probably not high enough to be disappointed with the 1969 crop. For one thing, foreign movies from *Satyricon* to *Women in Love* were now emerging in a steady stream to keep spirits high within the new economy of high visibility and low returns. Yet the foreign art movie had a shotgun approach of its own. Then as now, a certain important queerish genre of the art house/film festival product offered a something-for-everyone blend of intellectualism and ambiguity, mixed gender nudity, and an aura of recuperable marginality. The "exotic" articulation of taboo desire alongside its simultaneous disavowal teetered on a tightrope between the status of high culture and subversive subcultural chic. Gay cinephiles were offered a mixed package, just the right blend of the social justification derived from visibility alone and an adequate dose of well-motivated beefcake, all diluted by melodramatic catharsis and the open or dead-queer ending. The irreconcilability of subject and object continued, with Luchino Visconti's morbid Teutonic trilogy (*The Damned, Death in Venice,* and *Ludwig*) highlighting the rut that even the gay-authored art imports seemed unable to escape.

Amid both the art house trade-offs and the sexploitation rip-offs of the late sixties, it is no wonder that Warhol's unashamed nudes, swishy wit, and matter-of-fact documentation of gay lifestyles were a breath of fresh air. After all, positive image ideology was still limited to low-key griping by an increasingly anachronistic and film-illiterate Mattachine constituency and a gleam in the eye of the next generation of the liberation vanguard, still closeted in their white college dorms. Warhol's unapologetically bitchy queens and easy trade were more potent political icons than suicidal Rod Steigers, angst-ridden Continentals, and the new generation of clone consumers all at once, as Stonewall was to demonstrate. Here was a cinema where, as Viva understood on a deep spiritual level in *Cowboys,* the lilies of the field who toil and spin don't wear pants, where Holly Woodlawn could deliver *Trash's* great last line, "Joe let me suck your cock" with all the aplomb of Bette Davis, and where in *My Hustler* you could stare proudly for forty-five minutes at two towel-wrapped trade repeatedly applying deodorant.

The relationship of Warhol and his awakening gay audience on the eve of Stonewall was ultimately not unlike that of the two trade in *My Hustler*. In that epochal, allegorical skinflick, the men in the bathroom permanently unsettled the dynamic of gay subject and object—glancing and staring in the mirror at themselves and each other, orchestrating put-ons, come-ons, and takeoffs, and gaily teasing each other's furtively glimpsed cocks. As the contestation around Warhol six years after his death attests, the upshot of the cruise between the Sugar Plum Fairy and Paul America is still an open ending.

NOTES

■

For feedback on earlier drafts, I am grateful to José Arroyo, Ross Higgins, Steve Kokker, and Callie Angell, as well as to several participants of the "Politics of Pop" conference, Duke University, where this piece was first presented. I am especially indebted to Steve Kokker's A. W. resources and J. D'A. obsessions and to Richard Dyer, whose pioneering work in the field of gay cinema has been immeasurably helpful and with whom I hope this piece engages in fruitful dialogue. Thanks also for research help to Matt Hays and to Alan Miller and the Canadian Gay Archives, Toronto.

1   Andy Warhol and Pat Hackett, *POPism: The Warhol Sixties* (New York: Harcourt Brace Jovanovich, 1980), p. 294.

2   Ronald Tavel, Harry Fainlight, and Billy Linich, "Soundtrack of Andy Warhol's *Harlot*," *Film Culture*, no. 40 (Spring 1966); rpt. in *Andy Warhol Film Factory*, ed. Michael O'Pray (London: British Film Institute, 1989), pp. 86–93.

3   My use of the term "gay" for pre-Stonewall collective self-conceptions may seem anachronistic unless one remembers how widespread the word was in gay male vernacular and even publications of the sixties (the first of literally hundreds of periodicals with the word "gay" in the title—called *Gay*—appeared in Toronto in 1964). I use the term both as knowingly and as loosely as possible.

4   Robin Hardy was one of the first post-1987 critics to blow the whistle on the "sanitization" of Warhol's work across the board, in "Andy Warhol Goes Straight: How the Life of an Artist Who Liked the 'Swish' Is Being Whitewashed," *Advocate*, December 5, 1989, pp. 58–60.

5   I am thinking especially of Richard Dyer, *Now You See It: Studies on Lesbian and Gay Film* (London: Routledge, 1990), pp. 102–173; Tony Rayns, "Death at Work: Evolution and Entropy in Factory Films," in *Warhol Film Factory*, ed. O'Pray, pp. 160–169; Mark Finch, "RIO LIMPO: *Lonesome Cowboys* and Gay Cinema," in *Warhol Film Factory*, ed. O'Pray, pp. 112–117; R. Bruce Brasell, "*My Hustler:* Gay Spectatorship as Cruising," *Wide Angle* 14, no. 2 (April 1992): 54–64; Bryan Bruce and Gloria Berlin, "The Superstar Story," *Cineaction!* (Toronto), no. 7 (1986): 52–63; and Stephen Tropiano, "Joe Dallesandro—A 'Him' to the

Gaze: *Flesh, Heat,* and *Trash,*" *Spectator* (University of Southern California) 10, no. 1 (Fall 1989): 46–55. I would include excellent work by nongay critics as well, such as David E. James, "The Producer as Author," 136–145, and Peter Wollen, "Raiding the Icebox," 14–27, both in *Warhol Film Factory,* ed. O'Pray.

6 Warhol and Hackett, *POPism,* 11–13.

7 Dyer, *Now You See It,* 140 ff.

8 Thomas Waugh, "The Third Body," in *Queer Looks: Perspectives on Lesbian and Gay Film and Video,* ed. Martha Gever, John Greyson, and Pratibha Parmar (New York: Routledge, 1993).

9 Richard Dyer made a similar point in 1977, in particular about class difference, in reference to Pasolini: "The interpenetration of class and race with sexuality is widespread in Western culture. . . . Yet it does seem to be a more insistent feature of how gayness is imaged. It is true that gayness does permit the creation of milieux in which barriers of class and race can be bridged; but this is not what comes across in [Pasolini's] images of the adolescent and the older man, or the sub-proletarian *ragazzi* and the bourgeois admirer. Rather what is stressed is *inequality.* It is as if precisely the equality that homosexuality promises, of equality based upon the same social status of the partners (both women or men), has to be denied by insisting on built-in inequalities of class and age. This is partly because the heterosexual norm of inequality between partners exercises its influence over gay consciousness, so that some form of inequality has to be reinvented (there is a complex interplay in gay fiction between the characters acting out 'masculine' and 'feminine' roles and their class, race and age differences); . . . the images of men in Pasolini's work are scarred by an ideology that denies gayness its validity and its subversive implications." Paul Willemen, ed., *Pier Paolo Pasolini* (London: British Film Institute, 1977), p. 60. One hopes that we have arrived at a stage where the potential richness and energy of the dynamic of difference can be affirmed rather than only its potential complicity in oppression.

10 Valerie Solanas, *The SCUM Manifesto* (New York: Olympia Press, 1968), pp. 55–56.

11 I am borrowing the concept of the "vaginal" image of female sexuality from Richard Dyer's discussion of Marilyn Monroe as a construction of 1950s psychoanalytic and popular cultural discourses of the vaginal orgasm. Dyer, *Heavenly Bodies: Film Stars and Society* (London: British Film Institute/Macmillan, 1987), pp. 50–66.

12 Chief offenders are, of course, Molly Haskell, *From Reverence to Rape: The Treatment of Women in the Movies* (New York: Holt, Rinehart and Winston, 1974), p. 244; and Pauline Kael, for example, review of Cukor's *Rich and Famous, New Yorker,* October 26, 1981, rpt., Kael, *Taking It All In* (New York: Holt, Rinehart and Winston, 1984), pp. 247–248. But both follow on the mid-sixties "homosexual conspiracy" reading of the gay playwrights by Walter Kerr and others.

13 Parker Tyler, *Underground Film: A Critical History* (New York: Grove, 1969), p. 226.

14 Bruce and Berlin, "Superstar," p. 56.

15 The reader will notice that I switch from the term "hustler" to "trade" at this point, because this generic label encompasses a whole complex of class identification, self-image, cultural role-playing, and sexual behaviors (trade is never penetrated, orally or anally, and it never kisses), as opposed to the vocational connotation of "hustler" (male prostitute). I am

painfully aware that this does not solve all terminological problems, all the more so since at least one of my vernacular checkers does not agree that "trade" can be used as a noun to refer to an individual, as I insist on doing.

16 All dialogue has been transcribed by the author, unless otherwise noted.

17 Parker Tyler, *Screening the Sexes: Homosexuality in the Movies* (New York: Holt, Rinehart and Winston, 1972), p. 55.

18 I lay out this continuum tentatively in "Third Body."

19 Tropiano, "Dallesandro," p. 47.

20 Reader's narrative, *Straight to Hell: The Manhattan Review of Unnatural Acts* (New York), no. 50 (1981): 4.

21 Peter Gidal, "Warhol," *Films and Filming* 17, no. 8 (May 1971): 64–75.

22 Finch, "RIO LIMPO," p. 115.

23 Tropiano, "Dallesandro," p. 54.

24 Gary Indiana, "I'll Be Your Mirror," *Village Voice,* May 5, 1987; rpt. in *Warhol Film Factory,* ed. O'Pray, pp. 182–185.

25 Amy Taubin, "Hot Heads," review of the film special "Reel Sex," *Village Voice,* December 1990, p. 20.

26 For a detailed study of the physique cinema, see Thomas Waugh, "Hard to Imagine: Gay Erotic Cinema in the Postwar Era," *Cineaction!* (Toronto), no. 10 (October 1987): 65–72.

27 Gidal, "Warhol," pp. 64–75; James, "Producer as Author," pp. 141–142.

28 Finch, "RIO LIMPO," p. 112.

29 Joseph Gelmis, *The Film Director as Superstar* (Garden City, N.Y.: Doubleday, 1970), p. 66. Warhol's animated preoccupation with the genre is palpable in Gelmis's interview (p. 68):

> Have you seen any *beavers?* They're where girls take off their clothes completely. And they're always alone on a bed. Every girl is always on a bed. And then they sort of fuck the camera. . . . Yeah. You can see them in theaters in New York. The girls are completely nude and you can see everything. They're really great. . . . We go in for artier films for popular consumption, but we're getting there. Like, sometimes people say we've influenced so many other filmmakers. But the only people we've really influenced is that beaver crowd.
>
> The beavers are so great. They don't even have to make prints. They have so many girls showing up to act in them. It's cheaper just to make originals than to have prints made. It's always on a bed. It's really terrific.

30 Marcia Kramer, *Andy Warhol et al.: The FBI File on Andy Warhol* (New York: UnSub Press, 1988).

31 Advertisement for *Flesh, Los Angeles Advocate,* August 1969; advertisement for *Lonesome Cowboys, After Dark* (New York), undated, c. 1968.

32 *Manual v. Day* (Supreme Court 1962) declared that male nudes were no more obscene than equivalent female nudes, adding the new criterion to the legal definition of obscenity, that materials had to be "patently offensive." The 1967 Minneapolis case against the gay beefcake distributor Directory Services Incorporated drew considerable attention to its innovative judgments that (1) a gay target audience did not automatically imply obscenity, (2) eroticism could have redeeming social value, (3) community standards of a national scope were

applicable, and (4) minority rights were a legitimate concern in obscenity jurisprudence. This case did not set a national precedent but encouraged prosecutors to lay off homophobic crusades.

33 Compare the following passage: "I knew that we were probably going to have more trouble with the censors soon—at least if our movies kept getting attention—and I guess I must have known in the back of my mind that it would be a smart idea to have at least one really articulate performer in each movie. The legal definition of 'obscenity' had that 'without redeeming social value' phrase in it, and it occurred to me that if you found someone who could look beautiful, take off her clothes, step into a bathtub, and talk as intellectually as Viva did . . . , you'd have a better chance with the censors than if you had a giggly teenager saying, 'Let me feel your cock.' It was all just silly legal strategy, though, because to me they were all great, all just people being their real selves on camera and I liked them all the same." Warhol and Hackett, *POPism*, pp. 229–230.

34 Jonas Mekas's accounts of his arrests for the exhibition of Smith's *Flaming Creatures* and for Genet's *Un chant d'amour* appeared in his *Village Voice* columns of March 12 and 19, 1964, respectively, and are reprinted in Mekas, *Movie Journal: The Rise of a New American Cinema, 1959–1971* (New York: Collier, 1972), pp. 126–130. His commentary on the obscenity convictions of *Creatures* and Anger's *Scorpio Rising* appeared on June 18, 1964, and is reprinted in *Movie Journal* on pp. 141–144.

35 Anecdote recounted by Neal Weaver, "The Warhol Phenomenon: Trying to Understand It," *After Dark*, January 1969, p. 26.

36 The principal relevant works by Parker Tyler, dean of American critics of underground and gay cinema, are *Underground Film* and *Screening the Sexes*; Frank O'Hara's *Standing Still and Walking in New York* (San Francisco: Grey Fox, 1983) has several passing references to Warhol's films; Tony Rayns (leading gay British promoter of Warhol's films), "Andy Warhol Films Inc: Communication in Action. Interviews with Paul Morrissey and Joe d'Allesandro [sic]," *Cinema* (London), no. 6/7 (August 1970): 42–47; Rayns's review of *My Hustler, Monthly Film Bulletin* (London) 38 (June 1971): 123; David Ehrenstein (current film critic for the *Advocate*), "An Interview with Warhol," *Film Culture*, no. 40 (Spring 1966), and "Room Culture" (on *Chelsea Girls*), *Film Culture* 42 (Fall 1966); Richard Goldstein (current executive editor of the *Village Voice* and leading contributor on gay politics and culture), review of *Chelsea Girls, New York Journal Tribune* (date unknown, c. 1966), cited by Gregory Battcock; Gregory Battcock, performer in Warhol's *Horse* and columnist for the short-lived New York gay tabloid of the late sixties *Gay*, in *The New American Cinema* (New York: E. P. Dutton, 1967); Henry Geldzahler, subject of *Henry Geldzahler* (1964) and curator at the Metropolitan Museum of Art, wrote among other things "Some Notes on *Sleep*," in *Film Culture: An Anthology*, ed. P. Adams Sitney (London: Secker and Warburg, 1971); and Ed Hood (possessive "Dial-a-Hustler" customer in *My Hustler*), contributed a piece on Edie Sedgwick to *Film Culture*, no. 46 (Summer 1967).

37 Paul Morrissey, interviewed by Tony Rayns, "Andy Warhol Films Inc," pp. 42–47.

38 The Cinema Theatre had been the site of the seizure of *Scorpio Rising* in 1964.

39 Advertisement for the Park Theatre showing of *My Hustler, Los Angeles Advocate*, July 1968.

40 *Drum* (Philadelphia), September 1967, p. 23.

41 Warhol reviews in the *Los Angelos Advocate* include Bart Cody on *Bike Boy,* August 1968, p. 23; Jay Ross [Jay Rosenthal] on *Lonesome Cowboys,* January 1969, pp. 10, 21; and Jay Ross on *Flesh,* August 1969, pp. 9–10.

42 *After Dark,* January 1969; and *Films and Filming,* April 1971.

43 Lee Atwell, "Homosexual Themes in the Cinema," *Tangents* (Los Angeles), March 1966, p. 10.

44 Park Theatre audience survey reported in Jay Ross, "Gay Moviegoers Have Their Say," *Los Angeles Advocate,* January 1969, p. 21.

45 Weaver, "Warhol Phenomenon," p. 24.

46 Rayns, "Andy Warhol Films Inc," p. 45.

47 Weaver, "Warhol Phenomenon," quoting Morrissey, p. 29.

48 Cited in "Film Stuff" column, *After Dark,* March 1969.

MICHAEL MOON
Screen Memories, or, Pop Comes from the Outside: Warhol and Queer Childhood

"I was never embarrassed about asking someone, literally, 'What should I paint?' because Pop comes from the outside, and how is asking someone for ideas any different from looking for them in a magazine?"—Andy Warhol, *POPism*[1]

"I was promised an improved infancy."—Hart Crane, "Passage"[2]

From early on in his career until the end of his life, Andy Warhol sketched (and later photographed or filmed) innumerable images of male nudity, ranging from models in standard "artistic" poses to men masturbating and having sex with each other. Warhol's penchant for sketching and photographing other men's bodies and especially their genitals, one of the few constants in his career as an artist from his early days as an advertising artist and magazine illustrator until late in his lifetime, seems to have been an important aspect of his ability to structure and maintain his highly productive, innovative, and influential career. During the 1950s, as Warhol became increasingly successful as a commercial artist, he repeatedly attempted to gain recognition as a "fine" artist with a series of exhibitions of his drawings. These early gallery shows, which featured images of cupids, beautiful boys' faces, and penises festooned with bows and lipsticked "kiss marks," predictably attracted little positive attention from a New York art world completely taken up with the macho heroics of abstract expressionism (see figure 1).

During and after the years of his first fame as a Pop artist and underground filmmaker, Warhol produced masses of hard- and soft-core images—mostly photographic ones—of male nudes, but unlike other kinds of images he

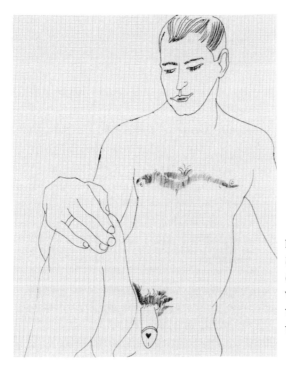

Figure 1. Andy Warhol, *Untitled (erotic drawing)* (c. 1957). ©1996 Andy Warhol Foundation for the Visual Arts/ARS, New York.

made routinely, he seems never to have found a way to use his "sex pictures" (his code word for them in his diaries is "landscapes") in his artistic production; only a slight trace of them ever found any place among his exhibited works.[3] In this essay I consider how we may understand Warhol's very early Pop paintings of cartoon and comic strip characters (mostly produced circa 1960) as representing not a total rupture with his flagrantly homoerotic art of the fifties but rather a continuation by other means of his fey but ferocious and, in some ways, ultimately successful war against the exclusion of swishiness and fagginess from the repertory of possible gestures that could be made and recognized in visual art.[4] Recent investigations of the relation between Warhol's sexuality and his art have tended to emphasize his representations of male object choices (for example, explicitly, in his early Pop portraits of Troy Donahue and Warren Beatty; in his 1964 film *Thirteen Most Beautiful Boys;* or, somewhat more obliquely, in his New York World's Fair installation of the same year, *Thirteen Most Wanted Men*).[5] In looking at some of the cartoon paintings that were among the key images through which Warhol established what I see as both a break with and a transformed continuation of his "fag" art of the fifties, I am concerned with his representations of a range of "queer" or "perverse" desires that include but are by no means restricted to male-male object choice.

The third son and youngest child of Ruthenian immigrants, Andy Warhol appears to have had a difficult childhood on several counts. Perceived as being passive, effeminate, physically awkward and weak, and sometimes weird to the point of uncanniness (this last a quality that would distinguish his adult persona, too), he was frequently harassed by other children. From early on, his mother seems to have attempted to compensate him for ill treatment from others by lavishing affection and attention on him. In the first chapter of *The Philosophy of Andy Warhol*, entitled "Love (Puberty)," Warhol dispatches the subject of his difficult albeit indulged early years in a couple of highly compressed paragraphs:

> I had had three nervous breakdowns when I was a child, spaced a year apart. One when I was eight, one at nine, and one at ten. The attacks— St. Vitus Dance—always started on the first day of summer vacation. I don't know what this meant. I would spend all summer listening to the radio and lying in bed with my Charlie McCarthy doll and my un-cut-out cut-out paper dolls all over the spread and under the pillow.
>
> My father was away a lot on business trips to the coal mines, so I never saw him very much. My mother would read to me in her thick Czechoslovakian accent as best she could and I would always say "Thanks, Mom," after she finished with Dick Tracy, even if I hadn't understood a word. She'd give me a Hershey Bar every time I finished a page in my coloring book.[6]

I propose to take this little story of Warhol's as a screen memory of sorts, as a scene (as Freud first theorized) which draws on actual figures and events from one's experience but which is also composed at least partly of imaginary and symbolic elements and in which the objects and events recalled become belatedly and retroactively charged with a set of meanings that simultaneously mask and reveal a network of formative perceptions and fantasies from and about one's early life. I propose at the same time to make the scene as a queered version of a "primal" one. Freud's primal scene is the traumatically anxious and frightening one of the infant's or small child's observing or hearing the sights and sounds of adults engaged in sexual acts.[7] Warhol rewrites the primal scene in the passage above to feature an all-male cast plus his mother. In this highly pastoral revision of a primal scene, anxiety and trauma are allayed so thoroughly as to raise the question of what is being held so resolutely at bay. This cartoon idyll of happy solitary play interrupted by frequent maternal attention is introduced, one must remember, as an account of what happened during what Warhol remembers as "three nervous breakdowns" he experienced between ages eight and ten. To dismiss this scene of childhood contentment as a mere wish fulfillment would be to miss what strikes me as its strong aura of aggressively suppressed and fearful defensiveness.

The peculiar version of queer-child pastoral that Warhol imagines himself performing as a little boy lying abed with his dolls and coloring book is a challenging and potentially rich site of interpretation. The presence of radio and comic strip characters as well as, on the child's part, the activity of coloring suggest that one thing we may have here is a belated and highly colored memory/fantasy about the mythical origins of the adult Warhol's having painted his way into becoming a Pop Art celebrity by making numerous images of (among other subjects) comic strip and cartoon characters. Put more broadly, analyzing the elements of this scene may help us better understand the intersecting histories of gay or protogay identity and mass culture in the early to middle decades of this century.

Some of the reasons for the appeal of this scene to the adult Warhol seem obvious: consigned to recuperation in bed, temporarily "safe" from rivalry with his elder brothers and the necessity of contact with other children, his father equally, providentially (and apparently permanently) absent (being away at work in or, in Warhol's class-effacing and class-ironizing locution, "on business trips to" the coal mines), Warhol represents his child self modestly luxuriating in an ideal set of conditions of work and leisure. In the (non-)person of his Charlie McCarthy doll, he has a surrogate male partner to share his bed with him, along with a set of presiding images to guarantee the alleged unspoiledness, that is, the sexual undifferentiatedness, of the scene, the virgin pages of "un-cut-out cut-out paper dolls" that litter the spread.

The main activities represented in the scene are "listening to the radio," listening to the mother read, and "coloring." The whole scene takes place under the aegis of a woman's voice; as Warhol mentions elsewhere in his *Philosophy:* "While I was little I used to listen to The Singing Lady on the radio all the time while I was in bed coloring."[8] The fluency or uninterrupted quality of both representations of this scene ("I would spend *all summer* listening to the radio and lying in bed," and "I used to listen to The Singing Lady on the radio *all the time*"; emphasis mine) is punctuated, but apparently not interrupted, by the unfluent sounds of Julia Warhola reading the comics to Andy in her (to him) incomprehensible accent.

It is perhaps the two closing references in the little anecdote, both to his mother, that are most highly charged and most densely encoded. If the child Andy claims not to "under[stand] a word" of her rendition of Dick Tracy, it may be because the name of the comic strip "dick" (that is, "detective") resonates obscenely in the imagined/remembered child's ear, and by extension in the mother's, not only with "dick" as the most ordinary vernacular term for "penis" but also because of the way the figure's surname resonates with what appears to have been the adult Warhol's most intensely invested mode of contact with other men's penises: photographing or drawing or "tracing" them. "Dick" is "trace-y" for Warhol in a double sense: it is a desired object to be "traced" in the sense of being detected and pursued and also in that of being captured by being drawn—and thereby kept at a safe and comfortable distance, but also still in potentially exciting proximity, in the relatively manageable form of a visual image and/or record. According to some of his early models, Warhol seems generally to have limited his own participation in many male-male "sex scenes" at which he was present from the fifties through the seventies to gazing at and "tracing," that is, visually recording, them.[9]

As with Julia Warhola's supposedly incomprehensible reading of Dick Tracy to her little son, her showering him with Hershey Bars can also be interpreted as fantasmatic material with its own pronounced, if encoded, erotic coloration. Like "Dick Tracy," the term "Hershey Bar" is another proper name from Warhol's childhood that is susceptible to a specifically sexual construction: at the time he was writing his *Philosophy,* "the Hershey highway" was current gay slang in Warhol's glossy disco circle and beyond it for the rectum and the sexual practices associated with it. Rather than seeing the punctuality ("regularity" is perhaps the appropriate term) with which the prized morsel (the Hershey Bar reward) is delivered up as the mother's, it may make more sense interpretively to see it as an adult's screen memory of himself as a child promptly delivering a stool to demonstrations of maternal

pleasure and encouragement. Watching and photographing other men "taking the Hershey highway" (among other sexual acts) as an adult in the
seventies, as Warhol was doing around the time he wrote this account of his
childhood, may have contributed to his impetus to make his representative
scene of early bliss close with an encoded anal exchange between himself
and his mother.

Ultra Violet, in her 1988 memoir *Famous for Fifteen Minutes,* reports a
conversation she had with Warhol that suggests that he himself saw this
scene of his childhood as standing in some significant relation to his subsequent sexual and social history. "When Andy was a sickly eight-year-old, he
was confined to bed all summer long. He listened to the radio in the company of his Charlie McCarthy doll," she begins, apparently having been
given by Warhol the same cartoon-style account of his childhood he provides in *Philosophy.* The following dialogue ensues between them:

> I ask, "Did you play with dolls?"
> "Gosh, no."
> "Who were your heroes?"
> "Dick Tracy. I Scotch-taped his photograph on the bedroom wall."
> "Why Dick Tracy?"
> "Sex appeal."
> "You just stared at him?"
> "I fantasized about Dick's dick."
> "What?"
> "I fantasized it was [a] lollipop." . . .
> Andy laughs. "Yes, Dick's lollipop." He adds, "I had two sex idols—
> Dick Tracy and Popeye." . . .
> "Did you also fantasize about Popeye?"
> "My mother caught me one day playing with myself and looking at a
> Popeye cartoon."
> "Why Popeye and Tracy?"
> "They were stars. So was Charlie McCarthy. I wanted to make it with
> stars. I fantasized I was in bed with Dick and Popeye. Charlie would rub
> against me and seduce me."[10]

It might be tempting to read the "censored" version of the scene that I quoted
from Warhol's *Philosophy* at the beginning of this essay as merely a secondary

version of an ontologically prior, "uncensored" scene of sexual fantasy that actually took place in the teller's childhood, as in the version Ultra Violet says Warhol told her. In my interpretation of the two versions of the scene, I prefer to maintain the tension between them rather than to dispel it by granting either some primary status. Indeed, it is the tension between the terms for the main elements of the two versions, heavily encoded in the first case and made thoroughly sexually explicit in the second, that gives the scene its powerfully ambiguous status as memory *and* fantasy, screen memory *and* primal scene. Without according either account primacy, I do want to examine more closely some of the ways in which the terms of the scene shift from one version to the other in this at least twice-told tale of Warhol's. One striking change is that social and sexual differences, kept resolutely at bay in the first version, have become sharply defined in the second. In it, differences of social class register imaginarily as differences of "magnitude": the other figures are established "stars," the underclass child Andy at most an aspiring (and intensely desiring) one. Similarly, generational difference divides the quasi-adult "stars" from the child who "want[s] to make it with [them]." Finally, in this more unbuttoned account of the fantasy/memory, the virginal pages of the paper-doll books, mute guarantors of sexual undifferentiatedness, have vanished, and "Charlie McCarthy" wantonly "rub[s] against . . . and seduce[s]" the child.

The mother's voice is also silenced in this eroticized version. Rather than a voice reading in an incomprehensible accent, she has become transformed into a figure of surveillance and prohibition—but her "catching" her son "playing with [him]self and looking at a Popeye cartoon" has no apparent effects or consequences as Warhol tells the story. When Warhol tells Ultra Violet his "cartoon-orgy" story, she briefly attempts to explain the odd little scene with "pop" psychology in a double sense of the word. She asks, "Were they [Tracy and Popeye] father images to you?" According to her, Warhol replied: "Don't know. I barely knew my father. He died when I was fourteen."[11]

It is unnecessary to follow the reductive interpretive trajectory of Ultra Violet's proposal about the figures of Warhol's fantasy (that is, that they were all simply "father images" for him), but it is worth noticing that from early on in the Pop movement, Warhol was aware of—and commented on at the time—the paternal signifiers lurking in both "Pop" and "dada," the antecedent movement from which Pop—especially in its Warholian form—was commonly considered to derive:

Dada must have something to do with Pop—it's so funny, the names are really synonyms. Does anyone know what they're supposed to mean or have to do with, those names? [Jasper] Johns and [Robert] Rauschenberg—Neo-Dada for all these years, and everyone calling them derivative and unable to transform the things they use—are now called progenitors of Pop. It's funny the way things change.[12]

In Warhol's reconstructions of the scene of his childhood, Tracy figures not only "dick" through his name but also "pop" through the delectable "lollipop" that Warhol claims to have fantasized was Tracy's phallus. "Popeye," whose sexual charge for the child Warhol is unspecified, also conspicuously figures "pop" through *his* name. "Pop" is also, of course, the name of the art movement of which Warhol became the biggest star, and in relation to which he first became famous, through being proclaimed by the mass media "the Prince of Pop" or "the Pope of Pop." Rather than reading the ubiquity of "pop" in Warhol's texts simply as a sign of his desire for his absent father, we will be able to attend to more of the meanings of those texts (both written and painted) if we also recognize the word's frequent functioning as a verb, "to pop up" or "to pop out."

Being "about to pop" was common sixties slang (among my freshman-year dormmates and more widely, I believe) for being about to ejaculate. Part of Warhol's devotion to the term "pop" surely derived from the endless series of double entendres the use of the word made possible between his art and social milieu and the phallic and climactic character of the cycle of adult-male sexual functioning from erection to ejaculation. From the "peelable" banana Warhol designed for the jacket of a Velvet Underground album to the "unzippable" fly he designed for the jacket of a Rolling Stones album to the ecstatic face of the fellatee at the "climax" of his film *Blow Job*, Warhol's art is full of ritual veilings and unveilings of the phallus. Throughout his painting and filmmaking of the sixties, Warhol continues to explore phallic sexuality in two different scenes: one in which it is highly visible and highly valued, and another in which it is only one kind among many other at least equally appealing possibilities. The centrality of the term "pop" in Warhol's production during the sixties may be taken as a sign both of a hypervaluation, on Warhol's part as well as of his culture as a whole, of the climactic character of adult sexuality, especially the specifically erectile and ejaculatory character of phallic sexuality, as well as of desires for and knowledges of ways to escape or "pop out" of the culture's relentless production of heterosexual desire focused around straight men and their phallic possession of the female. Warhol's utterance, "Pop comes from the outside," betokens not only the dependence of Pop Art on pop culture for its materials but also a recognition of the violently divided feelings of Warhol's version of Pop Art and pop culture about "Pop's" (that is, Dad's) explosively phallic sexuality.

Warhol's early Pop Art derives much of its energies from its contradictory emphases: one a fascinated devotion to sexuality at its most flagrantly phallic, and the other a no less marked concern with "marginal," nonphallic erotics (for example, the infantile erotics of withholding and releasing urine and feces, which I shall discuss a little further on in relation to two of Warhol's early Pop paintings). The revisionary queer power of much of his Pop cartoon work proceeds from its ability both to evoke and to a considerable degree to celebrate the phallic and also to subvert it comically and to disperse it across the range of abjected erotics I shall discuss in relation to a number of his early Pop paintings of cartoon characters.

Dick Tracy and Popeye (not to mention Charlie McCarthy) may seem odd or at least unexpected erotic choices for a child, but given the novelty and ubiquity of comic strip characters in U.S. culture of the thirties, the kind of fantasy attachments to such figures that Warhol had was probably quite common. Besides their extremely wide availability—as well as the never-to-be-underestimated vagaries of desire—other, more specific factors no doubt played a part in Warhol's early fantasy choices and his adult memories or fantasies about them. Consider, for example, that the graphic signature of Chester Gould's image of Dick Tracy is the literally "clean-cut," razor-sharp appearance of his facial profile—in (again, literally) clear-cut contrast with the "villains" of the strip and their "blank," disintegrative, or otherwise disfigured, repellent, and grotesque facial features (see figure 2). The potential of such a graphic schema is, of course, high for generating invidious narratives about the supposedly inevitably authoritarian, violent, and punitive relations of "clean-cut" men to other men; one can read out of Warhol's subsequent biography the complicated effects the general cathexis of "movie star good looks" on a mass scale in the thirties and thereafter had on his attitudes toward himself and other people and on his choices of erotic objects as an adult.

Yet Warhol seems to have gotten more out of Dick Tracy than unmitigated

Figure 2. Andy Warhol, *Dick Tracy* (1960). ©1996 Andy Warhol Foundation for the Visual Arts/ARS, New York.

reinforcement for his self-hating attachment to conventional good looks. In having fantasized as a child that "Dick's dick" was a "lollipop," Warhol proved himself able to find a fantasmatically sweet and pleasurable organ on the Tracy character's otherwise hard and sharply contoured body. The erotic appeal of Popeye to the boy Warhol provides another instance of a possible kind of resistance on the child's part to the brand of "hard and sharp" male good looks and behavior promoted by *Dick Tracy* and his Crimestoppers' Club and in some ways internalized by the child Warhol. No one is movie star handsome in *Popeye*; all the characters are drawn as grotesques, but (in contrast with Gould's practice in *Dick Tracy*) affectionately so. Popeye's facial profile, from sailor's cap to pipe clutched firmly in prognathous jaw, is repeated in the profile of his whole body, with its outsize forearms visually echoing the pugnacious curve of his chin (see figure 3). The appearance of his face and body mark him not only as working class but even within that general category as a transgressive outsider: in one sense, he's the "one-eyed

Figure 3. Andy Warhol, *Saturday's Popeye* (1960). ©1996 Andy Warhol Foundation for the Visual Arts/ARS, New York.

sailor," the rapacious phallus of male folklore. Popeye and his friends are cheerfully and aggressively lower class, their cartoon careers one long celebration of their ability to enjoy their "low appetites"—for each other, for food and drink, and, most of all, for spectacular brawling.

Yet within this carnivalesque milieu, Popeye is in one way an anomalous character, that is, in his relation to work and to technology in the industrial workplace of the earlier twentieth century. Indeed, Popeye's "sexiness" for the young Warhol may have inhered in part in his magical relation to physical strength and capacity for work, especially as these could be maximized by technology, as much as it did in Popeye's potentially queer (because he is the antithesis of a "proper" bourgeois male such as Dick Tracy) and prolie insouciance. One can readily imagine how appealing this combination of characteristics in a single figure might have been to a child with Warhol's anxious and ambitious relations to work, social class, and gender. The artist who famously proclaimed, "I want to be a machine," as Warhol did in the early sixties, may well have found a major, early fantasy model for himself in the figure of Popeye, who, as Michael Wassenaar has argued, played a uniquely complex role in mass culture representations of "man and machine" and specifically "man *as* machine" in the thirties and thereafter. Of the Popeye cartoons of Warhol's childhood in the thirties, Wasenaar writes: "Much like a metaphorical engineer, Popeye transforms himself in each of the Fleischer cartoons of Warhol's childhood in the thirties, Wassenaar writes: "Much like a metaphorical engineer, Popeye transforms himself in each of the Fleischer the engine—through which energy is transformed into work. As both regulator and regulated, engineer and machine, Popeye is a popular hero of the cybernetic."[13]

Dick Tracy and Popeye are the subjects of several of Warhol's first Pop experiments, as are Superman and Batman. Warhol embellished several versions of each of these images of his early Pop practice with repetitive crayon-stroke patterns, as if to signal that the two classes of figures (comic strip character and costumed comic book superhero) constituted one class of objects to the desiring child whose first art was "coloring." As we have seen, according to Warhol's own testimony, Dick Tracy and Popeye were both "sex symbols" to his child self. In recovering his memories of the sexiness that comic strip characters had had for him in childhood, Warhol assumed an attitude less marked by a coy and defensive knowingness than many of his contemporaries in the sixties, who affected to relish the kinky, fetishistic, and queer effects that the exploits of (for example) Batman and Robin continually produced while in many cases remaining committed to some version of a "liberated" heterosexuality for themselves.[14]

It is through the potential links that exist between the images of costumed superheroes and their potential erotic-fantasy value for children and adults that Warhol found one of his principal ways of radically refiguring the male-homoerotic in his earliest Pop paintings. In contrast with his numerous overtly erotic drawings of male friends and models in the pre-Pop work, his

Figure 4. Andy Warhol, *Superman* (1960). ©1996 Andy Warhol Foundation for the Visual Arts/ARS, New York.

portrayals of a figure such as Superman complicate the questions of what is erotically appealing about such a figure and how many kinds of desires can be served by a single, supposedly simple, cartoon image. Warhol and his fellow innovators of Pop had been among the first generation of children to participate in the early-childhood practice of fashioning "capes" and "disguises" out of towels and bathrobes and "flying" around the house with arms outstretched. Unlike the game of "Peter Pan," which had been current for a generation before and involved some of the same kinds of make-believe and which was more obviously rooted in the nursery condition of the strict limits exercised over children's powers, under which one could "fly" only as long as one refused to grow up, "playing superhero" was about fantasies of superpotency, of literally rising above the power of adults rendered suddenly puny and earthbound.

Although a superficial look at Warhol's *Superman* painting might suggest that it was merely a careful, uninflected copy of an image of the figure chosen at random, further inspection reveals numerous links between this work and the kinds of transformative labor the figure of Popeye represented in the popular culture of the 1930s. The figure of Superman hovers in the upper left-hand corner of the image, emitting a blast of air that fills the lower right-hand corner (see figure 4). Superman's "thought," "Good! A mighty puff of my super breath extinguished the forest fire!" is recorded in a balloon that Warhol has carefully copied and then partially obscured with white paint; the only immediately legible word in the picture is the great red "PUFF!" across its center. One set of gay male subculture meanings in which the painting may participate links it with *Blow Job,* the early film of Warhol made only about three years after this painting, which shows only the face and upper torso of a young man being fellated. Reversing the vertical visual logic of the film, the object of Superman's titanic "blow job" is below the lower border of the image—which is itself approximately six inches above the lower edge of the canvas, which is blank, except for a couple of paint drips. Although the figure of Superman is raised above the spectator's gaze and the lower back of his body is turned toward us, the picture does not represent the cleft of the buttocks, one of the conventional foci of male-homoerotic visual representation and one of the features of the male anatomy Warhol would have been most likely to emphasize in his pre-Pop homoerotic work. Indeed, Superman's trunks seem ovoid, even inflated, in a way that hardly conforms even to the loosely cartoony anatomy of the figure as ordinarily drawn; the trunks look more like a diaper or infant's rubber pants than like tight-fitting briefs over muscular adult-male buttocks.

Although in actual comic book art characters' body parts are generally indicated in only the most stylized manner, the depiction of the "superhero" body costumed in alternately flowing and fitted fabrics (cape and tights) conspicuously demarcated into separate regions has its own strongly sexualizing implications, as it does in this image by alternating red and blue garments, which highlight the chest, hips, buttocks, genital region, and feet. Despite (or perhaps because of) the way the figure's genital area and buttocks look somehow "diapered," concealed, and sealed off from the rest of the picture, its lower half is dominated by several massive columns of heavy "smoke" that look phallic and fecal at the same time; that the great flood of breath with which Superman extinguishes the forest fire is painted in a way that could also represent a great blast of water (the more usual way of putting out large fires) makes the image potentially one of urethral eroticism, too— so that several kinds of infantile erotic pleasure, available to so-called adult sexuality, too, although officially proscribed for it, are figured in the painting.

In a way, the painting simultaneously fulfills and dismisses the fearful prophecies of Fredric Wertham and other moralizing critics of comic books in the 1950s who feared (and so testified before government investigating bodies) that the early cathexis of costumed superheroes by child readers might produce a mass "pervert" culture of sadomasochistic fetishism.[15]

I was in junior high school during the years Warhol produced his early Pop paintings and can testify that pubescent boys were at the time still passing around their own crude cartoon drawings of Superman doing his superphallic thing, so to speak, usually to a prone and not quite recognizable Lois Lane. The hyperpotency of Superman and the literal defacement of Lois Lane in these drawings spoke volumes about both the phallic focus of our own newly imperative sexual desires and our collective although entirely unvoiced inability to imagine our desires inspiring any feelings in others besides fear and disgust. The image was one of many around which boys my age inducted ourselves with varying degrees of unwillingness into a scene of heterosexuality based on a restaging of the primal scene in which the imaginary object of our desires was at best faceless and at worst a victim of rape. I suspect that such fantasies and images had been formative for at least a generation at the time Warhol produced his revisionary image of a "superhero" of perverse, infantile pleasures.

Infantile eroticism bodes large in another of Warhol's initial Pop experiments: *Nancy* (1960) shows approximately a frame and a quarter of (presumably) a three- or four-frame sequence of the Ernie Bushmiller cartoon character (see figure 5). In the upper, "full" frame, Nancy, standing in front of her house, holds herself and shivers, "BRR   MY SNOW SUIT ISNT WARM ENOUGH — ILL PUT ON A SWEATER TOO." In the lower partial frame, all that is visible are the words "BRR   IM STILL." To understand the relation of this early Pop painting to the process of gay male encoding I have been analyzing, one might begin by recalling that "nancy" was (along with "fairy") one of the most common terms in circulation at the time of the painting's production, both inside and outside gay culture, for an effeminate and therefore presumptively homosexual man. In considering the range of sexualities the painting might represent, we should bear in mind the prevailing climate of homophobia and misogyny manifest in some of the dominant psychoanalytic and psychiatric discourse of the fifties and sixties. Take, for example, the widely cited work of such a prominent New York psychoanalyst of the

Figure 5. Andy Warhol, *Nancy* (1960). ©1996 Andy Warhol Foundation for the Visual Arts/ARS, New York.

period as Edmund Bergler, whose insistence on vaginal orgasm in heterosexual intercourse as an index of mental health in women ("Under frigidity we understand the incapacity of a woman to have a *vaginal orgasm during intercourse*," Bergler writes in his characteristically now-hear-this manner; a few lines later he foments, "The *sole criterion* of frigidity is absence of vaginal orgasm")[16] was as vehement as his parallel insistence on the necessity of psychiatric cure (what he calls "destruction of the perversion") for homosexuals.[17] Bergler and other "medical authorities" of his time took on what they saw as "sexual neurotics" in single groups in some of their books and articles and across the board, as it were, in other publications, as the title of a 1951 book of Bergler's attests: *Neurotic Counterfeit-Sex: Homosexuality, Impotence, and Frigidity.* The book's procedure, accurately articulated in the title, is to equate with each other the members of various groups of men and women who fail to achieve what Bergler and his colleagues see as a "healthy" and affirmative relation to heterosexual-male dominance. To deviate from this absolute standard is by definition to occupy one of the other positions, all of which are stigmatized as not only "neurotic" but also "counterfeit" (criminally false and deceptive) in the same gesture.

Besides those of the infantile pleasures we have already noticed, one of the other abjected positions Warhol explores in his early work—especially, perhaps, in *Nancy*—is that of the "frigid" woman; in this image he represents a transitional scene of thawing between her position and that of the similarly abjected gay male "nancy" and raises the question of whether there might not be strategic advantages in a gay man's energetically taking up the position of what may be the most misogynistic of twentieth-century psychiatric constructions, the frigid woman. "Frigid people really make it" became one of Warhol's favorite mottos, and although "frigidity" certainly admits of a wider range of meanings than simply "sexual unresponsiveness" (such as "habitually indifferent behavior" or "frostiness of manner"), there is a sense in which this putatively feminine sexual characteristic remains the "core" of the "frigid" identity he embraced as one of his chief public personae.[18]

Nancy was one of the first of Warhol's early Pop works to attract the attention and admiration of Ivan Karp of the Castelli Gallery. According to David Bourdon, what "grabbed" Karp about it on his first viewing was its "interrupted narrative sequence and its implication that Nancy remains out in the cold indefinitely."[19] Karp later spoke of the powerfully "chilling" effect of Warhol's early cartoon paintings, praising them for their "cold," "bleak," and "brutish" aspects—effects particularly conspicuous in *Nancy,* where the "frigid" effects the artist was producing in much of his work of the period are literally thematized: "outsider" Nancy tries to "warm up" but fails to and "stays frigid."[20]

Karp became an instrumental figure in explaining and defending Warhol's Pop work to art dealers and collectors as well as to the media, but considerations of gender and sexuality played no part in his or, to my knowledge, any other critic's theory of Pop until years afterward. Yet what Karp immediately recognized as some of the most notable qualities of a painting like *Nancy*— its "chilling" and "brutish" appearance, its "interrupted[ness]," its "freeze-frame" visual construction—all these characteristics require consideration in relation to the pathologized representations of feminine and gay male identity described above. As several lesbian and gay historians have amply demonstrated, gay people began "coming in from the cold" in large numbers in the fifties and sixties, began banding together socially and politically to reject the collective position that had been imposed on them of being officially "frozen out" of common life.[21] In the figure of Warhol's "Nancy," "STILL" freezing or frigid no matter how many garments she puts on, we have not only a picture of a frigid woman starting to thaw or melt but also an emblem of sorts for a strategic repudiation of "warm" models of gay male desire (of which the "warm" nudes of Warhol's late-fifties sketches could be said to represent literal exemplars) and gay male "community" and a similarly strategic embrace of an attributive femininity (or effeminacy) in its extremest (frigid) form (see figure 1, one of Warhol's conventionally homoerotic male nudes of the 1950s).

In a note to one of his major discussions of screen memories and memories of childhood, Freud interprets "frozenness" as a sign of the phallus. "From a dream of P.'s," he writes, "it appears that ice is in fact a symbol by antithesis for an erection: i.e. something that becomes hard in the cold instead of like a penis—in heat (in excitation)."[22] Warhol, too, attributed phallic significance to some of his more famously static or "frozen" Pop productions, such as his eight-hour-film of the top section of the Empire State Building, which he reportedly referred to as "an eight-hour hard-on," predictably linking its subject to one of the hunky costumed cartoon and serial heroes of his childhood: "The Empire State Building is a star. . . . It's so beautiful. The lights come on and the stars come out and it sways. It's like Flash Gordon riding into space."[23] We may recall from his narration of his memory of his childhood illness to Ultra Violet that "star" seems to have served him as a term both for the phallic object of desire ("dick," Dick Tracy, and so forth) and for the paradoxically "cold" source of light and identification. "Frozen" by their stardom into an imaginarily permanent state of "erection" or elevation above the field of desire, Warhol's cartoon "stars" are the symbolically saturated figures of his childhood to whom he ritualistically— and productively—returned when he undertook to produce a break between his identity and his work, as well as in his own relations to these phenomena.

Again, we may look to *Nancy* for a complex representation of some of the signs of infantile erotic desire and pleasure that I have discussed in relation to Warhol's *Superman*. Most of the left three-quarters of the painting (showing the exterior of Nancy's house) is what one might call a "muddy" or "urine" yellow, while the upper right-hand quarter of it is a cool "ice blue." This dual color scheme is interrupted two-thirds of the way down the canvas by the horizontal bank of "snow" in which Nancy stands, a patch of paint that extends from one side of the painting to the other and ranges in color from off-white to a dingy brownish white (significantly, the two speech balloons are painted in the same way the snowbank is). The three large patches of color that make up the painting are brought into particularly tense relation to each other in the figure of Nancy herself, who stands hunched stiffly forward from the shoulders, her knees flexed and held tightly together in a way that suggests she not only might be cold but also might have to pee; the ice-blue pants of her snowsuit heighten the subliminal effect of the pose of "frozen" discomfort, and their "puffy" and "stuffed" appearance suggest—as the similar appearance of the trunks did in *Superman*—that an infantile urethral erotics may be in play here. *Superman* is energized by the "mighty puff" of "super-breath" that also looks like a flood of water (or urine) loosed from on high; the energy of *Nancy* is withheld or held in in the crouching figure of Nancy, although the field of "urine" yellow that surrounds her hints at a release of energy and tension—from urethral retention—of a kind that doesn't do any "work" (as the "mighty puff" of "super-breath" does). I have been arguing that the cartoon figures in Warhol's early Pop are "symbolically saturated" ones, and here in a sense is a picture that is on one level all about saturation, of the literal kind everyone experiences in infancy and early childhood (and sometimes later, although the experience of "wetting one-self" as an adult is so highly stigmatized as hardly to make it into discourse except as a sign of intense abjection).[24] In the mid- to late seventies, Warhol made what he informally called "Piss Paintings"—later exhibited and sold as *Oxidation Paintings*—on canvases that had been specially prepared to register permanently the streams of urine directed onto them by the artist and some of his assistants, but an early Pop painting like *Nancy* experiments with literalizing urination in less direct fashion.

Nancy's boots are a blur of bright red, the same color as the bow in her hair; these are two of the painting's "hot spots," suggesting that Nancy is "hot" from head to toe at the same time that she's "STILL" (the painting's enacted but unspoken—because they are interrupted—words) "COLD" or even "FREEZING." The blurry, undelineated appearance of Nancy's boots marks them as a particularly highly liminal space in the painting, between heat and cold, frozen and liquid, body and landscape. The push-panel on the door behind her, the point of possible escape for her from the frigid scene she inhabits, is the painting's other bright red hot spot. Nancy's flesh-colored face, fiercely punctuated by her black porcupine hairdo, is the only small area of what one might call tonal neutrality in the little "war" among the red, blue, and yellow physical states (heat, cold, and urine or urination) that the painting depicts. It is notable that the way the painting represents the expression of intense concentration and resolve on Nancy's face is through a configuration of punctuation marks: her brows, the wrinkles of concentration between them, her eyes, nose, and mouth form a kind of typographical pun on a determined face, composed entirely of parentheses, quotation marks, hyphens, and periods. It is as if the missing punctuation from the sentence in the speech balloon over her head had migrated to her face, which registers for the viewer as a kind of complex exclamation mark.

This figure of a child's body, eroticized in terms of an infantile erotics that is subliminally represented as potentially dissipating its energies in a puddle of urine and/or thawing slush, is instead arrested, "frozen," and focused at a threshold moment of increasingly intolerable discomfort. The painting as a whole, like others of the early Pop work, itself functions as a kind of complex, hypergraphic punctuation mark, like the stars-inducing "punch" of the mighty first in *Saturday's Popeye* (1960) and *Popeye* (1961) or in the aforementioned cyclonic "PUFF!" of *Superman*. The affective burst that *Nancy* enacts is perhaps more rather than less powerful than Popeye's and Superman's "super"-virile actions because it is deferred indefinitely ("IM STILL"), represented as simultaneously being contained and becoming uncontained, like the thawed water emerging from the snow or the urine (already coloring most of the scene) threatening to escape from the body.

As we have seen him doing in the painting *Nancy* and as I believe we see him doing in much of the Pop painting of the early sixties and in his writing and other kinds of production most closely related to it (for example, his films), Warhol derived—from the most hieratic and highly stylized gestural moments ("the frozen moment") of operatic and balletic performance, of highbrow and middlebrow tragedy, of middlebrow melodrama and lowbrow cartoons—a cool, mechanical, antitragic, antigrandiose, anti-self-sacrificial moment of a kind that had a powerfully disruptive effect on the cultural pieties that underwrote much female and gay-male oppression and self-oppression in postwar culture.[25]

If "feelings" and "style" of some kinds do get eliminated from Warhol's early Pop work, other kinds of "feelings"—commonly despised ones, infantile and other kinds of proscribed ones—play lambently around the margins and, as we have just seen, sometimes at the center of his transformed practice. What Warhol spoke of at the time as the total elimination of "style" from his work is rather an elimination of what was generally considered to constitute style in midcentury United States: carefully cultivated technique employed in the painstaking transmission of a highly refined body of artistic conventions. In attempting, beginning about 1960, to rid his art of all conventional signs of the "piss-elegant" style he had pursued so fervently and single-mindedly in his pre-Pop art, Warhol discovered in the process of reengaging with the comic strip style and the comic-strip erotics of his childhood a field of representation that, however far removed from the explicit pre-Pop drawings of male nudes, is nonetheless valuable precisely for the ways in which it complicates and enriches notions of what constitutes queer artistic production.

NOTES

∎

I wish to thank Marcie Frank, Jonathan Goldberg, and Eve Kosofsky Sedgwick for invaluable counsel about this article. Thanks also to audiences at Duke University, Tulane University, and Williams College and to participants in the Mass Culture Workshop at the University of Chicago for stimulus and debate.

1   Andy Warhol and Pat Hackett, *POPism: The Warhol Sixties* (New York: Harcourt Brace Jovanovich, 1980), p. 116.

2   *The Complete Poems and Selected Letters and Prose of Hart Crane,* ed. Brown Weber (New York: Anchor Books, 1966), p. 21.

3   Victor Bockris, *The Life and Death of Andy Warhol* (New York: Bantam, 1989), provides numerous accounts, many of them based on the testimony of participants, of the artist's production of images of the male nude in several media throughout his career. On Warhol's sketching sessions of the fifties, see, for example, pp. 61–62; for accounts of his exhibitions of "boy drawings" of 1952, 1954, and 1956, see pp. 67–68, 78–79, and 84, respectively. For an account of some of Warhol's "Polaroid sex sessions" of the seventies, see Bob Colacello, *Holy Terror: Andy Warhol Close Up* (New York: HarperCollins, 1990), pp. 343–344. For a thoughtful analysis of some of the many ways in which Warhol's work of the fifties participated in gay male subcultural life in Manhattan and beyond, see Trevor Fairbrother, "Tomorrow's Man," in *"Success is a job in New York . . .": The Early Art and Business of Andy Warhol* (New York: Carnegie Museum of Art, 1989), pp. 55–74.

4   Warhol relates an anecdote in *POPism* that has become emblematic of his abject and anomalous relation to the New York art world at the end of the fifties; this is the often-cited tale of his asking his friend Emile de Antonio why Warhol's fellow artists and fellow fags Robert Rauschenberg and Jasper Johns routinely snubbed him. "You're too swish, and that upsets them," de Antonio informed Warhol. Interestingly, he adds that Rauschenberg and Johns were also put off by Warhol's collecting habits (already a conspicuous aspect of his persona) and his use of his own name in his commercial work (Rauschenberg and Johns designed windows for Tiffany's under a discrete pseudonym). Conspicuous consumption of other artists' work and conspicuous success as a commercial artist both seem to be taken as intensifications of Warhol's effeminate personal mannerisms by his anxious and relatively closeted contemporaries. See Andy Warhol and Pat Hackett, *POPism: The Warhol Sixties* (New York: Harcourt Brace Jovanovich, 1980), pp. 11–13.

5   See, for example, Kenneth E. Silver, who attempts to situate what he reads as "gay identity" both in relation to Warhol's art and that of a number of his gay contemporaries and predecessors in his wide-ranging article "Modes of Disclosure: The Construction of Gay

Identity and the Rise of Pop Art," in *Hand-Painted Pop: American Art in Transition, 1955–62,* ed. Russell Ferguson (Los Angeles: Museum of Contemporary Art, 1992), pp. 179–203; see especially Silver's exhaustive discussion of Rauschenberg's and Johns's response to Warhol, pp. 193–197. See also Richard Meyer's analysis of *Thirteen Most Wanted Men* in his article "Warhol's Clones," *Yale Journal of Criticism* 7, no. 1 (Spring 1994): 79–109.

6   Andy Warhol, *The Philosophy of Andy Warhol* (New York: Harcourt Brace Jovanovich, 1975), pp. 21–22.

7   For "Screen Memory" and "Primal Scene," see respective entries in Jean Laplanche and J.-B. Pontalis, *The Language of Psycho-Analysis,* trans. Donald Nicholson-Smith (New York: W. W. Norton, 1973). For a wide-ranging analysis of the place of "primal-scene" theories in the writings of Henry James, Freud, and Heidegger, see Ned Lukacher, *Primal Scenes: Literature, Philosophy, Psychoanalysis* (Ithaca: Cornell University Press, 1986).

8   Warhol, *Philosophy,* p. 84.

9   See references in note 1 above to accounts of Warhol sketching male-male sex scenes in the fifties in Bockris, *Life and Death of Andy Warhol,* and photographing them in the seventies in Colacello, *Holy Terror.*

10   Ultra Violet, *Famous for Fifteen Minutes: My Years with Andy Warhol* (New York: Avon, 1988), pp. 154–155. Note the author's "Disclaimer," p. v: "I have relied on memory, diaries, tapes, recorded phone calls, press clippings, books, magazines, interviews, and conversations to document what I bear witness to. Some conversations are reconstructed and are not intended, nor should they be construed, as verbatim quotes."

11   Ibid., p. 155.

12   "What is Pop Art?" interviews by G. R. Swenson with Andy Warhol and other painters, *Art News,* November 1963, p. 60.

13   Michael Wassenaar, "Strong to the Finich: Machines, Metaphor, and Popeye the Sailor," *Velvet Light Trap* 24 (Fall 1989): 23.

14   See Sasha Torres's essay on Batman in popular culture of the sixties in this volume.

15   Fredric Wertham, *Seduction of the Innocent* (New York: Holt, Rinehart and Winston, 1954), and Gillian Freeman, *The Undergrowth of Literature* (London: Nelson, 1967).

16   Edmund Bergler, quoted by Robert Anton Wilson, "Attitudes toward Sex, Modern," in *The Encyclopedia of Sexual Behavior,* ed. Albert Ellis and Albert Abarbanel (New York: Hawthorn, 1961), p. 190; emphases Bergler's.

17   Edmund Bergler, "Homosexuality and the Kinsey Report," in *The Homosexuals: As Seen by Themselves and Thirty Authorities,* ed. A. M. Krich (New York: Citadel, 1958), p. 233.

18   See, for example, Warhol's discussion of this motto in his *Philosophy,* p. 98.

19   David Bourdon, *Warhol* (New York: Harry N. Abrams, 1989), p. 82.

20   Of the terms in the first part of this sentence, "cold" is quoted in Bourdon; the rest of the terms are quoted from the interview with Karp in the British documentary on Warhol.

21   Among the key texts in the recent historiography of gay and lesbian social and political movements "before Stonewall" is *Before Stonewall,* directed by Greta Schiller and co-directed by Robert Rosenberg (1986) videocassette; Allan Berubé, *Coming Out under Fire: The History of Gay Men and Women in World War Two* (New York: Free Press, 1990); John D'Emilio, *Sexual Politics, Sexual Communities: The Making of a Homosexual Minority in the*

United States, 1940–1970 (Chicago: University of Chicago Press, 1983); Elizabeth Lapovsky Kennedy and Madeline Davis, *Boots of Leather, Slippers of Gold: The History of a Lesbian Community* (New York: Routledge, 1993); Stuart Timmons, *The Trouble with Harry Hay* (Boston: Alyson, 1990).

22 Freud, "Childhood Memories and Screen Memories," in *The Psychopathology of Everyday Life,* trans. Alan Tyson; ed. James Strachey (New York: Norton, 1960), p. 49 n. 2.

23 Warhol, quoted in Bockris, *Life and Death of Andy Warhol,* p. 154.

24 "Saturation" is Sándor Ferenczi's term for infantile sexual pleasure, in contrast with the cyclic and climactic qualities that characterize adult sexuality. See his essay "Confusion of Tongues between Adults and the Child" (1933), reprinted in Sándor Ferenczi, *Final Contributions to the Problems and Methods of Psychoanalysis,* ed. Michael Balint (New York: Brunner/Mazel, 1980), pp. 156–167.

25 Peter Brooks has written compellingly about the history and effects of "the frozen moment" of melodrama in nineteenth-century literary and theatrical culture in *The Melodramatic Imagination: Balzac, Henry James, Melodrama, and the Mode of Excess* (New Haven: Yale University Press, 1976).

JONATHAN FLATLEY
Warhol Gives Good Face:
Publicity and the Politics of Prosopopoeia

Suddenly we all felt like *insiders* because even though Pop was everywhere—that was the thing about it, most people still took it for granted, whereas we were dazzled by it—to us it was the new Art. *Once you "got" Pop, you could never see a sign the same way again.* And once you thought Pop, you could never see America the same way again.— Andy Warhol, *POPism*[1]

ndy Warhol had his own way of seeing the world. For Warhol, this *way of seeing*[2]—what he called "Pop"—had a transformative effect so powerful that once you "got it," you "could never see a sign the same way again," indeed "could never see America the same way again." In asserting that seeing and thinking "Pop" not only made everything look different but also allowed him and his queer friends to feel "suddenly" like "insiders," I believe that Warhol gives us an important insight into the attraction and potentially political energies of Pop. In this essay, I am interested in understanding how the Pop way of seeing is embodied in Warhol's paintings and films, how Pop achieves its effects, and what it means to "feel" like an insider.

It is likely that the word "insider" is a meaningful one for Warhol because of the currency enjoyed by the figure of the "outsider" in the fifties and early sixties, a currency owed in part to the 1956 publication of Colin Wilson's *The Outsider*,[3] where Wilson explored the effects of oppressive normativity in modern Western culture on different exemplary "outsiders." One of his theses is that "outsider" status, while signaling exclusion and "abnormality," also enables one to see structuring elements of society that are invisible to others.

By thinking in terms of "outsiders" and "insiders," fifties homosexuals like Warhol could access, before Stonewall and identity politics, a vocabulary that could express and even politicize the experience of being queer in a homophobic culture. In saying that Pop allowed him to feel like an insider, Warhol suggests that Pop was, among other things, a tactic for surviving in a homophobic world. But *how?* How does being "dazzled" by what everyone else takes "for granted" make Warhol and his friends feel like insiders? Warhol notes that "Pop Art took the inside and put it outside, took the outside and put it inside. The Pop artists did images that anybody walking down Broadway could recognize in a split second—comics, picnic tables, men's trousers, celebrities, shower curtains, refrigerators, Coke bottles—all the great things that the Abstract Expressionists tried so hard not to notice at all."[4] By taking the "images that anybody walking down Broadway could recognize in a split second" inside the canvas as the "new art," Warhol not only reversed the macho[5] abstract expressionist valorization of "all that abstraction and introspective stuff." Taking these public images as his palette also opened this "outside" world to appropriation and transformation, bringing himself and his friends inside it as active participants in this public image-space. In fact, eventually this reuse of already recognizable images literally made Warhol an art world insider. Pop gave *him* a public.

These two moves—the de-reification of mass culture images and the acquisition of a public persona—are what made Warhol feel like an insider. I want to think about these moves as constituting something of a survival strategy. After all, a faggy, pasty-white, working-class queer from Pittsburgh such as Warhol was as unlikely as anyone to find representations of himself, his desires, or his experiences "inside" the public sphere, especially in the fifties. If he was to make any use of the images around him, he was surely going to have to de-reify and develop a creative and imaginative relation to them. By all indications, it was while he was still a child that Warhol developed the skills that enabled him to gather the raw material—from comic strips, radio shows, coloring books, and Hollywood celebrities—with which he managed and imaginatively created an identity.[6] It is noteworthy that these skills translated into an art movement that recognized as its starting point the necessity of taking public images as the kind of raw material of our culture, material that could not be ignored, especially by those it excluded. Warhol's persistent, career-long exploration of what we might call the "poetics of publicity" can be seen in part to rise from the need to mourn his own absence from the public sphere.

Warhol knew what it was like to be refused access to publicity—in the most basic sense of appearance before others—because of his unwillingness to disavow his effeminacy, his homosexuality, and his admiration of the male body. It is well known, for example, that his 1956 attempt to get his own show at the Tanager Gallery was rejected because his affectionate portraits of boys were too indiscreet, too unabashed in their homoerotic sexiness,[7] and that in the early sixties Warhol was spurned by other New York artists such as Robert Rauschenberg and Jasper Johns, as well as mainstream art circles, for being "too swishy." And, even after Warhol gained art world respectability— not, of course, for his homoerotic work but as the "pope of Pop" and as avant-garde film director—he and his friends remained vulnerable to homo- phobic attacks. About this, Warhol writes:

> Naturally the Factory had fags; we were in the entertainment business and—That's Entertainment. Naturally, the Factory had more gays than, say, Congress, but it probably wasn't even as gay as your favorite TV police show. . . . I think the reason we were attacked so much and so vehemently was because we refused to play along and be hypocritical and covert. That really incensed a lot of people who wanted the old stereotypes to stay around. I often wondered, "Don't the people who play these image games care about all the miserable people in the world who can't fit into stock roles?"[8]

If it were homosexuality as a *practice* that was the subject of the attacks, Warhol recognizes, then all Hollywood would be as vulnerable as the Fac- tory ("the Factory . . . probably wasn't even as gay as your favorite TV police show."). The unease at the source of the attacks concerned the *public display* of a sexuality that was not a straight male one, the way that Warhol "refused to play along and be hypocritical and covert." To have access to the public, to *be* public, whether as a politician or a TV actor, one had to fill a *stock role,* stock roles that were more available to some than to others.

What Warhol astutely notes is that the ability to be a specific person with a specific body and specific desires is in tension with the ability to be ab- stracted into a public person, a process he aptly describes as "fitting into a stock role." It's just that some specific people fit into stock roles better than others. Or as Michael Warner puts it, "Some particularities, such as white-ness and maleness, are already oriented to the procedure of abstraction."[9] Others, as in Warhol's observation, like homosexual men who wanted to get jobs as TV actors, might be *tolerated,* but only so long as they could occupy a stock bodily role, at least temporarily—or at least publicly if not "privately."

Warner suggests that we think about these mechanisms of our public sphere in terms of the dialectic between *negativity* and *embodiment,* between being public and being a body. Identification with a "disembodied public subject" who is parallel to your private person has its attractions, even neces-sities. Warhol recognized that one needs to be publicly representable—that one needs at least to be able to *imagine* that one is representable—in order to feel like one *is* at all.[10] As David Wojnarowicz puts it: "Sexuality defined in images gives me comfort in a hostile world. They give me strength. I have always loved my anonymity and therein lies a contradiction because I find comfort in seeing representations of my private experiences in the public environment."[11] When we acquire a public persona or identify with public bodies, we participate in "utopias of self-abstraction" that enable us to feel as if we have transcended our particularity. We gain a certain kind of anonymity in identifying with a body that could in principle be anybody's body. More-over, seeing bodies that are like our own in public spaces assures us that we won't be excluded from publicity because of our bodies, that we will not be marked, excluded, refused.

At least in part, the disembodied public self is attractive for what it enables one to see that one is *not:* to be public is to transcend particularity, embodi-ment, and domesticity, the spaces where the disenfranchised have histor-ically been made to dwell. In U.S. culture, authority and "insideness" is connected with the privilege to suppress and protect the body.[12] For those who have not been able to transcend their specific corporeality in the ab-stract realm of citizen, their hyperembodiment serves as a continual obstacle to power and pleasure. Thus, women, African Americans, and other minor-itized persons who had been historically unable to participate in the political public sphere have had to find other ways to access publicity.

One important way Warhol accessed publicity was through the creation of queer versions of what Nancy Fraser has called *subaltern counterpublics.* Fraser argues that the idea of *the* public has been limiting and inaccurate insofar as a singular public has often served as a mechanism of exclusion and has rarely been a meeting place of social equals. She thus uses counterpublic to indicate parallel discursive arenas where members of subordinated social groups invent and circulate counterdiscourses, so as to "formulate oppositional interpretations of their identities, interests and needs."[13] For Warhol, a counterpublic like the Factory is valuable not only because it enables "oppositional interpretations" but also because it enables the appearance and visibility of alternative sexual practices. Thus, Warhol says, "If a man sees two guys having sex, he finds out one of two things: either he's turned on or turned off—so then he knows where he stands in life."[14] The Factory was a counterpublic insofar as it was a place and a space where you *could* see two men having sex. Likewise, part of the utopian impulse behind his homoerotic films, paintings, drawings, and photos was the desire to turn galleries, museums, movie theaters, art studios, and other places into queer counterspaces. What was disturbing to some and nourishing and exciting for others was the way that Warhol resisted being fit into stock roles by changing, mocking, or exploding them while at the same time cleverly and persistently promoting himself in the public eye.

But like other minoritized subjects, Warhol sought not only to create counterpublics but also to access the elements of publicity present in aspects of everyday life such as consumption, spectatorship, and fandom.[15] Warner writes, "As the subjects of publicity—its 'hearers,' 'speakers,' 'viewers' and 'doers'—we have a different relation to ourselves, a different affect, from that which we have in other contexts."[16] Throughout his career, Warhol explored the ways that we could be hearers, speakers, viewers, and doers of publicity, even when our presence is not permitted, let alone desired, in the public sphere. In this essay, I will argue that even if Warhol was not always successful (for example regarding the AIDS epidemic) in his manipulation of the "poetics of publicity," he nonetheless offers us valuable insight into its logic and mechanics, values and dangers.

Warhol saw that the poetics of publicity were also those of mourning. To become public or feel public was in many ways to acquire the sort of distance from oneself that comes with imagining oneself dead. The "self-negativity" that we experience by imagining ourselves as "public" might be seen as something like attending your own funeral. You got to see yourself reified, eulogized, coherent, whole—and you get to see other people recognizing you.[17] The connection between recognition, mourning, and funerals was always a major interest of Warhol. In, for example, the early *Jackie* and *Marilyn* paintings, Warhol draws attention to the homology between the face-giving that portraiture accomplishes and the work of representing or memorializing involved in mourning.

Many of Warhol's persistent interests—portraiture, celebrity, consumption, pornography, and disasters—can be usefully understood together in terms of prosopopoeia, the fiction of a voice beyond the grave. It is the trope that ascribes face, name, or voice to the absent, inanimate, or dead; it means literally to give or create (*poeia*) a face or person (*prosopon*), to person-ify. As the medium of face intelligibility and recognition, prosopopoeia is the trope of fame and shame alike.

In his essay "Autobiography as De-facement," Paul de Man described prosopopoeia as the trope through which "one's name is made as memorable and intelligible as a face."[18] For de Man, the fact that autobiography as much as the epitaph trades on the trope of prosopopoeia suggests the impossibility of making a generic distinction between the two. Instead, the moment of face-giving can be thought about as a figure of understanding or cognition, the specular moment involved in *any* attempt to address another, read a text, or recognize oneself. Thus, autobiography is interesting not because it reveals reliable information about the self but insofar as, when we think about it in terms of prosopopoeia, it illustrates the *impossibility* of self-identity and the fact that the giving of face, to the extent that it must presuppose an absence, always also entails a de-facing. Likewise, portraiture, especially in the case of Warhol, is not interesting in the commentary it provides about its subjects (though his portraits usually do that too) but to the degree that it illustrates the incoherencies internal to recognizability, address, mourning, and identity. Or as Gertrude Stein put it: "It is not extremely difficult not to have identity but it is extremely difficult the knowing not having identity. One might say it is impossible but that it is not impossible is proved by the existence of masterpieces which are just that."[19]

In Warhol's work, both the commodity and the celebrity, the advertisement and the elegy are situated in the prosopopoetic economy, an economy that defaces as it gives face, that produces anonymity even as it enables recognition, and does not distinguish between the dead and the living. Through his engagement with prosopopoeia—in the Campbell soup cans, the elegiac portraits of the just-dead Marilyn Monroe and a mourning Jackie Kennedy, and the gruesome pictures of disaster victims—Warhol learned how to mourn his own absence from the already recognizable world of public images; Warhol learned how to give *himself* a face. Like any commodity, however, this did not come without cost.

FACE VALUE
■

"I can certainly say that I never began to live, until I looked upon myself as a dead man."—J.-J. Rousseau, *Confessions*[20]

The intimate relation between portraiture and mourning did not go unobserved by Warhol's contemporaries or his sitters. Indeed, they knew that the epitaph-like quality of Warhol's portraits was precisely the source of their value. Jasper Johns is reported to have said to Holly Solomon on seeing Warhol's portrait of her, "Hi Holly, (kiss) how does it feel to be dead?"[21] (see figure 1). She gloated in reply, "Long after I'm dead, it will be hanging," acknowledging that the portrait renders her dead insofar as it turns her into an objet d'art, a "Warhol," and therefore not only bestows on her the aura of celebrity but insures that she will be remembered long after her death. Like a visual elegy or epitaph, it preserves her best look for posterity. As David Bourdon remarks, "The commissioning of a Warhol portrait was a sure indication that the sitter intended to achieve posthumous fame,"[22] for to become the subject of a Warhol portrait was to participate in the fame of Warhol's other sitters and of Warhol himself. Yet, for the sitter, becoming an objet d'art is, after all, becoming an *object,* or more nearly a commodity, brand "Warhol." The less sanguine suggestion of Johns's question ("How does it feel to be dead?") concerns the effect that the portrait has on the *living* Solomon, that is, How does it feel to be a commodity, to be valued as a person only insofar as you are taken for a thing? and How does it feel to be famous, a *public* figure?

In dramatizing these issues so explicitly, Warhol's portraits departed radically from a portrait tradition in which a portrait was valuable inasmuch as it was a representation of the *individuality* of the person portrayed.[23] We can see this in the puzzled and often hostile reaction of art critics to his portraits. Even though the portraits received a degree of art world legitimacy with a Whitney exhibit, "Portraits of the Seventies," the commissioned portraits remained the special objects of critical vitriol, frequently cited as the most

Figure 1. Andy Warhol, *Holly Solomon* (1966). ©1996 Andy Warhol Foundation for the Visual Arts/ARS, New York.

vulgar example of Warhol's having "sold out" or "prostituted" himself. Even sympathetic critics such as Benjamin Buchloh found the portraits interesting precisely as one of Warhol's most "corrupted and debased moments."[24] Like much of Warhol's art, these portraits occasioned anxiety about the status of art, about the artist, and about the confusion of things with persons.

These were issues which Warhol had been addressing since his early celebrity portraits and which were in fact implicit in his silkscreening technique. This method, which relied on the reproduction of a photograph to create the desired "assembly-line effect," did not require a live sitter. As Warhol noted: "With silkscreening, you pick a photograph, blow it up, transfer it in glue onto silk, and then roll ink across so the ink goes through the silk but not through the glue. That way you get the same image, slightly different, each time. . . . My first experiments with screens were heads of Troy Donahue and Warren Beatty, and then when Marilyn Monroe happened to die that month, I got the idea to make screens of her beautiful face—the first Marilyns."[25] Since the starting point of the process is a photograph—one that was often touched up—and not a person, Warhol did not "represent" faces, he "produced" them or, to use the term popularized by Baudrillard, "simulated" them.[26] The work of art is conceived of not in relation to a "real person" but in relation to the process of reproducibility itself, and so we can say that Warhol worked from a *model* rather than an "original." The "person" disappears from the process as if she had never existed.

Warhol portraits literally "gave" his sitters their "best look." Because Warhol had a firm belief in, as he put it, "plastic surgery," "low lights and trick mirrors,"[27] Warhol erased wrinkles, cut off double chins, removed zits, and made eyes brighter and lips fuller. His portraits, in all their stylized brilliance, do not refer to any "real" face but instead to an ideal model, the "star." Brooke Hayward, who, like her husband Dennis Hopper, commissioned a portrait (see figure 2), described what we might call the "aesthetic ideology" behind Warhol's portrait "style": "Andy conceived of his portraits as idealized versions of his sitters. In my case, Andy always had this conceit that I should have been a movie star, which no doubt is why he chose, of all the Polaroids, the most glamourous pose and rendered it in classic Easter egg colors. By using all those powerful colors, all reality is swept away."[28] In an astute set of observations, Hayward notes Warhol's "conceit that [she] should have been a movie star," drawing the connection between her portrait and Warhol's long-standing interest in celebrity portraits. Hayward's remark is funny, too, though, because Warhol had a conceit that *everyone* should be a superstar. "If everybody's not a beauty, then no one is."[29] By "giving face," in that famous "Warhol" way, Warhol reproduced the star effect for all his sitters, at the same time that he drew attention to the constructed, anonymous identity of all the stars.[30]

Hayward suggests that in the commissioned portraits, as in the celebrity portraits, the "beauty effect," or "idealization" was achieved through Warhol's use of color and pose. In persistently painting "poses" rather than persons, Warhol undermines any attempt to read his painting as expressive (of the artist's creativity or emotions) or interpretive (of the sitter's character or inner nature); it minimizes the artist's "artistry," emphasizing instead the

Figure 2. Andy Warhol, *Brooke Hopper* (1973). ©1996 Andy Warhol Foundation for the Visual Arts/ARS, New York.

already existing artificiality of "reality." In a wide range of his paintings—the celebrity portraits, the *Statue of Liberty,* or the *Ladies and Gentlemen* portraits of black drag queens—we can see that Warhol was interested in already-made-up faces, obviously fictional identities, containers or signs of something else. So, for Brooke Hayward, he chose "the most glamorous pose" and used a color that evoked "classic Easter egg" associations. In this way, as Hayward notes, "all reality is swept away." The portrait is something like a glossy mask, an idealized, fixed version of oneself, to which one is always faced with the task of "living up." While Solomon's best look is preserved on the canvas, it is a look she can never match. Solomon will forever after—as if in fact she *were* dead—be haunted by her portrait. In refusing to sit for any more portraits, Dorian Gray said: "There is something fatal about a portrait. It has a life of its own."[31]

In fact, as Warhol suggests in noting that Marilyn's death gave him the idea "to make screens of her beautiful face," the posthumous portrait is the ideal one. (And, in fact, Warhol did accept commissions for at least two posthumous portraits.) The *idea* of the screened face is incompatible with the existence of the living face; to make screens of someone's face requires the ability to imagine that the person is dead, to mourn, as it were, in advance of death. Thus, for another example, Warhol claimed that it was the rumors of Liz Taylor's deathly illness on the set of *Cleopatra* in 1962 that gave him the idea to do a series of portraits of her.

This mournful structure of the portraits is also the mechanism that enables his fan identification with the celebrity. These sexy, powerful, and glamorous Hollywood divas were attractive to Warhol as a fan, something that seems especially apparent in a painting such as *Gold Marilyn Monroe* (1962), which depicts Marilyn like a saint in an icon. To begin with, they gained fame and fortune precisely through an unabashed relation to their sexuality. In addition, Marilyn Monroe occupied a somewhat special status because she not only was a movie star and a popular icon but also had crossed over from commercial entertainment to become the coveted object of high-culture adulation as the subject of a famous Willem de Kooning painting (*Woman 1*, 1950–52), as the wife of Arthur Miller, and a participant in the glamour of the Kennedy presidency. It was a crossover that Warhol, a successful commercial artist, was himself trying to make at the time.[32] So these portraits were not only works of mourning but also (or more nearly therefore) embodiments of the fantasies of identification specific to the fan. Indeed, it is the ability to imagine mourning for celebrity divas such as Marilyn or Liz that allows us to feel like we may incorporate their diva-ness, their relation to publicity. For Warhol, this kind of identification *was* the work of mourning.

We might say that Warhol's portraits occupy an aporia between prosopopoeia and *hypogram*. The Greek word *hypographein,* which means "to underscore by means of makeup the features of a face," was the basis of Ferdinand de Saussure's term "hypogram," which was the figure that "underscored a name, a word, by trying to repeat its syllables, and thus giving it another, artificial mode of being added, so to speak to the original mode of the word."[33] While the hypogram denotes the existence of a stable face that can

be "embellished, underscored, accentuated or supplemented by the hypogram . . . *prosopon-peia* means to *give* a face and therefore implies that the
original face can be missing or nonexistent."[34]

On the one hand, Warhol's portraits have the appearance of being like
hypograms, decorative makeup jobs that are unable to "signify" anything in
themselves. On the other, the supplementary act of underscoring, *by means
of makeup,* the features of a face, turns out not to be simple addition, "increase," or improvement but in fact a display of the radical instability of
recognizability. Prosopopoeia may be a fictive voice, but as Jacques Derrida
has remarked, it is a voice "which haunts any said real or present voice."[35]
The hypogramic quality of Warhol's portraits quickly slides to the prosopopoetic, inflecting *all* our face recognitions with an uncanny sense of the
fictive. As Dorian Gray came tragically to understand, our portraits haunt *us.*
Warhol's portraits remind us that *recognition*—of the famous and the everyday alike—is contingent on our ability to *remember* the image of a person in
the same way *as if* we were mourning her. There is no recognition, indeed no
face, as it were, *before* the portrait.

Judith Butler has reminded us that Freud theorized that all identifications
are made in response to a loss of some kind and that "they involve a certain
mimetic practice that seeks to incorporate the lost love within the very identity of the one who remains."[36] In his earlier writings, Freud conceived of an
opposition between (1) the work of *mourning,* which entailed a de-cathexis
from the lost love object in accordance with "reality" so that the love object
could be replaced with others, and (2) *melancholia,* which was a failure to
mourn, characterized by a hallucinatory preservation of the lost love in the
ego, variously characterized as "incorporation," "introjection" or "identification."[37] Later, however, Freud suggests that the "identification" associated
with melancholia may be "the sole condition under which the id can give up
its objects."[38] "Hallucination" is necessary to come to terms with "reality,"
which suggests that the distinction was suspect to begin with. It was certainly suspect for Warhol; as he said, "I don't know where the artificial stops
and the real begins."

In an extension of the above Freudian understanding, Jacques Lacan characterized the "work of mourning" as a masquerade, remarking that "the
function of the mask . . . dominates the identifications through which refusals of love are resolved."[39] Commenting on Lacan, Butler writes, "The mask is

taken on through the process of incorporation which is a way of inscribing and then wearing a melancholic identification in and on the body. . . . Dominated through appropriation, every refusal fails, and the refuser becomes part of the very identity of the refused, indeed becomes the psychic refuse of the refused."[40] Warhol's failures to fit stock roles—his refusals— turned themselves into the scene and seen of his art. His incorporations through the mask allowed him to feel inside a realm of publicity from which he had been refused access. Warhol's melancholic way of seeing, though it dwelled on loss and refusal, was the opposite of *depressing.*

After all, Warhol's identification with fame worked. He became in fact identified with Monroe and her fame, literally: the *Marilyns* were "Warhols." As these faces became "Warhols," *his* name became as recognizable as was Marilyn's face. And, in turn, he was able to make his own face famous. Early in Warhol's career, Ivan Karp gave him now famous advice: "You know people want to see *you.* Your looks are a certain part of your fame—they feed the imagination."[41] He could have said, They need to see your face to consume and incorporate you.

Warhol made good use of his own visage in feeding the public imagination. In the *Myths* (1981) series (see figure 3), for example, by placing his own portrait alongside a collection of faces from the cultural imaginary (including Superman, Uncle Sam, the Mammy, Dracula, and others), Warhol represents both the myth*making* role that the artist plays and the mythical status of the artist in our culture. This gesture at once points out and maximizes his own fame, underscoring the absolutely cartoonlike character of it, the comic book element of our daily acts of recognition. One thing Warhol does by titling this self-portrait *The Shadow* is recall us to a childhood scene of listening to a radio superhero voice and of fantasmatically identifying with that voice. But it is also important that, like other superheroes that were the subject of Warhol's art (Superman or Batman, for example), the Shadow is a figure whose *visibility* is in a dependent relation to his *anonymity. The Shadow* allegorizes Warhol's fantasy that like the Shadow, he could move into the public precisely as someone *hidden,* that publicity would work like a screen, shielding him at the same time that it presents him.[42] Like a *prosthesis,* his self-portraits extended his person into the public sphere, the realm of fame, giving the public a product on which to feed its imagination. "So you should always have a product that's not just 'you' . . . [so] you don't get stuck

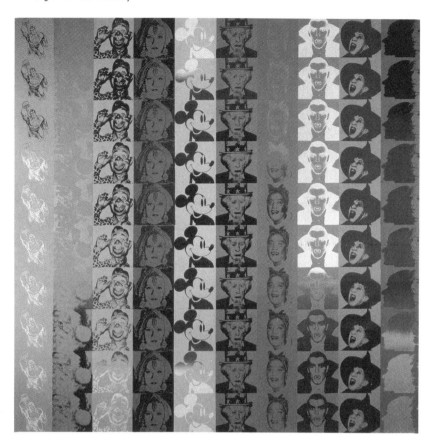

Figure 3. Andy Warhol, *Myths* (1981). ©1996 Andy Warhol Foundation for the Visual Arts/ARS, New York.

thinking your product is you and your fame, and your aura."[43] The trick, as Stein reminded us above, is to remember that you don't have an identity. Though you may need a public self, its value is precisely the negativity, not the "self-identity," it affords. As Warhol suggests in his camouflage self-portraits, his public persona is also like a *prophylaxis,* protective, an armor that could take the abuse that might have otherwise been directed at his person. It disembodied him, separated out his image from his body. By having a product that was not "him," he was able to occupy both sides of the dialectic between bodily positivity and public self-abstraction—something that was otherwise strictly impossible for the gay man whose appearance in public was strictly policed. Warhol liked to find ways to have his body, so to speak, and eat it too.[44]

Warhol's interest in the face-giving and face-taking that characterizes our public sphere and his desire to *manage* these prosopopoeias regarding his own person successfully can be seen not only in his portraits but also in his art that explicitly takes the commodity form as its subject: his work in the advertising industry, his early Pop paintings of consumer products, and later series like *Ads,* among other work. Warhol's 1960 *Before and After* (see figure 4) provides a good place to see the homology between the prosopopoeias of Warhol's portraits and of the commodity aesthetics that underwrite advertising and consumption. Seen in the context of his interest in portraiture, *Before and After* is an allegory of his portraits and the face-giving they perform. As such it could also be an advertisement for his portrait service. Indeed, the nose-job ad that Warhol reproduced in characteristic deadpan fashion is the paradigmatic advertisement, promising what all commodities do—a better

Figure 4. Andy Warhol, *Before and After* (1960). ©1996 Andy Warhol Foundation for the Visual Arts/ARS, New York.

you, a new face. The Warhol portrait is then the quintessential commodity: in purchasing the Factory-produced portrait, the sitter receives what all commodities promise, a reified, public self. Significantly, Warhol is offering this commentary not as an outside critic of commodity culture but as someone who himself wants to redeem that promise. In this sense, *Before and After* is also an ironic commentary on Warhol's own desires. As a self-proclaimed consumer of and believer in cosmetic surgery and his own portrait service, he knew very well the attractions of the prosthetic self, the public face. Warhol often drew on the prosopopoetic element of the commodity, emphasizing the similarities in the structure of the portrait and the commodity.

Since Marx, analysts of capitalist culture have noted that reification and personification are, so to speak, two sides of the same coin. In Marx's analysis, the commodity form offers the solution to the problem posed by the incommensurability between use value and exchange value. Seen as use value, the produced object is something that is produced by people to satisfy human needs. For these objects to be exchangeable, however, they must be abstracted into a universal scale of value. Thus the otherwise incommensurable—diamonds and land, labor and food, shoes and animals—can be bought and sold. This is reification. From the point of view of activity of production, people must relate to their labor not in terms of the specificity or use of the activity itself but instrumentally, only insofar as that labor can be sold for money. Thus the laborer has an alienated relation to the object she produces; it offers no recognition back to her as an embodiment or objectification of her. It is this process, of course, that allows for the accumulation of surplus value, by masking the use value of the labor that the worker sells to the capitalist, by making it appear as if the source of value is a thing rather than a social relation. In short, through the substitution of the seemingly *objective* characteristics of objects for the *social* characteristics of the labor that produced the object, the "products of labor become commodities, sensuous things which are at the same time supra-sensible or social."[45]

Thus, what from the point of view of production has been a reification—the turning of human activity into an abstract thing—from the side of consumption is a personification. As Marx writes, "If commodities could speak, they would say this: our use-value may interest men, but it does not belong to us as objects. What does belong to us as objects, however, is our value. Our own intercourse as commodities proves it. We relate to each other merely as exchange-values."[46] The essence of commodity fetishism is the ascription to objects the characteristics of persons, precisely insofar as the commodity is a transformation of human social relations into an abstract thing. Or, as Walter Benjamin argued, the commodity aura can "endow any soup can with cosmic significance but cannot grasp a single one of the human connections in which it exists."[47] Therefore, commodities appear to speak to one another because they must seem to be the source of their own value; value is seen to come from the objects rather than the social relations that enable their production. The personification of exchange value is literalized most clearly perhaps in the portraits that adorn our money, one of the many forms of everyday portraiture that made its way into Warhol's art.

The commodity must be able to appear to talk not only to other commodities but also to the consumer. As Benjamin put it, "If the soul of the commodity which Marx occasionally mentions in jest existed, it would be the most empathetic ever encountered in the realm of souls, for it would have to see in everyone the buyer in whose hand and house it wants to nestle."[48] The commodity offers the consumer recognition and comfort. Often, the commodity fetish works in the form of the trademark, a "second skin," that, in Lauren Berlant's gloss of W. F. Haug, "enables the commodity to appear to address, to recognize, and thereby to 'love' the consumer."[49] What the consumer purchases is self-mediation, self-negativity. The promise of consumption is always the promise of the face-lift, of a self that is protected, more recognizable because it is abstracted.[50]

If authority, or "insidedness" (to return to Warhol's term), in U.S. culture is connected with the privilege to suppress and protect the body, then we can understand how the recognition and love offered by the commodity is, as Berlant argues, especially comforting for women, African Americans, and other minoritized persons who had been historically unable to participate in the political public sphere. Consumption offers the limited possibility of managing one's embodiment: "Be somebody with a body," offers one advertisement Warhol appropriated in a 1980s painting. The ways that consumption promises this negotiation of embodiment and abstraction is, I think, immediately understandable to anyone who finds (as I do) shopping a potent antidepressant. Part of the affective payback of consumption is the way that in consuming a product we can identify ourselves with everyone else who consumes that product; we access another mode of universalizing our-

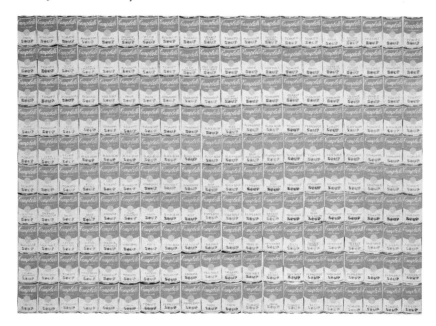

Figure 5. Andy Warhol, *Two Hundred Campbell's Soup Cans* (1962). ©1996
Andy Warhol Foundation for the Visual Arts/ARS, New York.

selves and our desires. Warhol noted that "you can be watching TV and see
Coca-Cola, and you know that the President drinks Coke, Liz Taylor drinks
Coke, and just think, you can drink Coke, too. . . . All the Cokes are the same
and all the Cokes are good."[51]

One of the most striking effects of Warhol's engagement with commodity
aesthetics is the way that Warhol made Campbell's *his* trademark, *his* prosthetic second skin. Ivan Karp remarked that Warhol's "full face portraits" of
soup cans insured that "tomato soup will never be just tomato soup again."
Instead, the Campbell's soup can has become a "symbol that is universally
recognized" as Warhol's own.[52] In doing this Warhol cannot help but give the
lie to the idea that value is produced by the product itself. But at the same
time, Warhol's paintings testify to the enormous and unavoidable power of
the commodity fetish, a power he wishes to garner and to make available for
others to appropriate. In this light, I like to think of *Two Hundred Campbell's
Soup Cans* (see figure 5) as something like a memento mori, a reminder that
the trademark always also mourns as it promises recognition, that it de-faces
as it gives face.

REPRESENTING DISASTER IN THE AGE OF AIDS

■

Warhol had a real eye for disaster, a canny sense of its attraction. His most famous paintings after the celebrity portraits are probably those from the *Disaster Series:* electric chairs, race riots, suicides, gruesome car crashes, funerals, atomic bombs, Jackie mourning. He brought these paintings together with his portraits of Marilyn and Liz in an exhibit that he called *Death in America,* stating: "My death series was divided into two parts, the first one famous deaths and the second one people nobody ever heard of. . . . It's not that I feel sorry for them, its just that people go by and it doesn't really matter that someone unknown was killed. . . . I still care about people but it would be much easier not to care, it's too hard to care."[53] Warhol's disasters remind us where mourning happens and where it does not: while both celebrities' deaths and disaster victims are in a sense eulogized by the mass media coverage they receive, it is a eulogy that has nothing to do with the specificity of the people who have died. The prosopopoeias in mass media coverage of disasters are always in some sense anonymous; it (usually) doesn't matter who the dead are. What matters is that the embodied spectacle of their death is presented to a mass audience for consumption.

In *Tunafish Disaster* (1963) (see figure 6), Warhol gives us a good illustration of this spectacle. Here, Warhol reproduces the photograph and text from a newspaper story about two women who were killed by botulism-contaminated tuna. Pictured are the captioned portraits of the disaster victims and the murderous A&P tuna can. By taking his images from the newspaper, Warhol makes it clear that what his painting represents is not at all the event of the disaster but rather our consumption of it. And one can see how it would have been an attractive image for Warhol, literally yoking the disaster together with the portrait and the commodity form, providing us the chance to speculate on their shared structure, especially when we place this work next to the Marilyns, Jackies, and the Campbells. As it stutters across the canvas, the caption "Seized shipment: did a leak kill . . ." announces that the promises of comfort and recognition held out by the commodity here failed disastrously. But, the image also seems to remind us that this danger always lurks within the prosopopoetic promise: the ideal publicity is always in a sense posthumous. As another genre of mass publicity that mediates between embodiment and abstraction, the disaster gives the audience the

Figure 6. Andy Warhol, *Tunafish Disaster* (1963). ©1996 Andy Warhol
Foundation for the Visual Arts/ARS, New York.

chance to identify with the disembodied space of public witnessing, to enter a kind of fantasy of self-abstraction by mourning somebody else's body.[54] Warhol's *Disaster Series* underscores the ways that logic of the disaster is a logic of consumption. And just as the "did a leak kill" caption echoes like an eerie anticipation of anxieties about prophylaxis in the age of AIDS, *Tunafish Disaster* looks in retrospect like a depressing prediction of the ease with which the mass public sphere could assimilate AIDS as *disaster,* the to-be-consumed rather than a crisis to be addressed or as losses to be mourned.

That the trade-in for a better, abstracted self that is the attraction of consumption is always done on someone else's terms, with someone else's images, becomes a special problem when these images fail to address you, indeed exclude you. Take, for example, the discourse around AIDS, where the discourse is addressed to a decidedly de-gayed "general public." In this instance, "it is heartbrakingly accurate to speak of the prophylaxis held out by mass publicity to those who will identify with its immunized body."[55] The creation of this prophylaxis is the primary function of what Simon Watney has called the "spectacle of AIDS," part of which is the construction of the "AIDS victim," who is "usually hospitalized and physically debilitated, 'withered, wrinkled, and loathsome of visage'—the authentic cadaver of Dorian Gray. This is the *spectacle of AIDS. . . .* It is the principle and serious business of this spectacle to ensure that the subject of AIDS is 'correctly' identified and that any possibility of positive sympathetic identification *with* actual people with AIDS is entirely expunged from the field of vision."[56] The spectacle of AIDS produces the person with AIDS as someone with whom no one could possibly identify, the loss of whom need not be mourned. The exclusion of gay men from the "public" to which all "signs" regarding AIDS are directed makes it even more than usually difficult for people with AIDS to manage and protect their own sense of embodiment. "In this sense, the gap that gay people register within the discourse of the general public might well be an aggravated form—though a lethally aggravated form—of the normal relation to the general public."[57] In other words, while we all negate our bodily specificity to enter the public sphere, when your body is made into a barrier to publicity, the rupture between embodiment and abstraction becomes glaringly clear.

In "Portraits of People with AIDS," Douglas Crimp considers the kinds of images produced by the liberal imperative to "give AIDS a face," to "bring AIDS home."[58] These images, Crimp notes, both brutally invade and brutally maintain privacy. Privacy is invaded insofar as their most private feelings and thoughts have been exposed and deployed for their spectacle value. It is maintained to the extent that "the portrayal of these people's personal circumstances never includes an articulation of the public dimension of the crisis, the social conditions that made AIDS a crisis and continue to perpetuate it as a crisis. People with AIDS are kept safely within the boundaries of their private tragedies."[59] The problem is not so much one of faceless statistics; faces have been ceaselessly provided by the media. But they are always depoliticized abstractions: portraits of people with AIDS are consistently conflated with "portraits of the human condition." The people in the portraits Crimp discusses could not be gay men whom we, the viewers, identify with or find sexy or mourn the losses of. Both Crimp and Watney point out how around AIDS, both mourning and political action—exemplary public acts—run into the minoritizing and abstracting forces of the public sphere.[60]

Given Warhol's history of depicting disasters and dwelling on the elements of mourning and embodiment in mass culture, one might expect that he would have registered some kind of intelligent response to AIDS. For the most part, as is well known, the public responses he made to the epidemic were phobic ones, even as his friends and lovers died. His failure to address AIDS surely stemmed in part from his phobic and shame-filled relation to illness. But I think that the failure in this instance of his familiar appropriation of public prosopopoeias to offer him any protection or comfort might also signal that the brutality of the mass public sphere had perhaps taken him by surprise, in a kind of preemptive attack from which he never recovered. He had no rejoinder to the mass public sphere, which, as Crimp and Watney show, makes a gay-specific and affirmative mourning extremely difficult. Warhol's singular painting that treats the theme, *AIDS/Jeep/Bicycle* (see figure 7), which was not exhibited during Warhol's life (perhaps because it was incomplete or the beginning of a collaborative project), is remarkable because it contains no address, no faces, no mechanism for managing the gap between the embodied and the abstract. Instead, there is only absence. The bicycle and the Jeep are riderless. It is Warhol's most melancholic painting in the depressing sense, registering a failure to mourn, an inability to appropriate some form of publicity that might comfort him.

Despite Warhol's shame-filled failure in the face of AIDS, Warhol's insights into the logic of our public sphere have been successfully taken up by AIDS activists. ACT UP and Gran Fury, for example, have been energized by ef-

Figure 7. Andy Warhol, *AIDS/Jeep/Bicycle* (c. 1985). ©1996 Andy Warhol
Foundation for the Visual Arts/ARS, New York.

fective strategies such as taking the world of public images as their palette, appropriating already recognizable images to mock or challenge them,
and shamelessly putting themselves in the public eye. One need only look
through *AIDS Demo Graphics* to see the echoes of Pop in the keen graphic
sensibilities of AIDS activism (see figures 8, 9, 10, and 11).[61] It is not only Pop's
demonstration of the value and necessity of publicity that seems influential
here but also Pop's formal devices, the emphasis on faces, fame, recognizability, repetition, and reappropriation.

GIVING FACE AS GIVING HEAD
■

"The erotic, rather than being a heightened version of sense experience, is a figure
that makes such experience possible."—Paul de Man, "Hypogram and Inscription"[62]

I want to conclude this consideration of Warhol's interventions in publicity
by drawing attention to his skill at finding glamour, publicity, and sexiness in
places where there may initially appear to be none. In particular, I want to

Figure 8. Andy Warhol, *Front and Back Dollar Bills* (1962). ©1996 Andy Warhol Foundation for the Visual Arts/ARS, New York.
Figure 9. Andy Warhol, *Vote McGovern* (1972). ©1996 Andy Warhol Foundation for the Visual Arts/ARS, New York.

reflect on his efforts to cope with the dearth of representations of male homoeroticism in the public world.

Warhol's 1963 film *Blow Job* addresses the constructed nature of the "erotic" and the productive quality of the camera and, by implication, our vision. The film is a thirty-minute close-up of a man's face while he, we are promised by the title, is fellated (see figure 1 in Waugh, this volume). In a sense, it is another of Warhol's anonymous portraits; the actor (according to various reports) is a hustler who agreed to act in the film after an actor friend of Warhol's didn't show up for the filming. The reactions to the Factory screening of the film, as described by Ultra Violet, focus mainly on the frustrating sense that all the action is taking place "offscreen."[63] Likewise, most of the critical work that discusses the film considers it in terms of the *exclusion* that the camera performs by displacing the action from our field of vision. On one level, to be sure, what is seen is displaced by what is imagined. But the "exclusion" of the "actual" blow job has a productive effect as well. The

Figure 10. Gran Fury, *Wall Street Money* (1988).

Figure 11. Donald Moffett, *He Kills Me* (1987). Courtesy of the artist.

promise enacted by the title leads us to read the pleasure of the blow job into the face. The offscreen blow job that is in the realm of "fantasy" because we cannot see it places the on-screen face also in the realm of the "fantasy." Precisely in the way that we are led to imagine that each tilt of the head and squinting of the eyes means something more than itself, *Blow Job* foregrounds how all face-reading is a matter of "feeding the imagination."[64]

Blow Job, like the portraits, highlights the extent to which anything that we project behind the face, the meaning or recognizability we give it, is "hallucinatory" and "real" at once. Because it is impossible to tell if the person is "actually" being fellated, Warhol's film, as David James notes, "makes performance inevitable, [as it] constitutes being as performance."[65] The experience of watching *Blow Job* is then not one of voyeurism (as it has sometimes been read)[66] but a lesson in how the camera (and visuality itself) displaces the distinction between life and art, the real and the fantasy. James argues that "rather than unfolding in ignorance of the camera's presence or

Figure 12. "*The Andy Warhol Diaries*, March 13, 1978: 'The Post has a picture of Halston and Ken Harrison. But all I could look at was the way Ken Harrison was holding his glass. . . .'" Vinnie Zuffante, photograph from New York Post, (1978). Courtesy of the Artist.

unaffected by it, the spectacle in Warhol's films is produced by and *for* the camera. . . . As the recording apparatus mechanically transforms life into art, it constitutes the space of its attention as a theater of self-representation. . . . The defining condition of voyeurism—'repetitive looking at unsuspecting people' is precluded."[67] Warhol is not an outsider looking in; his look, in fact, creates the image. The performance is done with an acute awareness of and relation to being seen. Warhol teaches us that the potentially minoritizing and exclusive world of images—this "real" world—can be haunted by the fictive, because it always already was.

We can see how the transformative effects of Warhol's look affected him even on a very day-to-day level in the following passages from *The Andy Warhol Diaries*. On Monday, March 13, 1978, Warhol registers his reaction on seeing a picture of his friend Ken Harrison in the weekend *Post* (see figure 12). The photo reminded Warhol of pictures he had of Harrison naked, pictures that were probably like this image from the series *Sex Parts* (see figure 13), which contains some of the many images of male genitalia that Warhol sketched, painted, and photographed throughout his career: "The Post has a picture of Halston and Ken Harrison. But all I could look at was the way Ken Harrison was holding his glass. Because I have nude pictures of him with Victor." If you look at the two images, you can see how the picture of Ken Harrison holding his glass at the left of the *Post* photo might remind Warhol of a drawing like the one from *Sex Parts*. They resemble each other not only because the hand holding the glass in the *Post* photo looks like the hand holding a man's penis in the *Sex Parts* drawing but also, in each image, the hand intrudes into the picture from outside the frame; the disembodied (and, in the *Sex Parts* image, anonymous) hand reaches into the picture and grabs. I would like to think of these images as a kind of allegory for Warhol's own reaching into the photo to rescue an otherwise invisible and quite sexy subtext from it, an allegory for Warhol's perpetual gesture toward the fantasy of blurring the distinctions between inside and outside, life and art, audience and artist.

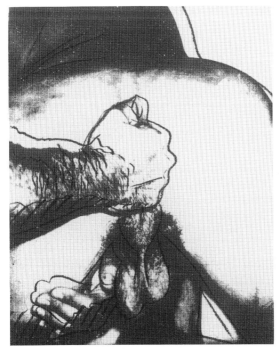

Figure 13. " '. . . Because I have nude pictures of him with Victor.' " Andy Warhol, *Sex Parts* (1978). ©1996 Andy Warhol Foundation for the Visual Arts/ARS, New York.

This heroic act of rescuing sexiness and pleasure from the daily *Post* is, for me, the paradigmatic Pop gesture, a perfect example of how Warhol's Pop way of seeing enabled him to feel like an insider, to reinhabit and reinvent the image world around him. If it could neither totally reverse the minoritizing powers of the public sphere nor abolish homophobia, it was nonetheless a way of seeing that allowed him to recognize his friends and in so doing to make his daily news a little less sad and little more sexy.

NOTES
■

For their critical responses, encouragement, and advice, I thank Fredric Jameson, Carol Mavor, José Muñoz, Michael Moon, and Eve Kosofsky Sedgwick. For close readings of earlier drafts of this essay that significantly affected the final draft, I thank Jennifer Doyle and Janice Radway.

1   Andy Warhol and Pat Hackett, *POPism: The Warhol Sixties* (New York: Harcourt Brace Jovanovich, 1980), p. 39; emphasis mine.

2   A phrase made popular by John Berger's *Ways of Seeing* (London: BBC and Penguin Books, 1972), where Berger forwarded the simple yet powerful thesis that because every image embodies a way of seeing and each viewer brings to the image her own way of seeing, we must think about vision itself as a kind of culturally, ideologically, and historically specific *representation*. Berger takes this gesture from Walter Benjamin, in particular his work on Baudelaire and his essay "Art in the Age of Mechanical Reproduction," in which Benjamin discusses at length the effects mechanical reproduction have had on the way we perceive "art" and the world. In *Illuminations* (New York: Schocken, 1969).

3   Colin Wilson, *The Outsider* (London: Pan Books, 1956). For more on the importance of Wilson's book for Warhol's milieu, see Fred Lawrence Guiles, *Loner at the Ball* (London: Black Swan, 1990), pp. 121–122.

4   Warhol and Hackett, *POPism*, p. 4.

5   There are many accounts of the machoness, misogyny, and homophobia of the abstract expressionists. John Giorno, the man who was sleeping in *Sleep* and Warhol's lover at the time, writes in the recent and excellent *You Got to Burn to Shine* (New York: High Risk Books, 1994): "The art world was homophobic, and an everpresent threat. Anyone who was gay was at a disadvantage. An artist overtly with a boyfriend was at a complete disadvantage, and could ruin his career. De Kooning, Pollock, Motherwell, and the male power structure were mean straight pricks. No matter their liberal views, they deep down hated fags. Their disdain dismissed a gay person's art. On top of it, those guys really hated Pop Art. . . . I am a witness to their being cruel to Andy Warhol. Andy got around homophobia by making the movie *Sleep* into an abstract painting: the body of a man as a field of light and shadow" (132–133).

6   For more detailed discussions of Warhol's childhood, see Simon Watney's and Michael

Moon's essays in this volume. See also the biographies by Guiles (mentioned above) and Victor Bockris, *The Life and Death of Andy Warhol* (New York: Bantam, 1989).

7   According to Philip Pearlstein, Warhol's former roommate who was already exhibiting at the Tanager and who brought Warhol's work to the attention of the gallery: "He submitted a group of boys kissing boys which the other members of the gallery hated and refused to show." Warhol and Pearlstein had a falling out after that. This story is recounted in David Bourdon, *Warhol* (New York: Harry N. Abrams, 1989), p. 51. See also Guiles, *Loner at the Ball*, pp. 121–125.

8   Warhol and Hackett, *POPism*, pp. 222–223.

9   See Michael Warner, "The Mass Public and the Mass Subject," in *The Phantom Public Sphere*, ed. Bruce Robbins (Minneapolis: University of Minnesota Press, 1993), p. 252.

10   In a somewhat different register, Judith Butler has made a similar argument. She writes: "I can only say 'I' to the extent that I have first been addressed, and that address has mobilized my place in speech; paradoxically, the discursive condition of social recognition precedes and conditions the formation of the subject: recognition is not conferred on a subject, but constitutes that subject. . . . The 'I' is thus a citation of the place of 'I' in speech, where that place has a certain priority and anonymity with respect to the life it animates. Recognition, paradoxically, comes before the self." Judith Butler, *Bodies That Matter: On the Discursive Limits of "Sex"* (New York: Routledge, 1993), pp. 225–226.

11   David Wojnarowicz, *Close to the Knives: A Memoir of Disintegration* (New York: Vintage, 1991), p. 120.

12   Indeed, it might be argued that the ideal of the public sphere is attractive *only* insofar as it is exclusive, insofar as there are always persons around who are forced to be only embodied, bodies that "summarized the constraints of positivity . . . from which self abstraction can be liberating." Warner, "Mass Public," p. 239. See also the brilliant discussion of publicity and embodiment in Lauren Berlant's "National Brands/National Bodies: *Imitation of Life*," in *Phantom*, ed. Robbins, pp. 173–208.

13   Nancy Fraser makes this argument in "Rethinking the Public Sphere: A Contribution to the Critique of Actually Existing Democracy," in *Phantom*, ed. Robbins, pp. 1–32. The idea of "counterpublics" is one of the ways Fraser adapts Jürgen Habermas's theory of the public sphere to describe more accurately contemporary democracies. See Habermas, *The Structural Transformation of the Public Sphere* (Cambridge: MIT Press, 1991). My own thoughts about publicity and the public sphere in this context have also been influenced by Hannah Arendt, esp. *The Human Condition* (Chicago: University of Chicago Press, 1958). For Arendt, appearance in a public sphere gives one a "feeling for reality" that can come only from being seen and heard. She notes how, in ancient Rome, a life not lived among others, not *inter homines esse*, was no life at all. For Arendt, "Appearance—something that is being seen and heard by others as well as by ourselves—constitutes reality." In Arendt's view, this is, in part, because action and appearance in public produce stories, witnesses and audiences who will narrativize one's speech and action. For more on Arendt, see Lewis P. Hinchman and Sandra K. Hinchman, eds., *Hannah Arendt: Critical Essays* (Albany: State University of New York Press, 1994) and the excellent bibliography there; and Dana Villa, *Arendt and Heidegger: The Fate of the Political* (Princeton: Princeton University Press, 1995).

14   Warhol and Hackett, *POPism*, pp. 222–223. Also see George Kateb, *Hannah Arendt, Politics, Conscience, Evil* (Totowa, N.J.: Rowman and Allanheld, 1983).

15   This is closer to what Oskar Negt and Alexander Kluge have called publicity as a "horizon of experience," in *The Public Sphere and Experience,* trans. Peter Lbanyi, Jamie Daniel, and Assenka Oksiloff (Minneapolis: University of Minnesota Press, 1993). They suggest that the public sphere is a model for understanding contemporary mass media culture better than are Frankfurt School ideas of "mass culture." In their view, the idea of the public, of appearing in a space where we can be seen by and interact with a plurality of others, mediates the ways that we think about our experience and our selves in late capitalist culture. On Negt and Kluge's contribution to the theory of the public sphere, see Miriam Hansen's "Foreword" to this translation and her "Early Cinema, Late Cinema: Permutations of the Public Sphere," *Screen* 34, no. 3 (Autumn 1993). See also Fredric Jameson, "On Negt and Kluge," in *Phantom,* ed. Robbins, pp. 42–74.

16   Warner, "Mass Public," p. 234.

17   Interestingly, along these lines, Arendt notes that "the curse of slavery consisted not only in being deprived of freedom and visibility, but also in the fear of these obscure people themselves 'that from being obscure they should pass away leaving no trace that they have existed.'" In a footnote, she continues citing from R. H. Barrow's *Slavery in the Roman Empire,* noting with interest that one thing the Roman colleges provided besides "good fellowship in life and the certainty of a decent burial . . . [was] the crowning pleasure of an epitaph; and in this last the slave found a melancholy pleasure." Barrow, *Slavery in the Roman Empire* (London: Methuen and Colt, 1928) p. 168, cited by Arendt, *Human Condition,* p. 55.

18   Paul de Man, "Autobiography as De-facement," in *The Rhetoric of Romanticism* (New York: Columbia University Press, 1984), pp. 75–76.

19   Gertrude Stein, "What Are Master-pieces and Why There Are So Few of Them," reprinted in *The Gender of Modernism,* ed. Bonnie Kime Scott (Bloomington: Indiana University Press, 1990), p. 499.

20   Jean-Jacques Rousseau, *The Confessions of Jean-Jacques Rousseau* (New York: Modern Library/Random House, 1975), p. 236.

21   In David Bourdon, "Andy Warhol and the Society Icon," *Art in America,* January/February 1975, p. 42.

22   Bourdon, *Warhol,* p. 324.

23   Hans-Georg Gadamer serves as an exemplary and influential defender of this position. See *Truth and Method* (New York: Crossroad, 1986), esp. pp. 119–142. For Gadamer, the portrait is an intensification of what he calls the "picture." This is the opposite of a copy, which only *refers* or points back to the original and in so doing cancels itself out. By picture he means that which "says something about the original" and as such has an existence of its own, but an existence that is inextricably tied to the original. Through the portrait—the picture *par excellence*—the individual experiences what Gadamer calls "an increase in being." For an extended discussion of portraiture that takes this Gadamerian understanding as its starting point, see Richard Brilliant, *Portraiture* (Cambridge: Harvard University Press, 1991), esp. the "Introduction."

24 Benjamin Buchloh, "The Andy Warhol Line," *The Work of Andy Warhol,* ed. Gary Garrels (Seattle: Bay Press, 1989), p. 63. He describes the seventies portraits as follows: "It is hard to imagine a more accurate collection and depiction of the unique fusion of *arriviste* vulgarity and old-money decadence, the seamless transition from the powers that produce and control corporate culture to those that govern American high cultural institutions than the endless number of commissioned portraits of the American ruling class of the last decade." Buchloh's argument is that these "corrupted and debased moments" are parodic anticipations of art world trends which enable Warhol to have a distance and provide a commentary on changes "to which other artists were still blindly subjected."

25 Warhol and Hackett, *POPism,* p. 22.

26 Jean Baudrillard, *Simulations* (New York: Semiotext(e), 1983). "Here it is a question of a reversal of origin and finality, for all the forms change once they are not so much mechanically reproduced but *conceived from the point-of-view of their very reproducibility,* diffracted from a generating nucleus we call the model" (100). For comment on Warhol specifically, see also pp. 136, 144, and 158–159.

27 Andy Warhol, *The Philosophy of Andy Warhol* (New York: Harcourt Brace Jovanovich, 1975), pp. 51 and 63.

28 Quoted in Bourdon, *Warhol,* p. 324.

29 Warhol, *Philosophy,* p. 62.

30 For more on this, see Simon Watney's "The Warhol Effect," also in *Work of Andy Warhol,* ed. Garrels. "By the mere fact of contingency with such figures as Marilyn Monroe, Elizabeth Taylor, Jackie Kennedy, Mao, and so on, *anyone* can assume celebrity status. It is on this simple yet sophisticated principle that his commissioned portraits depended" (119).

31 Oscar Wilde, *The Picture of Dorian Gray* (London: Penguin, 1985), p. 147.

32 Thomas Crowe intelligently discusses similar themes in "Saturday Disasters: Trace and Reference in Early Warhol," *Art in America,* May 1987.

33 Paul de Man, "Hypogram and Inscription," in *The Resistance to Theory* (Minneapolis: University of Minnesota Press, 1986), p. 44.

34 Ibid.

35 Jacques Derrida, *Memoires for Paul de Man* (New York: Columbia University Press, 1988), p. 26.

36 Judith Butler, "Imitation and Gender Insubordination," in *Inside/Out,* ed. Diana Fuss (New York: Routledge, 1991), p. 26.

37 Sigmund Freud, "Mourning and Melancholia" (1917), in *General Psychological Theory,* ed. Philip Rieff (New York: Collier Books, 1963), esp. pp. 165–166.

38 Sigmund Freud, *The Ego and the Id* (New York: Norton, 1960), p. 19. Judith Butler offers a helpful gloss on this in her discussion of the "melancholia of gender" in *Gender Trouble* (New York: Routledge, 1990): "The identification with lost loves characteristic of melancholia becomes the precondition for the work of mourning. . . . Strictly speaking, the giving up of the object is not a negation of the cathexis, but its internalization and, hence, preservation" (62).

39 Cited in Butler, *Gender Trouble,* p. 48, and Jacques Lacan, *Feminine Sexuality,* ed. Juliet Mitchell and Jacqueline Rose (New York: W. W. Norton, 1985), p. 85.

40   Butler, *Gender Trouble,* p. 50.

41   Warhol and Hackett, *POPism,* p. 17.

42   In this respect, the self-portraits are analogous to the *Marilyns* in particular. One of Warhol's best early critics, Mary Josephson, wrote, "Marilyn's face, like Warhol's, is quintessentially surface; but its peculiar anguish lies in the fact that, since there was nothing behind Marilyn's face either, the anguish is experienced on the surface, that is, uncomprehendingly." Josephson, "Warhol: The Medium as Cultural Artifact," *Art in America,* May/June 1971, pp. 40–46.

43   Warhol, *Philosophy,* p. 86.

44   Apropos star consumption and the long close-ups of faces in his films, Warhol said, "I did this because people usually just go to the movies to see the star, to eat him up, so here at last is a chance to look only at the star for as long as you like no matter what he does and eat him up all you want to." Quoted by Benjamin Buchloh, "Andy Warhol's One-Dimensional Art: 1956–1966," in *Andy Warhol: A Retrospective,* ed. Kynaston McShine (New York: Museum of Modern Art, 1989), p. 53.

45   Karl Marx, *Capital,* vol. 1, trans. Ben Fowkes (New York: Penguin/New Left Review, 1976), p. 165.

46   Ibid., pp. 176–177.

47   Walter Benjamin, "A Short History of Photography," in *One Way Street and Other Writings,* with an introduction by Susan Sontag, trans. Edmund Jephcott and Kingsley Shorter (London: NLB, 1979), p. 255.

48   See Walter Benjamin, *Charles Baudelaire: A Lyric Poet in the Era of High Capitalism,* trans. Harry Zohn (London: NLB, 1973), p. 55.

49   Berlant, "National Brands/National Bodies," p. 186.

50   This mechanism of workaday advertisement and consumption was smartly captured by Theodore Dreiser in *Sister Carrie* (New York: Bantam Classics, 1958), p. 82:

> Fine clothes were to her a vast persuasion; they spoke tenderly and Jesuitically for themselves. When she came within earshot of their pleading, desire in her bent a willing ear. The voice of the so-called inanimate! Who shall translate for us the language of the stones?
>
> "My dear," said the lace collar she secured from Partridge's, "I fit you beautifully; don't give me up."
>
> "Ah, such little feet," said the leather of the soft new shoes; "how effectively I cover them. What a pity they should ever want my aid."

The attraction of the shoes for Dreiser's Carrie is understandably great: the shoes (as fetish par excellence) not only offer to recognize Carrie as a woman but also promise to cover and comfort her, to perform the same prosthetic and prophylactic function that the public self might perform for the unmarked white male body.

51   In Warhol, *Philosophy,* pp. 100–101. The topic of repetition is also obviously important and interesting here. In paintings like *Thirty Are Better Than One* (repetitions of the Mona Lisa), the *Marilyn* diptych, or *100 Coke Bottles,* the repetition of the same image in the same painting makes repetition itself the subject of the painting. Repetition may have been especially attractive to Warhol as another way to negotiate the tension between embodi-

ment and abstraction. As Michel Foucault has noted vis-à-vis Warhol, as repetition enables recognition, it undermines identity: "A day will come when, by means of similitude relayed indefinitely along the length of a series, the image itself, along with the name it bears, will lose its identity. Campbell, Campbell, Campbell, Campbell" (*This Is Not a Pipe* [Berkeley: University of California Press, 1983], p. 54). Only when something is repeatable, abstractable, can it acquire value. (Likewise, Judith Butler has pointed out that it is paradoxically only by repeating a set of gestures and behaviors that are already "universal" that we acquire our specific gender identities.) See "Imitation and Gender Insubordination" and *Bodies That Matter.*

52 Bourdon, *Warhol,* p. 90.

53 In Buchloh, "Andy Warhol's One-Dimensional Art," p. 53.

54 See Warner's discussion of disasters in "Mass Public," pp. 248–253.

55 Ibid., p. 252.

56 Simon Watney, "The Spectacle of AIDS," in *AIDS: Cultural Analysis, Cultural Activism,* ed. Douglas Crimp (Cambridge: MIT Press, 1988), p. 78.

57 Warner, "Mass Public," p. 252.

58 Douglas Crimp, "Portraits of People with AIDS," in *Cultural Studies,* ed. Lawrence Grossberg, Cary Nelson, and Paula Treichler (New York: Routledge, 1992), pp. 117–133.

59 Ibid., p. 120.

60 For more on this, see Douglas Crimp, "Mourning and Militancy" in *October* 51 (Winter 1989), and Simon Watney, *Policing Desire* (Minneapolis: University of Minnesota Press, 1987), esp. the "Introduction."

61 Douglas Crimp, with Adam Rolston, *AIDS Demo Graphics* (Seattle: Bay Press, 1990).

62 de Man, "Hypogram and Inscription," p. 53.

63 Ultra Violet, *Famous for Fifteen Minutes: My Years with Andy Warhol* (New York: Avon, 1988), pp. 31–36.

64 This is a variation on the famous "Kuleshov effect."

65 David James, *Allegories of Cinema* (Princeton: Princeton University Press, 1989), p. 69. Another interesting and intersecting reading of *Blow Job* is offered by John Giorno, who sees it as a meditation on and a celebration of anonymous sex. See *You Got to Burn to Shine,* pp. 146–147.

66 See, for example, Stephen Koch, *Stargazer: Andy Warhol's World and His Films* (New York: Praeger, 1973), pp. 47–51.

67 Ibid., pp. 67–68.

EVE KOSOFSKY SEDGWICK
Queer Performativity: Warhol's
Shyness/Warhol's Whiteness

The jokes that mean the most to you are the ones you don't quite get; that's one true fact I've figured out over the years. Another is, The people with the most powerful presences are the ones who aren't all there. Like going to hear Odetta at the Cookery some years ago and having her—I don't know what was going on with her—in the middle of one song, *still singing,* wander off for a brief tour of the restaurant kitchen, her machinelike, perseverating voice winding from its distance outward toward the excruciated and rapt audience: now *that* was *presence:* presence like the withdrawal of a god.

Andy Warhol had presence of that revelatory kind—revelatory not in the sense that it revealed "him" but rather that he could wield it as a sharp, insinuating heuristic chisel to pry at the faultlines and lay bare the sedimented faces of his surround. As with Odetta at the Cookery, excruciation—the poetics, politics, semiotics, and somatics of shame—provided the medium for this denuding sculpture at once so intimate, so public. Shame, in Warhol's case, as crystallized in a bodily discipline of florid shyness:

> There are different ways for individual people to take over space—to command space. Very shy people don't even want to take up the space that their body actually takes up, whereas very outgoing people want to take up as much space as they can. . . .
>
> I've always had a conflict because I'm shy and yet I like to take up a lot of personal space. Mom always said, "Don't be pushy, but let everybody know you're around." I wanted to command more space than I was

commanding, but then I knew I was too shy to know what to do with the attention if I did manage to get it. That's why I love television. That's why I feel that television is the media I'd most like to shine in.[1]

From shame to shyness to shining—and, inevitably, back, and back again: the candor and cultural incisiveness of this itinerary seem to make Warhol an exemplary figure for a new project, an urgent one I think, of understanding how the dysphoric affect shame functions as a nexus of production: production, that is, of meaning, of personal presence, of politics, of performative and critical efficacy. What it may mean to be a (white) queer in a queer-hating world, what it may mean to be a white (queer) in a white-supremacist one, are two of the explorations that, for Warhol, this shyness embodied.

Both *POPism* and *The Philosophy of Andy Warhol* include extended arias specifically on the shy and, *not* incidentally, on the queer and on the white, in which the illusion of Warhol's presence gets evoked in a shimmeringly ambiguous, shame-charged linguistic space of utterance and address. In *POPism*, in a scene from the Factory in 1966, Warhol describes Silver George impersonating Andy Warhol over the phone:

> "You want me to describe myself?" Silver George was saying. He looked at me as if to say, "You don't care if I do this, right?" I asked who it was and when he said it was a high school paper I motioned for him to go ahead.
>
> "Well, I wear what everybody else around the Factory wears," he said, looking over at me as a reference. "A striped T-shirt—a little too short—over another T-shirt, that's how we like them . . . and Levi's . . ." He listened for a few moments. "Well, I would call myself—youthful-looking. I have a slightly faggy air, and I do little artistic movements. . . ." I looked up from painting. I'd thought all they wanted was a fashion description, but it didn't matter. . . .
>
> "Well, I have very nice hands," he said, "very expressive. . . . I keep them in repose or touching each other, or sometimes I wrap my arms around myself. I'm always very conscious of where my hands are. . . . But the first thing you notice about me is my skin. It's translucent—you can really see my veins—and it's gray, but it's pink, too. . . . My build? Well, it's very flat, and if I gain any weight, it's usually all in my hips and stomach. And I'm small-shouldered and I'm probably the same dimension at my waist as I am at my chest. . . ." Silver George really had

momentum now. . . . "And my legs are very narrow and I have tiny little ankles—and I'm a little birdlike from my hips down—I sort of narrow in and taper down toward my feet. . . . 'Birdlike,' right . . . and I carry myself very square, like a unit. And I'm rigid—very conservative about my movements; I have a little bit of an old-lady thing there. . . . And my new boots have sort of high heels, so I walk like a woman, on the balls of my feet—but actually, I'm very . . . hardy. . . . Okay?

. . . "No, it was no trouble." . . .

When Silver George hung up, he said they were really thrilled because they'd heard I never talked and here I'd just said more to them than anybody they'd ever interviewed. They'd also said how surprised they were that I could be so objective about myself.[2]

What Warhol does in publishing this account in 1980 under his own name—his own and Pat Hackett's, not to let things get too oversimplified!—is a bit like what he's done in *Philosophy* in 1975, retelling a phone conversation between himself, as "A," and one of the several interlocutors he brings together under the designation "B":

"Day after day I look in the mirror and I still see something—a new pimple. If the pimple on my upper right cheek is gone, a new one turns up on my lower left cheek, on my jawline, near my ear, in the middle of my nose, under the hair on my eyebrows, right between my eyes. I think it's the same pimple, moving from place to place." I was telling the truth. If someone asked me, "What's your problem?" I'd have to say, "Skin."

"I dunk a Johnson and Johnson cotton ball into Johnson and Johnson rubbing alcohol and rub the cotton ball against the pimple." . . .

"When the alcohol is dry," I said, "I'm ready to apply the flesh-colored acne-pimple medication that doesn't resemble any human flesh I've ever seen, though it does come pretty close to mine. . . . So now the pimple's covered. But am I covered? I have to look into the mirror for some more clues. Nothing is missing. It's all there. The affectless gaze. The diffracted grace . . ."

"What?"

"The bored languor, the wasted pallor . . ."

"The what?"

"The chic freakiness, the basically passive astonishment, the enthralling secret knowledge . . ."

"WHAT??"

"The chintzy joy, the revelatory tropisms, the chalky, puckish mask, the slightly Slavic look . . ."

"Slightly . . ."

"The childlike, gum-chewing naivete, the glamour rooted in despair, the self-admiring carelessness, the perfected otherness, the wispiness, the shadowy, voyeuristic, vaguely sinister aura, the pale, soft-spoken magical presence, the skin and bones . . ."

"Hold it, wait a minute, I have to take a pee."

"The albino-chalk skin. Parchmentlike. Reptilian. Almost blue . . ."

"Stop it! I have to pee!"

"The knobby knees. The roadmap of scars. The long bony arms, so white they look bleached. The arresting hands. The pinhead eyes. The banana ears . . ."

"The banana ears? Oh, A!!!"

"The graying lips. The shaggy silver-white hair, soft and metallic. The cords of the neck standing out around the big Adam's apple. It's all there, B. Nothing is missing. I'm everything my scrapbook says I am."

"*Now* can I go pee, A? I'll only be a second."[3]

I can't do justice to the comic sublimity of these passages, in which an uncanny and unmistakable presence wills itself into existence in the flickering, holographic space of Warhol's hunger to own the rage of other people to describe him—to describe him as if impersonally, not to say sadistically. The effect of this shy exhibitionism is, among other things, deeply queer. ("Remember the 50s?" Lily Tomlin used to ask in a comedy routine. "Nobody was gay in the 50s; they were just shy.") Some of the infants, children, and adults in whom shame remains the most available mediator of identity are the ones called shy. And *queer,* as I've suggested elsewhere, might usefully be thought of as referring in the first place to this group or an overlapping group of infants and children, those whose sense of identity is for some reason tuned most to the note of shame.

What it is about them (or us) that makes this true remains to be specified. I mean that in the sense that I can't tell you now what it is—it certainly isn't a single thing—but also in the sense that, *for them,* it remains to be specified, is always belated. (I'd remark here on how frequently queer kids are *queer* before they're *gay*—if indeed they turn out gay at all.) As I've pointed out elsewhere,[4] the shame-delineated place of identity doesn't determine the consistency or meaning of that identity, and race, gender, class, sexuality, appearance, and abledness are only a few of the defining social constructions that will crystallize there, developing from this originary affect their particular structures of expression, creativity, pleasure, and struggle. Yet I'd venture that queerness in this sense has, at this historical moment, *some* definitionally very significant overlap—though a vibrantly elastic and temporally convoluted one—with the complex of attributes today condensed as adult or adolescent "gayness."[5] Everyone knows that some lesbians and gay men could never count as queer, and other people vibrate to the chord of queer without having much same-sex eroticism or without routing their same-sex eroticism through the identity labels "lesbian" or "gay." Yet many of the performative identity vernaculars that seem most recognizably "flushed" (to use James's word) with shame-consciousness and shame-creativity do cluster intimately around lesbian and gay worldly spaces: to name only a few, butch abjection, femmitude, leather, pride, sm, drag, musicality, fisting, attitude, zines, asceticism, Snap! culture, diva worship, florid religiosity—in a word, *flaming.*

And activism.

It seems clear enough that Warhol can be described as a hero of certain modern possibilities for embodying the transformations of "queer" shyness and for amplifying its heuristic power to expose and to generate meaning. Warhol's career offers seemingly endless ways of exploring the relation of queer shame/shyness to celebrity; to consumer culture; to prosopopoeia, the face and the portrait.

But Warhol's shyness is, along with a heuristic of being queer, also a heuristic of being "white." As such, it radically complicates any simple reappropriation of shame/shyness as being in a particular or given relation to a political telos. (And this makes sense to me: even if I just introspect about my own shyness and the politics it has made possible, the politics it has made necessary, the politics it has made prohibitively difficult, I see that it has been powerfully formative, and to very complex effect.) No one is as white as Warhol: he offers himself, willy-nilly but also with a certain defiant deliberation, as the literalizing allegory of whiteness, of the "flesh color" "that doesn't resemble any human flesh I've ever seen, though it does come pretty close to mine." Whiteness and shame are closely intertwined for Warhol—as maybe for anyone involved, at any angle, in the exacerbated race relations around urban space, civil rights, sexuality, and popular culture in the United States by the early 1960s. The exponentially increased salience of the stigma of "black" skin also concomitantly made the representational status of "white" skin vastly more problematical. To the extent that the stigma process signals the presence of a shame dynamic, to the extent also that shame definitionally functions doubly as both florid contagion *across* the skin sac and florid "self"-consciousness as delimited *by* the skin sac: to that extent, whatever a person's ideological politics of race might be, that person, even if "white," if shame-prone, is likely to inhabit a self at least partly constituted *as* a self by shame of the skin. Go back to those two long arias: remember how the skin, the whiteness of the skin (as an index of color or no color, of luminescence, of transparency/opacity, and of the natural/unnatural) is central in both those scenes of embarrassingly/hilariously alienated subjectivity.

There is a history, at least a century long, of racist uses of shame and the blush specifically as related to skin color and race.[6] It derives from Darwin: shame getting equated with "ability to" blush (meaning here to *be seen to* blush), which is then made to constitute the exact differential between "white" and "nonwhite" peoples, treated as being "the same as" the differential between more and less evolved species, that is, between fully and not-quite-fully human. Yet Warhol's pallor—whether because it represents his childhood illness or his self-described "bad chemicals" or because it represents an immigrant and specifically ethnic, working-class origin—is precisely *not* transparent to the blush of "the human." His *un*blushing white skin, in its very allegorical excessiveness, resists being normalized or universalized. In Warhol's face *the blush,* per se, is figured only in the hysterically condensed form of that wandering pimple; it's a "beauty problem." Because of the intractable literality of his whiteness, Warhol's physical instruments for efflorescing his shame/shyness, paradoxically, are therefore the race-transcending ones of the dippy musculature, the Shirley Temple mannerisms, the averted gaze. What Warhol allows to be called his "faggy air" is also the air of his literalizing shame of whiteness. Yet it is not an "air" available for identification only to white people (think of Michael Jackson)—in fact, as José Muñoz has suggested in his essay on Warhol's relation to Jean-Michel Basquiat and Basquiat's identifications with him (this volume), this demeanor may even be *more* resonant for nonwhite (gay) men with their particular histories of expertise in negotiating indignity with dignity.

Warhol's casual and more-than-casual racism: how to situate it in this connection? I would just briefly call special attention here to his distinctive (and, of course, in some ways profoundly limiting) strategy of "childlikeness." It's especially clear when he uses "childlikeness" as tone in which, again, to literalize race as color. A logic implicit in his language appears to me to go something like this: as his chalk-and-silver pallor is to the racial construct called "whiteness," so *the color brown,* and things colored brown, is to the racial construct called "blackness." I associate this tacit homology with the highly undisarming "candor" of his embarrassed relation to chocolate, and even to excrement. Significantly, both represent gay/homophobic signifiers even at the same time as they can be used as racial/racist ones. For instance, Michael Moon has written about Warhol's childhood memory (found in *Philosophy*) of receiving a Hershey Bar from his mother "every time I finished a page in my coloring book."[7] At the time *Philosophy* was written, Moon points out, " 'the Hershey highway' " was current gay slang . . . for the rectum, and for . . . the range of sexual practices—rimming (analingus), fucking, fisting, and scat—associated with it. . . . Watching and photographing other men 'taking the Hershey highway' (among other kinds of sexual activities) as an adult in the seventies . . . may have contributed to his impetus to make his representative scene of early bliss close with an encoded anal exchange between himself and his mother."[8]

The embarrassment in Warhol's writing that surrounds the figure of "the maid," apparently related to the embarrassment that surrounds dealing with excrement, is a subject on which Warhol likes to dilate. In the mode of advice to a new president:

> I've always thought that the President could do so much here to help change images. If the President would go into a public bathroom in the Capitol, and have the TV cameras film him cleaning the toilets and saying "Why not? Somebody's got to do it!" then that would do so much for the morale of the people who do the wonderful job of keeping the toilets clean. . . . He should just sit down one day and make a list of all the things that people are embarrassed to do that they shouldn't be embarrassed to do, and then do them all on television.[9]

But where does this embarrassment really live? Is it the origin or is it the destination, the pretext for or the truth of the imitable, whiny, plangent, infantine embarrassment of privilege? Two pages later in *Philosophy,* the problem of shame has come to seem Warhol's own:

I'm still thinking about maids. It really has to do with how you're raised. Some people just aren't embarrassed by the idea of somebody else cleaning up after them. . . . It's so awkward when you come face to face with a maid. I've never been able to pull it off. Some people I know are very comfortable looking at maids . . . but I can't handle it. When I go to a hotel, I find myself trying to stay there all day so the maid can't come in. I make a point of it. Because I just don't know where to put my eyes, where to look, what to be doing while they're cleaning. It's actually a lot of work avoiding the maid, when I think about it.[10]

What is structuring Warhol's style of interaction here is a racially mapped exacerbation and transgression of the double-binding, shame-proliferating "taboo on interocular experience" (as Silvan Tomkins puts it): "There are universal taboos on looking too directly into the eyes of the other because of the likelihood of affect contagion [in this case, specifically shame contagion], as well as escalation. . . . The taboo is not only a taboo on looking too intimately but also on exposing the taboo by too obviously avoiding direct confrontation."[11] And when the elaborated traces of these foundational shame strategies cross the path of a present-day politics of stigma and devaluation, perhaps few of us will be left with our flesh uncrawling.

When I was a child [Warhol concludes] I never had a fantasy about having a maid, what I had a fantasy about having was candy. . . . And now I have a roomful of candy all in shopping bags. So, as I'm thinking about it now, my success got me a candy room instead of a maid's room. As I said, it all depends on what your fantasies as a kid were, whether you're able to look at a maid or not. Because of what my fantasies were, I'm now a lot more comfortable looking [and no doubt the overdeterminedness of this particular choice need not excessively surprise us!] at a Hershey Bar.[12]

To sum up, shame, like other affects, is not a discrete intrapsychic structure but a kind of free radical that (in different people and also in different cultures) attaches to and permanently intensifies or alters the meaning of— of almost anything: a zone of the body, a sensory system, a prohibited or indeed a permitted behavior, another affect such as anger or arousal, a named identity, a script for interpreting other people's behavior toward oneself. Thus, one of the things that anyone's character or personality *is* is a record of the highly individual histories by which the fleeting emotion of shame has instituted far more durable, structural changes in one's relational and interpretive strategies toward both self and others.

Which means, among other things, that therapeutic or political strategies aimed directly at getting rid of individual or group shame, or undoing it, have something preposterous about them: they may "work"—they certainly have powerful effects—but they can't work in the way they say they work. (I am thinking here of a range of movements that deal with shame variously in the form of, for instance, the communal *dignity* of the civil rights movement; the individuating *pride* of "Black is Beautiful" and gay pride; various forms of nativist *ressentiment;* the menacingly exhibited *abjection* of the skinhead; the early feminist experiments with the naming and foregrounding of *anger* at being shamed; the incest survivors' movement's epistemological stress on *truth-telling* about shame; and, of course, many many others.) The forms taken by shame are not distinct "toxic" parts of an identity that can be excised; they are instead integral to and residual in the processes by which identity itself is formed. They are available for the work of metamorphosis, reframing, refiguration, *trans*figuration, affective and symbolic loading, and deformation; but are unavailable for effecting the work of purgation and deontological closure.

NOTES

Thanks to Hal Sedgwick for the Odetta story.

This essay is part of a larger project on shame, performance, and performativity. Some of its language overlaps with another, related essay of mine that emerges from the same project, "Queer Performativity: Henry James's *Art of the Novel*," *GLQ* 1, no. 1 (Summer 1993): 1–16.

1   Andy Warhol, *The Philosophy of Andy Warhol* (New York: Harcourt Brace Jovanovich, 1975), pp. 146–147.

2   Andy Warhol and Pat Hackett, *POPism: The Warhol Sixties* (New York: Harcourt Brace Jovanovich, 1980), pp. 199–200.

3   Warhol, *Philosophy,* pp. 7–10.

4   Eve Kosofsky Sedgwick, "Queer Performativity: Henry James's *Art of the Novel*," *GLQ* 1, no. 1 (Summer 1993): 1–16.

5   Quoted from ibid., p. 13.

6   On this, see, for example, James Ridgeway, *Blood in the Face* (New York: Thunder's Mouth, 1990); and Mary Ann O'Farrell's essay "Dickens's Scar: Rosa Dartle and *David Copperfield*,"

which she was kind enough to share with me in manuscript and which has considerably influenced my work here.

7   Warhol, *Philosophy,* p. 18.

8   Michael Moon, "Screen Memories, or, Pop Comes from the Outside," this volume.

9   Warhol, *Philosophy,* p. 100.

10 Ibid., p. 102.

11 Silvan S. Tomkins, *Affect, Imagery, Consciousness,* 4 vols. (New York: Springer, 1962–92), 3 (1991): 9.

12 Warhol, *Philosophy,* pp. 102–103.

JOSÉ ESTEBAN MUÑOZ

Famous and Dandy Like B. 'n' Andy:
Race, Pop, and Basquiat

DISIDENTIFYING IN THE DARK

■

I always marvel at the ways in which nonwhite children survive a white
supremacist U.S. culture that preys on them. I am equally in awe of the
ways in which queer children navigate a homophobic public sphere
that would rather they did not exist. The survival of children who are
both queerly and racially identified is nothing short of staggering. The obstacles and assaults that pressure and fracture such young lives are as brutally
physical as a police billy club or the fists of a homophobic thug and as
insidiously disembodied as homophobic rhetoric in a rap song or the racist
underpinnings of Hollywood cinema. I understand the strategies and rituals
that allow survival in such hostile cultural waters, and I in turn feel a certain
compulsion to try to articulate and explicate these practices of survival.
These practices are the armaments such children and the adults they become
use to withstand the disabling forces of a culture and state apparatus bent on
denying, eliding, and, in too many cases, snuffing out such emergent identity
practices. Sometimes these weapons are so sharply and powerfully developed that these same queer children and children of color grow up to do
more than just survive. And sometimes such shields collapse without a
moment's notice. When I think about Andy Warhol, I think about a sickly
queer boy who managed to do much more than simply survive. Jean-Michel
Basquiat, painter and graffitero, a superstar who rose quickly within the
ranks of the New York art scene and fell tragically to a drug overdose in 1988,

is for me another minority subject who managed to master various forms of cultural resistance that young African Americans need to negotiate racist U.S. society and its equally racist counterpart in miniature, the eighties art world.[1]

These practices of survival are, of course, not anything like intrinsic attributes that a subject is born with. More nearly, these practices are learned. They are not figured out alone, they are informed by the examples of others. These identifications with others are often mediated by a complicated network of incomplete, mediated, or crossed identifications. They are also forged by the pressures of everyday life, forces that shape a subject and call for different tactical responses. It is crucial that such children are able to look past "self" and encounter others who have managed to prosper in such spaces. Sometimes a subject needs something to identify with, sometimes a subject needs heroes to mimic and in which to invest all sorts of energies. Basquiat's heroes included certain famous black athletes and performers, four-color heroes of comic books, and a certain very white New York artist. These identifications are discussed in a recent recollection of the artist by Yo MTV Raps! host Fab Five Freddy:

> We [also] talked about painting a lot. And that was when Jean-Michel and I realized we had something in common. There were no other people from the graffiti world who knew anything about the painters who interested us. Everybody was interested by comic book art-stuff sold in supermarkets with bright colors and bold letters. Jean-Michel discovered that my favorite artists were Warhol and Rauschenberg, and I found out that Jean-Michel's favorite artists were Warhol and Jasper Johns. Which was great because we could talk about other painters as well as the guys painting on trains.[2]

In this nostalgic narrative, identification with highbrow cultural production, coupled with a parallel identification with the lowbrow graphic genre of the comic book, is what sets Basquiat apart from the rest of the subculture of early eighties New York graffiti artists. This double identification propelled Basquiat into the realm of "serious" visual artist. This powerful and complex identification is what made the movement from talking *about* Warhol to talking *to* Warhol so swift for Basquiat.

For Basquiat, Warhol embodied the pinnacle of artistic and professional success. One does not need to know this biographical information to understand the ways in which Basquiat's body of work grew out of Pop Art. But biographical fragments are helpful when we try to understand the ways in which this genius child from Brooklyn was able to meet his hero and gain access and success in the exclusive halls of that New York art world where Warhol reigned. At the same time, a turn to biography is helpful when we try to call attention to the white supremacist bias of the eighties art world and the larger popular culture that the Pop Art movement attempted to capture in its representations. Although it should be obvious to most, there is still a pressing need to articulate a truism about Pop Art's race ideology: next to no people of color populate the world of Pop Art, as either producers or subjects. Representations of people of color are scarce and, more often than not, worn-out stereotypes. Warhol's work is no exception: one need only think of the portrait of a Native American, which is titled *American Indian,* the drag queens of *Ladies and Gentlemen,* and the Mammy from the *Myths* series. The paintings reproduce images that are ingrained in the North American racist imagination. There is no challenge or complication of these constructs on the level of title or image. Pop Art's racial iconography is racist. A thesis/ defense of these images is an argument that understands these representations as calling attention to and, through this calling out, signaling out the racist dimensions of typical North American iconography. I find this apologetic reading politically dubious insofar as it fails to contextualize these images within the larger racial problematics of Pop Art.

With this posited, I will swerve back to the story this paper wants to tell, the story of how a black child of Haitian and Puerto Rican parents from Brooklyn becomes famous like Andy Warhol. The line I want to trace is one that begins with identifying with one's heroes, actually becoming like one's role model, and then moving on. This line is not easy to follow inasmuch as it is neither linear nor in any way straight. It is, in fact, a very *queer* trajectory. There are some identifications that the culture not only reinforces but depends on. An example of this would be the way in which some young black males identify with famous black athletes and entertainment media stars. Such a normativized chain of associations transmits valuable cultural messages while at the same time, depending on the identifying subject, it reinforces traditional ideas of "masculinity." Other identifications are harder to trace: how does this young African American identify with a muscular red, blue, and gold and yes, white, "superman," not to mention the pastiest of art world megastars?

In what follows I will consider these different identity-informing fixations and the ways in which they resurfaced in Basquiat's body of work. Central to this project is an understanding of the process of "disidentification" and its significance to Basquiat's artistic practices. I understand the survival strategies that subjects such as Basquiat and Warhol utilize as practices of disidentification. The psychoanalysts J. Laplanche and J.-B. Pontalis define "identification" as a "psychological process whereby the subject assimilates an aspect, property or attribute of the other and is transformed, wholly or partially, after the model the other provides. It is by means of a series of identifications that the personality is constituted and specified."[3] A disidentifying subject is unable to identify fully or to form what Freud calls that "just-as-if" relationship. In the examples I am engaging, the obstructive factor that stops identification from happening is always the ideological restrictions of a set identificatory site. In the case of Basquiat, it was often a specifically racialized normativity that foreclosed any easy identification.

The French linguist Michel Pecheux extrapolates a theory of disidentification from Marxist theorist Louis Althusser's influential theory of subject formation and interpellation. "Ideology and Ideological State Apparatuses" was among the first articulations of the role of ideology in theorizing subject formation. For Althusser, ideology is an inescapable realm in which subjects are called into being or "hailed," a process he calls "interpellation." Ideology is the imaginary relationship of individuals to their real conditions of existence. The location of ideology is always within an *apparatus* and its practice or practices, such as the state apparatus.[4] Pecheux built on this theory by describing the three modes in which a subject is constructed by ideological practices. In this schema the first mode is understood as "identification," where a "Good Subject" chooses the path of identification with discursive and ideological forms. "Bad Subjects" resist and attempt to reject the images and identificatory sites offered by dominant ideology and proceed to rebel, to "counteridentify" and turn against this symbolic system. The danger that Pecheux sees in such an operation would be the counterdetermination that such a system installs, a structure that validates the dominant ideology by reinforcing its dominance through the controlled symmetry of "counterdetermination." Disidentification is the third mode of dealing with dominant ideology, one that neither opts to assimilate within such a structure nor strictly opposes it; rather, disidentification is a strategy that "works on and against dominant ideology."[5] Instead of buckling under the pressures of dominant ideology (identification, assimilation) or attempting to break free of its inescapable sphere (counteridentification, utopianism), this "working on and against" is a strategy that tries to transform a cultural logic from within, always laboring to enact permanent structural change while at the same time valuing the importance of local or everyday resistance struggles.

Judith Butler gestures to the uses of disidentification when discussing the failure of identification. In *Bodies That Matter*, Butler parries with Slavoj Žižek, who understands disidentification as a breaking down of political possibility, "a factionalization to the point of political immobilization."[6] Butler counters Žižek's charge by asking the following question of his formulations: "What are the possibilities of politicizing *dis*identification, this experience of *misrecognition*, this uneasy sense of standing under a sign to which one does and does not belong?" Butler answers her query by writing, "It may be that the affirmation of that slippage, that the failure of identification is itself the point of departure for a more democratizing affirmation of internal difference."[7] Both Butler's and Pecheux's accounts of disidentification put forward an understanding of identification as never being as seamless or unilateral as the Freudian account would suggest.[8] Both theorists construct the subject as a subject *inside* of ideology. Their models permit one to examine theories of the subject who is neither the "Good Subject," who has an easy or magical identification with dominant culture, nor the "Bad Subject," who imagines herself outside of ideology. Instead, they pave the way to an understanding of a "disidentificatory subject" who tactically and simultaneously works on, with, and against a cultural form.

As a practice, disidentification does not dispel those ideological contradictory elements; rather, like a melancholic subject holding onto a lost object, it works to hold onto this object and invest it with new life. Eve Kosofsky Sedgwick, in her work on the affect, shame, and its role in queer performativity, has explained as follows:

> The forms taken by shame are not distinct "toxic" parts of a group or individual identity that can be excised; they are instead integral to and residual in the processes by which identity itself is formed. They are available for the work of metamorphosis, reframing, refiguration, *trans*figuration, affective and symbolic loading and deformation; but unavailable for effecting the work of purgation and deontological closure.[9]

To disidentify is to read oneself and one's own life narrative in a moment, object, or subject that is not culturally coded to "connect" with the disidentifying subject. It is not to pick and choose what one takes out of an identification. It is *not* to evacuate willfully the politically dubious or shameful components within an identificatory locus. Rather, it is the reworking of those energies that does not elide the "harmful" or contradictory components of any identity. It is an acceptance of the necessary introjection that has occurred in such situations.

Disidentification for the minority subject is a mode of *recycling* or reforming an object that has already been invested with powerful energy. It is important to emphasize the transformative restructuration of that disidentification. With this notion of disidentification posited, I will be suggesting that it is simply not enough to say that Basquiat identified with his subject matter or "heroes," be they Batman or Warhol. Beyond that, it is not enough to say that Basquiat identified with the movement we understand as Pop Art or any of its derivatives. Which is not to say that he rejected these previous cultural players, forms, and practices. Instead, he acknowledged and incorporated their force and influence; *transfigured,* they inform his own strategies and tactics in powerful ways.

The mode of cultural production I am calling disidentification is indebted to earlier theories of revisionary identification. These foundational theories emerged from fields of film theory, gay and lesbian studies, and critical race theory. While these different fields do not often branch into one another's boundaries, they have often attempted to negotiate similar methodological and theoretical concerns. The term "revisionary identification" is a loose construct that is intended to hold various accounts of tactical identification together. "Revisionary" is meant to signal different strategies of viewing, reading, and locating "self" within representational systems and disparate life worlds that aim to displace or occlude a minority subject. The string that binds such different categories is a precariously thin one, and it is important to specify the different critical traditions' influence to my own formulations by surveying some of the contributions they make to this project.

My thinking about disidentification has been strongly informed by the important work of critical race theorists, who have asked important questions about the workings of identification for minority subjects within dominant media. Michele Wallace has described the process of identification as one that is "constantly in motion."[10] The flux that characterizes identification for Miriam Hansen when considering female spectatorship and identification is then equally true of the African American spectator in Wallace's article. Wallace offers testimony to her own position as a spectator:

> It was always said among Black women that Joan Crawford was part Black, and as I watch these films again today, looking at Rita Hayworth in *Gilda* or Lana Turner in *The Postman Always Rings Twice,* I keep thinking "she is so beautiful, she looks black." Such a statement makes no sense in current feminist film criticism. What I am trying to suggest is that there was a way in which these films were *possessed* by Black female viewers. The process may have been about problematizing and expanding one's racial identity *instead* of abandoning it. It seems important here to view spectatorship as not only potentially bisexual but also multiracial and multiethnic. Even as "The Law of the Father" may impose its premature closure on the filmic "gaze" in the coordination of suture and classical narrative, disparate factions in the audience, not equally well indoctrinated in the dominant discourse, may have their way, now and then, with interpretation.[11]

The story that Wallace tells substantiates the theory of disidentification that is proposed in this essay. The wistful statement that is persistent in Wallace's experience of identification, "she is so beautiful, she looks black," is a poignant example of the transformative power of disidentification. In this rumination, the Eurocentric conceit of whiteness and beauty as being naturally aligned (hence, straight hair is "good hair" in some African American vernaculars) is turned on its head. Disidentification, like the subjective experience described in the above passage, is about expanding and problematizing identity and identification, not abandoning any socially prescribed identity component. Black female viewers are not merely passive subjects who are possessed by the well-worn paradigms of identification that the classical narrative produces; rather, they are active participant spectators who can mutate and restructure stale patterns within dominant media.

In the same way that Wallace's writing irrevocably changes the ways in which we consume films of the forties, the work of novelist and literary theorist Toni Morrison offers a much needed reassessment of the canon of American literature. Morrison has described "a great, ornamental, prescribed absence in American literature,"[12] which is the expurgated African American presence from the North American imaginary. Morrison proposes and executes strategies to reread the American canon with an aim to resuscitate the African presence that was eclipsed by the machinations of an escapist variant of white supremacist thought that is intent on displacing nonwhite presence. The act of locating African presences in canonical white literature is an example of disidentification employed for a focused political process. The mobile tactic (disidentification) refuses to follow the texts' grain insofar as these contours suggest that a reader play along with the game of African elision. Instead, the disidentificatory optic is turned to shadows and fissures within the text, where black presences can be liberated from the protective custody of the white literary imagination.

One of queer theory's major contributions to the critical discourse on identification is the important work that has been done on cross-identification. Sedgwick, for example, has contributed to this understanding of decidedly queer chains of connection by discussing the way in which lesbian writer Willa Cather was able to both disavow Oscar Wilde for his grotesque homosexuality and uniquely invest in and identify with her gay male fictional creations: "If Cather, in this story, does something to cleanse her own sexual body of the carrion stench of Wilde's victimization, it is thus (unexpectedly) by identifying with what seems to be Paul's sexuality not in spite of but *through* its saving reabsorption in a gender-liminal (and very specifically classed) artifice that represents at once a particular subculture and culture itself."[13] This example is only one of many within Sedgwick's oeuvre that narrates the nonlinear and nonnormative modes of identification with which queers predicate their self-fashioning. Butler has recently amended Sedgwick's reading of Cather's cross-identification by insisting that such a passage across identity markers, a passage that she understands as being a "dangerous crossing," is not about being *beyond* gender and sexuality.[14] Butler sounds a warning that the crossing of identity may signal erasure of the "dangerous" or, to use Sedgwick's word when discussing the retention of the shameful, "toxic." For Butler, the danger exists in abandoning the lesbian or female in Cather when reading the homosexual and the male. The cautionary point that Butler would like to make is meant to ward off reductive fantasies of cross-identification that figure it as fully achieved or finally reached at the expense of the point from which it emanates. While Sedgwick's theorizations around cross-identification and narrative crossing are never as final as Butler suggests, the issues that Butler outlines should be heeded when the precarious activity of cross-identification is discussed. The tensions that exist between cross-identification as it is theorized in Sedgwick's essay and Butler's response to that writing represent important spaces in queer theory that have been insufficiently addressed, in my estimation. The theory of disidentification that I am putting forth is response to the call of that schism. Disidentification, as a mode of understanding the movements and circulations of identificatory force, would always foreground that lost object of identification, establishing new possibilities while at the same time echoing the materially prescriptive cultural locus of any identification.

Operating within a very subjective register, Wayne Koestenbaum, in his moving study of opera divas and gay male opera culture, discusses the ways in which gay males can cross-identify with the cultural icon of the opera diva. Koestenbaum writes about the identificatory pleasure he enjoys when reading the prose of opera divas' auto/biographies:

> I'm affirmed and "divined"—made porous, open, awake, glistening—by a diva's sentences of self-defense and self-creation.
>
> I don't claim to prove any historical facts; instead, I want to trace connections between the iconography of "diva" as it emerges in certain publicized lives, and a collective gay subcultural imagination—a source of hope, joke, and dish. Gossip, hardly trivial, is as central to gay culture as to female cultures. From skeins of hearsay, I weave an inner life; I build queerness from banal and uplifting stories of the conduct of famous fiery women.[15]

A diva's strategies of self-creation and self-defense, through the crisscrossed circuitry of cross-identification, do the work of enacting self for the gay male opera queen. The gay male subculture that Koestenbaum represents in his prose is by no means the totality of queer culture, but for this particular variant of a gay male life world, such identifications are the very stuff on which queer identity is founded. In his memoir Koestenbaum explains the ways in which opera divas were crucial identificatory loci in the public sphere before the Stonewall rebellion, which marked the advent of the contemporary lesbian and gay rights movement. He suggests that before a homosexual civil rights movement, opera queens were some of the few pedagogical examples of truly grand-scale queer behavior. The opera queen's code of conduct was crucial to the closeted gay male before gay liberation. Again, such a practice of *transfiguring* an identificatory site that was not meant to accommodate male identities is to a queer subject an important identity-consolidating hub, an affirmative yet temporary utopia. Koestenbaum's disidentification with the opera diva does not erase the fiery females that fuel his identity-making machinery; rather, it lovingly retains their lost presence through imitation, repetition, and admiration. After focusing on the theoretical underpinnings of disidentification, I will turn to the disidentification that is central to Basquiat's project. In what follows, I suggest the ways in which Basquiat and Andy served as divas for each other, divine creatures who inspired and enabled each other through queer circuits of identifications.

SUPERHEROES AND SUPREMACISTS

■

Only now is cultural studies beginning to address the tremendous impact of superheroes, cartoons, and comic books in contemporary culture. Basquiat, like Warhol, was fascinated by the persistence and centrality of these characters in the cultural imaginary. Warhol, Roy Lichtenstein, and others blew up such images, calling attention to the art that goes into creating these seemingly artless productions. They zoomed in on every zip dot and gaudy color that made these characters larger than life. Michael Moon and Sasha Torres have forcefully explained the powerful homosocial and homosexual charges that animate these characters in our contemporary cultural mythologies.[16] Although I do not want to foreclose similar inquiries into Basquiat's identification with such images, I want to investigate another salient characteristic of these graphic figures: race. By examining the origins and aesthetics of the superhero, I will suggest that the twentieth-century myth of the superhero was, in its earliest manifestation, a disidentifying cultural formation that informed Pop Art and its legacy.

The American icon Superman first appeared in *Action Comics* #1 in June 1938. It is important to contextualize this first appearance alongside early-twentieth-century racist imaginings of a race of supermen. In their history of the comic book superhero, Greg McCue and Clive Bloom outline some of the cultural forces that helped form the Man of Steel.

The multitude of supermen in the air was not limited to adventures. In the early twentieth century, America was becoming aware of Nietzsche's *ubermensch* [superman] from *Thus Spoke Zarathustra*. Shaw's allusion to the idea in Man and Superman had made "superman" the translation of choice, replacing "over-man" or "beyond-man." Two young Jewish men [Superman's creators, Jerry Siegel and Joe Schuster] in the united states [*sic*] at the time could not have been unaware of an idea that would dominate Hitler's National socialism. The concept was certainly well discussed.[17]

McCue and Bloom allude to a connection between the creators' status as Jews and the transfiguration of the anti-Semitic possibility encoded within the popular notion of a "superman." I would push their point further and suggest that the young writer and artist team not only was "aware" of all the notions of supermen saturating both North American and European culture but also actively strove to respond to it by reformulating the myth of superman outside of anti-Semitic and xenophobic cultural logics. The writers go on to suggest the character's resemblance to other important figures within the Judeo-Christian tradition: "Superman, as a religious allusion, has been indicated as a contributing factor in his creation and continued popularity. The infant Kal-El's [who would eventually grow up to be Superman] space ship can be seen as a modern day cradle of Moses on the cosmic Nile."[18] I suggest that within the myth of Superman, a myth that Basquiat and Warhol both utilized in extremely powerful ways, a disidentificatory kernel was already present. The last son of Krypton is not only a popularized *ubermensch* but, at the same time, the rewriting of Moses, who led the Jews out of Egypt and through such obstacles as the Dead Sea and the desert. For the young Jewish comic creators and the countless fans who consumed their work, the dark-haired alien superman was a powerful reworking and re-imagining of a malevolent cultural fantasy that was gaining symbolic force.

If one decodes the signifiers of Jewish ethnicity that are central to the superman's mythic fabric, it becomes clear that in working through the Superman character, its creators were able to intervene in another phobic anti-Semitic fantasy that figured the Jew's body as weak and sickly. Sander Gilman has addressed this issue in *The Jew's Body*, in which he describes the need of the racist science of eugenics to figure morphological difference when discussing the Jew's difference. Such discourses fed the scientific discourse during the Nazi era. Gilman explains the ways in which the Jew's body as weak and sickly was first registered and discusses the Zionist call for a new Jewish body, which was proposed as an antidote to this stereotype: "Elias Auerbach's evocation of sport as the social force to reshape the Jewish body had its origins in the turn-of-the-century call of the physician and Zionist leader Max Nordau for a new 'Muscle Jew.' This view became the commonplace of the early Zionist literature which called upon sport, as an activity, as one of the central means of shaping the new Jewish body."[19] With Gilman's valuable historical analysis posited, we can begin to understand the unique process of ethnic disidentification, a process, once again, of transfiguration and reorganization on the level of identification. Siegel and Schuster displaced dominant racist images of the Jew as pathological and weak by fusing together the dangerous mythologies of the *ubermensch* with something like Nordau's fantasy of the "muscle Jew." The Superman character held onto both these images, like lost objects that could not be dispelled no matter how hateful or self-hating their particular points of origin might be. What is left at the end of this disidentificatory process is a new model of identity and a newly available site of identification.

The eighties saw a painful resurgence of white supremacist activity in the subcultural models of the skinhead and neo-nazi. With this in mind I want to consider Basquiat's rewriting/reimagining of Superman.[20] His painting titled *Action Comics* is a reproduction of the original cover art for *Action Comics #1.* Stylistically, the painting strays from the earlier Pop practice of reproducing and magnifying the hyperreal perfection of these images.[21] Basquiat's Superman is stripped of its fantasy aura of white male perfection. Instead of faultless lines, we encounter rough and scrawl-like lines that translate this image to the graphic grammar of a child's perception. The disidentificatory strokes here retain the vibrancy of this fantasy of wanting to be Superman, of wanting to be able to accomplish awe-inspiring feats that only the Man of Steel can accomplish, without retaining the aestheticism of the image. In this painting Superman is, in a manner of speaking, brought back to his roots. Basquiat's rendition of the character and of the classic cover art works to resuscitate the disidentificatory force of the character's first incarnation and appearance.

The same childlike technique is deployed in Basquiat's rendition of Batman and Robin, titled *Piano Lesson.* The title implies the disidentificatory locus of such production, a space that might be imagined as the mandatory childhood piano lesson, a moment when fantasizing about superheroes is a tactic to transcend the boredom of childhood. Batman and Robin appear as

Figure 1. Jean-Michel Basquiat, *Television and Cruelty to Animals* (1983).
©1996 Artists Rights Society (ARS), New York/ADAGP, Paris.

though they are being rebuilt in the painting. The familiar superheroes'
bodies are fragmented and incomplete. Such a representation connotes the
revisionary and transformative effect of disidentification. The half-finished
figures connote *process*, which is exactly how the *process* of disidentification
should be understood.

This disidentificatory impulse is even more prominent in a later painting.
The 1983 *Television and Cruelty to Animals* (see figure 1) presents a mangled
menagerie of cartoon characters. The canvas is populated by a large moose
head that we might imagine as Bullwinkle, a stray black eight ball, the
familiar Superman insignia, a curious conflation of that insignia and the bat
signal, and two crossed-out swastikas. We can say the barrage of images
represents a Pop media overload that characterizes postmodern North Amer-

ican childhood and adulthood. But I am more interested in the word images found near the top right-hand section of the painting. Here we see the phrase "Popeye versus the Nazis" written with a shaky black oil stick. This double-voiced articulation explicates the schoolyard fantasies of which mythological figure is mightier, "who can beat whom up." More important, it reveals the ideologies of white supremacy that are never too distant from the "good guys" of this collective imaginary. Ideologies that Basquiat's disidentificatory process brings into a new visibility. Ideologies that can be, like the Batman insignia in *Television and Cruelty to Animals,* temporarily crossed out. The superhero insignia is just one of many of the symbols in contemporary culture that Basquiat worked with; other types of signifier on which the artist focused were those that indicated ownership, such as the trademark sign and the copyright symbol. I will now turn to Basquiat's disidentification with the commodity form and its signifiers.

BRAND BASQUIAT
■

In the previous section I pointedly called attention to Basquiat's disidentification with the cartoon genre. That disidentification was certainly more radical than but not altogether dissimilar from the disidentification that characterized Pop Art's first wave. The variance is the intensity of the disidentificatory impulse and its relation to the image's aesthetic "realism." A 1984 collaboration between Warhol and Basquiat sharply contrasts these strategies (see figure 2). The right side of the canvas displays the classic Pop disidentificatory stance. This strategy was described by Lucy Lippard as the tension that is produced due to the narrow distance between the original and the Pop Art piece.[22] Warhol's Arm & Hammer symbol on the right has the appearance of a seamless reproduction. But the relationship to the original design or "model" is strictly disidentificatory. In Warhol's distinctly postmodern practice, the image's disjunctive relocation calls attention to the trace of human labor, personified in the rolled-up worker's arm that has always been central to the design. This strategy disrupts the normative protocols of the commodity form. Susan Stewart explains the workings of the commodity system in her important study of outlaw representational strategies: "For it is the nature of the commodity system, of its compelling systematicity per se, to replace labor with magic, intrinsicality with marketing, authoring with ush-

Figure 2. Andy Warhol and Jean-Michel Basquiat, *Arm & Hammer* (1984). ©1996
Andy Warhol Foundation for the Visual Arts/ARS, New York/ADAGP, Paris.

ering."[23] The refiguration of the trademark on Warhol's side of the canvas
interrupts the erasure of labor by calling attention to the trademark's very
inscription, one that, when properly scrutinized, reveals the thematics of
labor that the commodity system works to elide.

Basquiat deals with the same subject matter but approaches a critique of
the commodity form from a vastly different perspective that is still, within
the terms of this analysis, disidentificatory. The circular center in Basquiat's
half of the painting is occupied by a dime that features a black man playing
the saxophone. This image calls attention to the often effaced presence of
black production. An intervention like this interrogates the ways in which
the United States is, at base, a former slave economy that still counts on and
factors in the exploitation and colonization of nonwhite labor. And this is
especially true in the arenas of cultural labor. Basquiat's intervention does
more than call attention to the artifice and "constructedness" of these images.
Basquiat's half of the painting explodes a racial signifier that is often erased in
the empire of signs that is the world of U.S. advertising.

Although the compulsive need to periodize different stages and levels of
modernity is often the quickest route to stale and static conceptual grids, I do

find some of Paul Gilroy's theorizations around the "pre-modern" in modernity a useful apparatus for contemplating the black horn-blowing body in the center of Basquiat's half of the painting. In an essay whose title asks the provocative question, "Whose Millennium Is This?" Gilroy writes:

> Benjamin says that remembering creates the chain of tradition. His concern is with "perpetuating remembrance," and here, this modern black consciousness shares something with his blend of Jewish eschatology and Marxism. They converge, for example, in a concern with dissonance, negativity, redemption, and aesthetic stress on pain and suffering. Looking at modern black art and the social relations that support it can reveal how this remembering is socially and politically organized in part through assertive tactics which accentuate the symbolism of the pre-modern as part of their anti-modern modernism.[24]

The black face, starkly juxtaposed to the white arm, displays the vastly different cultural habitus of the two artists. The face, cartoonish and primitive, but primitive not in a contrived jungle fashion but with the primitivity of childhood, harkens back to a "pre-" moment that might be understood as pre-modern but is also pre- the congealing of subject formation. Its reference point is black music, which, as Gilroy has argued, is a key signifying practice within black Atlantic culture: "Music and its attendant rituals provide the most important locations where the unspeakable and unwriteable memory of terror is preserved as a social and cultural resource."[25] In the same way that shame cannot be expurgated in Sedgwick's understanding of the affect shame's relation to identity formation, this terror, this "unspeakable" terror that Gilroy identifies as being central to diaspora aesthetics and cultural practices, must, like the melancholic subject's lost object, be retained in the matrix of identity and its representations. Basquiat's figure, a shirtless, crudely sketched black male who plays a saxophone, is a melancholic reverberation that vibrates through the contemporary Pop Art project. Its "sound" evokes and eulogizes a lost past, a childhood, and a memory of racial exploitation and terror.

In Basquiat's disidentificatory project, one encounters a proliferation of trademarks and copyright symbols. Such symbols remind the viewer that the history of consumer culture on which Basquiat is signifying is an economy that was, in no small part, formulated on the premise that the ownership of other human beings was entirely possible. The quotidian dimensions of the

Figure 3. Jean-Michel Basquiat, *Quality Meats for the Public* (1982).
©1996 Artists Rights Society (ARS), New York/ADAGP, Paris.

commodity form are continually called attention to in paintings such as
Quality Meats for the Public (see figure 3), where the words swine, poultry, or
animated pig are trademarked. As Lauren Berlant, in an essay on national
brands and the racialized body, reminds us: "A trademark is supposed to be a
consensual mechanism. It triangulates with the consumer and the commodity, providing what W. F. Haug calls a 'second skin' that enables the
commodity to appear to address, to recognize, and thereby to love the consumer."[26] I want argue that the Basquiat brand trademark disrupts the tri-
angulating mediation of consumer and commodity. It does so by producing
an effect that Greg Tate has described, when writing about Basquiat's painting, as "an overloaded sensorium counterattacking the world via feedback
loop."[27] If all the world's swine and poultry are exposed as always already
trademarked, the special imaginary relationship that the trademark mediates
is then short-circuited. The second skin is skinned.

Near the end of his too brief career, Basquiat began employing the trademark IDEAL. IDEAL, as used in his 1987 painting *Victor 25448* (see figure 4),
clearly represents the national toy brand, but one is also left to think that the
statement is reflective of the trademark's status as "consensual mechanism"
that makes the commodity object the *ideal* for which the consumer is always
shooting. The particular plight of the black male consumer is embodied in
the black figure stumbling and falling in the direction of the floating ideal
symbols. The black male's flailing limbs and "x'd-out" eyes are descriptive of
the figure's betrayal by the "consensual mechanism" contract. IDEAL is, of
course, also reflective of Basquiat's own participation in such a process.
Indeed, none of his paintings can be understood as counteridentifications,
including straightforward attacks, on commodity culture's iconography insofar as he, too, deals in such practices. The "I" in ideal is a Basquiat who also
"deals" like an art dealer or drug pusher in the same consumer public sphere.
He is, as I have argued earlier, working on and against a cultural pattern, a
pattern that he, through his disidentificatory process, can transfigure.

Stewart has forcefully argued that the connections to be made between
"real" graffiti writers and graffiti artists like Basquiat who showed their work
in galleries instead of subway trains are nearly nonexistent. I will argue that
his mass proliferation of the copyright and trademark sign works in similar
ways as the "tags" of the urban graffiti writers she discusses. I make this claim
in part because Basquiat began, as the testimony of Fab Five Freddy attests,
as a graffiti artist on the trains and derelict walls of abandoned buildings in

Figure 4. Jean-Michel Basquiat, *Victor 25448* (1987). ©1996 Artists
Rights Society (ARS), New York/ADAGP, Paris.

New York City. Stewart explains that the graffiti writer's use of the brand
name has a disruptive effect on the symbolic economy of the commodity
system:

> They have borrowed from the repetitions of advertising and commercial
> culture as antiepitaph: the names' frequent appearance marks the stub-
> born ghost of individuality and intention in mass culture, the ironic
> restatement of the artist as "brand name." Graffiti celebrates the final
> victory of the signature over the referent, by making claims on the very
> subjectivity invented by consumerism. In this sense they have gone
> beyond pop art, which always took on the abstractions of the exchange
> economy solely as a matter of thematic.[28]

Basquiat's repetitions of trademarks, brand names, figures, and words set up
a parallel commodity system that, using the logic of Stewart's argument,
produces an individual subject who disidentifies (restructures) the social
holding pattern that is the mass-produced subject. Specificities, like race,
that are meant to be downplayed or whitewashed in consumer culture rise to
the forefront of his production. I do not detect a victory of consumerism in
Basquiat's project in the ways in which Stewart sees the graffiti writer's project as being a triumph over consumer capitalism. Instead, I see Basquiat's
practice as a strategy of disidentification that retools and is ultimately able to

open up a space where a subject can imagine a mode of surviving the nullifying force of consumer capitalism's models of self.

Stewart's charge that Pop Art, because of its location and complicity within consumerism, has made its critique operational only on the level of iconography and thematics is ultimately too sweeping an indictment. The notion that one is either co-opted by consumerism or fighting the "real" fight against it poses a reductive binarism between representation and "reality." If Stewart's locution is uncontested, the work of making queer culture in a homophobic world, as in the case of Warhol, or representing black male youth culture in places where it has been systematically erased (like the SoHo gallery) would register only as the rumblings of bourgeois society's assimilation machine. In the next section I will explore the role of fame, assimilation, and the politics of disidentification that were central to the work of both Basquiat and Warhol.

FAMOUS
■

This section is concerned with questions of Warhol's and Basquiat's interpersonal identifications and their collaborations as both celebrities and artists, and with the thematic of fame that concretely links these two personas. Before considering Basquiat's unstable identifications, disidentifications, and counteridentifications with Warhol, I want to gloss some of the ways in which Jean-Michel meant much to Andy. First the art. In 1984 Warhol explained that "Jean-Michel got me into painting differently, so that's a good thing." Indeed if we look at Warhol's work after his collaboration with Basquiat, we see a renewed interest in painting by hand, which he had done little of, beyond some abstract backgrounds, since 1962. Warhol's star status was equally revitalized by Basquiat. Few would deny that making appearances with hot young art world superstars such as Basquiat and Keith Haring upped Andy's glamour ratings. Basquiat also provided Andy's infamous diary with many a juicy gossip tidbit. The following passage from Saturday, May 5, 1984, recounts a story that is uncharacteristically sentimental for Warhol:

> It was a beautiful and sunny, did a lot of work. Called Jean-Michel and he said he'd come up. He came and rolled some joints. He was really nervous, I could tell, about how his show was opening later on at Mary

Boone's. Then he wanted a new outfit and we went to this store where he always buys his clothes. He had b.o. We were walking and got to Washington Square Park where I first met him when he was signing his name "SAMO" and writing graffiti and painting T-shirts. That area brought back bad memories for him. Later on his show was great, though, it really was.[29]

In this passage we hear a bit of the complexity of Warhol's identification with Basquiat. Warhol's sensitivity to Basquiat's "bad memories" of his seedy days as a graffiti artist selling hand-painted T-shirts in Washington Square Park might very well echo his own discomfort with his past, his own inability to reconcile completely that past with his present. The mention of joints further signifies with Andy's later disavowal of the crazy people and drug addicts who populated the Factory days. We also hear Warhol's bitchy "b.o." comment that served to temper his identification with Basquiat. But finally Basquiat's victory at Mary Boone is for the older artist both an identification with Warhol's former early successes and a victory for Warhol because of his, at the time, current investment in the twenty-four-year-old artist. There is also a much more poignant identification that Warhol records in the diaries, an August 5, 1984, outing to a party at the Limelight for Jermaine Jackson. The bouncers at the door are described as "dumb Mafia-type of guys who didn't know anyone." After being rejected at the door, Basquiat turned to Warhol and exclaimed, "Now you see how it is to be Black."[30]

Basquiat's formal disidentification—his simultaneous working with, against, and on Warhol's production—is uniquely thematized in a collaboration with Warhol that depicts one of Warhol's motorcycle images and one of Basquiat's distinctive distorted figures (see figure 5). The enlarged image of the motorcycle from a newspaper ad is an image that Warhol repeated throughout his mid-1980s black-and-white and Last Supper series. The black figures that Basquiat contributes to the frame work once again to show the black presence that has been systematically denied from this representational practice. These primitive jet-black images look only vaguely human and bare sharp fangs. Through such representations Basquiat ironizes the grotesque and distortive African American presentations in consumer culture. In this canvas, as in many of the other Warhol collaborations, the smooth lines of Warhol's practice work as *a vehicle* for Basquiat's own political and cultural practice.

Figure 5. Jean-Michel Basquiat and Andy Warhol, *Untitled* (c. 1984-1985). ©1996 Andy Warhol Foundation for the Visual Arts/ARS, New York/ADAGP, Paris.

My essay's title is a riff taken from the Disposable Heroes of Hiphoprisy. In their 1992 song "Famous and Dandy like Amos 'n' Andy," the fictional characters are an entry point into a hip hop meditation on the history of black media representation and the price of fame for African Americans. These are, of course, important thematics for Basquiat. (Basquiat used and trademarked names of characters from the early radio and TV show in some of his paintings.) To be sure, fame is of tremendous import for both of this essay's subjects, but a comparison of one of Basquiat's famous black athlete images with Warhol's portraits illustrates the world of difference between these two disidentificatory impulses and the aesthetic effects they produce. Warhol's portraits of Liza, Marilyn, Liz Taylor, Elvis, and so on are not so much portraits of celebrities as they are of fame itself. Although it can be argued that Basquiat's paintings also treat fame as a subject, his formulations enact the disturbing encounter between fame and racist ideology that saturates North American media culture. The famous Negro athlete series reflects the problem of being a famous black image that is immediately codified as a trademark by a white entertainment industry. The deployment of the word "Negro" is a disidentification with the racist cultural history that surrounds

Figure 6. Jean-Michel
Basquiat, *Untitled* (1981).
©1996 Artists Rights
Society (ARS), New York/
ADAGP, Paris.

the history of both sports in the United States and the contested lives of
African Americans in general. The simplicity of the following image exposes
these dynamics of being famous and ethnically identified in U.S. culture (see
figure 6): we see a trinity of three images, a hastily scrawled black head, a
crown symbol that accompanied most of the paintings in this series and a
baseball. The controversy that ensued in 1992 when the owner of one major
league baseball team, Marge Sholtz, referred to one of her players as "a
million dollar nigger" makes a point that Basquiat was making in this series:
the rich and famous black athlete is not immune to the assaults of various
racisms. Within such racist imaginings, the famous black athlete is simply
equated with the ball and other tools of the trade. Basquiat interrupts this
trajectory by inserting the crown symbol between the man and the object.
The crown was an image that Basquiat has frequently used to symbolize the
rich history of Africans and African Americans. The crown, or the title of
"King," is, as Stewart explains, a title used to designate the supremacy of
graffiti artists who were best able to proliferate and disseminate their tags.

Fab Five Freddy explained Basquiat's famous Negro artist series in the following way: "And like a famous Negro athlete, Jean-Michel slid into home.
He stole all three bases, actually, and then slid into home. Home being Mary
Boone's gallery."[31] I want to engage this metaphor further and speculate that
home base was also embodied in Basquiat's relationship with Warhol. The
painting *Dos Cabezas* (see figure 7) depicts two rough sketches of both

artists' faces lined up side by side, on an equal level. It also translates Andy's head into Spanish, setting up a moment of interculturation that is typical of both Basquiat's work and other examples of disidentification that can be found in U.S. culture.

The ways in which these two artists cross-identified, disidentified, and learned with and from each other also suggest the political possibilities of collaboration. The relationship of queerness and race is often a vexed and complicated one within progressive political arenas. When these identity shards are positioned as oppositional, they often split and damage subjects whose identifications vector into both identificatory nodes. Often the models and examples set by Pop Art in general and Andy Warhol in particular influenced Basquiat in innumerable ways. And, in turn, Basquiat rejuvenated both Pop Art and Warhol by exploding racial signifiers that had been erased, obstructed, or rendered dormant by the discourse. I want to make the point that these disidentificatory cultural practices and the coterminous interpersonal identificatory crossings and crisscrossing that Basquiat made with Warhol and Warhol with Basquiat were indispensable survival practices for both these marginalized men.

MELANCHOLIA'S WORK
■

My theoretical understanding of disidentification has been, as I have stated above, informed by the structure of feeling that is melancholia. In this final section I will further investigate the relationship of melancholia to disidentification within Basquiat's work, in an effort to make these connections more salient. I want to consider a photograph of Jean-Michel Basquiat (see figure 8). The portrait was one of the last photographs taken by James Van der Zee, the famous Harlem-based studio photographer whose career spanned five decades. The younger artist seems strangely comfortable in the gilded Edwardian trappings of Van der Zee's studio. His look away from the camera and the heaviness of his head, being held up by his hand, connotes this certain quality of melancholia. I look at this image and feel the call of mourning. I reflect on the subject's short and tragic life in the New York avant-garde scene, his early death from a drug overdose, the loss of this artist, and all the paintings that were left undone. In this final stage of his career, Van der Zee produced many portraits of important African Ameri-

cans, including Muhammad Ali, Romare Bearden, Lou Rawls, Eubie Blake, Ruby Dee and Ossie Davis, and Max Robinson, the first African American to land a position as a national newscaster. Robinson died of complications due to AIDS. To look at his portrait now is indeed to summon up the dead, to put a face and voice on the countless black bodies that have been lost in the epidemic.[32] Basquiat, who died of a drug overdose the same year as Robinson, also embodies this moment of crisis in communities of color where young men are mercilessly cut down by the onslaught of the virus, the snares of a too often deadly drug addiction, and a U.S. criminal justice system that has declared open season on young male bodies of color.

Basquiat understood the force of death and dying in the culture and tradition around him; his art was concerned with working through the charged relation between black male identity and death. He, like Van der Zee, understood that the situation of the black diaspora called on a living subject to take

Figure 7. Jean-Michel Basquiat, *Dos Cabezas* (1982). ©1996 Artists Rights Society (ARS), New York/ ADAGP, Paris.
Figure 8. James Van der Zee, *Jean-Michel Basquiat* (1982).

their dying with them. They were baggage that was not to be lost or forgotten because ancestors, be they symbolic or genetically linked, were a deep source of enabling energy that death need not obstruct.

Disidentification, as I have suggested above, shares structures of feeling with Freudian melancholia, but the cultural formations I am discussing are not, in the Freudian sense, the "work of mourning." Laplanche and Pontalis describe the work of mourning as an "intrapsychic process, occurring after the loss of a loved object, whereby the subject gradually manages to detach itself from this object."[33] The works of mourning here offer no such escape from the lost object. Rather, the lost object returns with a vengeance. It is floated as an ideal, a call to collectivize, an identity-affirming example. Basquiat saw the need to call up the dead, to mingle the power of the past with the decay of the present. bell hooks has recently commented on Basquiat's paintings of famous Negro athletes (see figure 9): "It is much too simplistic to

Figure 9. Jean-Michel Basquiat, *Untitled (Sugar Ray Robinson)* (1982). ©1996 Artists Rights Society (ARS), New York/ADAGP, Paris.

a reading to see works like *Jack Johnson* or *Untitled* (Sugar Ray Robinson), 1982, and the like, as solely celebrating black culture. Appearing always in these paintings as half-formed or somehow mutilated, the black male body becomes, iconographically, a sign of lack and absence."³⁴ hooks is correct to shut down any reading that suggests these twisted shapes are anything like purely celebratory. But I do take issue with her reading of "lack" in the work. The lines that Basquiat employs are *always* crude and half-formed, and while they do signify a radical lack of completeness, they also hearken back to a moment when a child takes a pencil to paper and, in a visual grammar that is as crude as it is beautiful, records the image of a beloved object, of a person or thing that serves as a node of identification, an object that possesses

Figure 10. Jean-Michel Basquiat, *CPRKR* (1982). ©1996 Artists Rights Society (ARS), New York/ADAGP, Paris.

transcendent possibilities. The power of this black painting has to do with the masterful way lack and desire are negotiated. The painting itself stands in for another lost object, childhood. The famous Negro athletes series works as a disidentification with the stars of an era when black representations were only the distorted images of athletes and the occasional performer that the white media deemed permissible.

Jazz great Charlie Parker was another of Basquiat's heroes, and Basquiat produced a creation that works as gravestone/mourning shrine for a lost hero (see figure 10). Again the lines are, as bell hooks would put it, half-formed. In these half-formed lines we find a eulogy of great power and elegance. The structure (a tied together wooden pole structure) records Parker's name and gives his place of death (Stan Hope Hotel) and the month and day he was memorialized at Carnegie Hall. The artist bestows royal status on the musician by renaming him Charles the First. Such a shrine is not as elegant and gilded as James Van der Zee's tributes to the dead. But this option is not available to Basquiat because the hurried pace of postmodernity no longer allows for the wistful and ethereal spaces of Van der Zee's portraits. Basquiat's objects also display the impulse to mourn, remember, and flesh out, but such achieved through different strategies than those of the portrait photographer. Basquiat's paintings effect this mourning through urgency, speed, and frantic, energized lines.

One of the artist's last finished paintings, *Riding with Death* (1988) (see figure 11), poses the black male body as death's horseman, riding and manip-ulating the pale specter. Many critics have read this painting in the light of Basquiat's death and found it ironic and delusional. I want to read *Riding with Death* under the pressure of the epidemics that now massacre millions of people of color. I want to read the painting as a call to do what Basquiat was able to do in his practice: to acknowledge and respond to the power of death and the dead in our lives. The black body mounting the white skeleton is brown and fleshed out in ways that many of his black male figures are not.[35] But the body is also highly abstracted, the face is crossed out by black scrawl, the hands and arms are only traces in black oil stick. This incompleteness is also true of the skeleton, which is missing a torso. The skeleton is a bright white that is almost illuminated by the gray-green background. Its whiteness is reminiscent of Warhol's own overwhelming whiteness. This whiteness can then stand in for a fantasy of black bodies not being burdened and mastered by whiteness, a fantasy space where the artist asserts his own agency in the

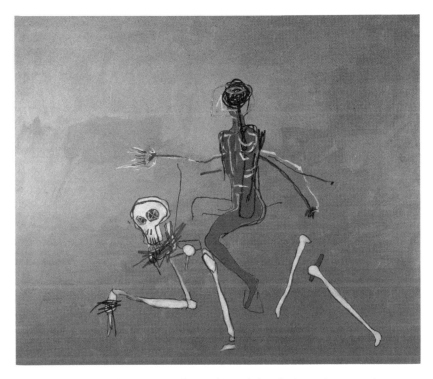

Figure 11. Jean-Michel Basquiat, *Riding with Death* (1982). ©1996 Artists Rights Society (ARS), New York/ADAGP, Paris.

relations of power in which he is imbricated because of his associations with the mainstream art world. I am not suggesting that whiteness is simply white people or the "white establishment." Instead, I read this painting as being about the complicated function of disidentification where oppressive, shameful, and sometimes dangerous cultural influences and forces are incorporated, mediated, and transfigured.

bell hooks has written that "Basquiat paintings bear witness, mirror this almost spiritual understanding. They expose and speak the anguish of sacrifice. It is amazing that so few critics discuss configurations of pain in his work, emphasizing instead its playfulness, its celebratory qualities."[36] hooks is right, again, to point out the problems in the artist's critical reception. To look at Basquiat as a ludic painter is to put the mask of the minstrel show on him. Like hooks, I see the pain and anguish in his productions, but to this I would add a powerful impulse in the artist's work to record a black life world that is complex and multilayered.[37] *Riding with Death* is an excellent example; in it we see black bodies tarrying with death and destruction. But Basquiat's images do more than connote the destruction of the black body. They also strategize survival and imagine assertions of self in a cultural sphere that is structured to deny visibility to such bodies.

hook's greatest reservation about Basquiat's body of work is what she understands as his gender trouble: "What limits body in Basquiat's work is the construction of maleness as lack. To be male, caught up in the endless cycle of conquest, is to lose out in the endless cycle of fulfillment. Significantly, there are few references in Basquiat's work that connect him to a world of blackness that is female or a world of influences and inspirations that are female."[38] Because Basquiat chose to represent black males almost exclusively and almost always in crisis, hooks figures the masculinity depicted in his oeuvre as lack primarily because of the absence of the female.[39] This line of argument echoes a previous theoretical maneuver by Hortense Spillers, who, in her influential essay "Mama's Baby, Daddy's Maybe: An American Grammar," argues that African American culture in the United States has been misnamed as matriarchal by manifestations of white male patriarchy such as the "Moynihan Report."[40] The "Moynihan Report" figured the black family as dysfunctional because of what was perceived as the weakness of black male role models and the dominance of the black woman.[41] Spillers challenges this cultural myth by arguing that "when we speak of the enslaved person, we perceive that the dominant culture, in a fatal misunderstanding, assigns a matriarchist value where it doesn't belong: actually misnames the power of the female regarding the enslaved community. Such naming is false because the female could not, in fact, claim her child, and false once again, because 'motherhood' is not perceived in the prevailing social climate as a legitimate procedure of cultural inheritance."[42] I want to call on Spillers's valuable appraisal of the way in which dominant culture figures an overabundance of black womanhood as *the* problem when discussing the status of African Americans within U.S. culture. I am suggesting that hooks's thesis is a reversal of the very same logic that the "Moynihan Report" disseminated in 1965. This inversion (African American men as lack instead of African American women as excess) still subscribes to the ideology of black men and black masculinity as "an absence and a negation." It also positions black women as something of a magical excess that can correct the failings of black men. The point made by hooks thus seems like a reversal of psychoanalysis's understanding of woman as lack—once again, an inversion that seems just as unproductive. Representing the complicated and dire situation of black masculinity in U.S. culture is important cultural work that should not be disavowed as a limitation. It is also important to note that the logic of hooks's argument relies on a presumption that if the artist incorporated more female influences and inspirations (assuming a spectator or critic can ever *know* what such forces might be), his lack would be filled. This formulation potentially reinscribes a heterosexist fantasy that the fulfilling of a normative male and female dyad would flesh out the incompleteness of the artist's production. While I do not mean to imply that no need exists for potentially productive alliances across gender (and sexuality) that can be formed in the African diaspora, I nonetheless see problems with hooks's formulation. The danger lies precisely at the point when any enslaved person, to use Spillers's description of people of color in the United States, is understood as incomplete because they chose to deal with the specificities of their gender and race coordinates without involving the opposite sex. I wish to suggest that such gender normative thinking, when not checked for its heterosexist presumptions, leads to politically unproductive ends.

There was a certain quality of melancholia intrinsic to the African American male cultural worker, a quality that was absolutely necessary to navigate his way through a racist and genocidal landscape. Which is not to say that mourning and genocide are salient thematics in the cultural production of African American women.[43] But it is to say that a recent history of African American masculinity would read like Van der Zee's funeral book.[44] And this is especially true of Basquiat's painting. The shrines, altars, and portraits that Basquiat produced are not limited to the status of works of mourning. I want to suggest that within them is the potential to become meditative texts that decipher the workings of mourning in our culture. They are melancholic echoes, queer reverberations, that make possible an identity or cluster of communal identifications that are presently under siege.

NOTES

■

1   While the racism that Basquiat encountered in the eighties art world (or even now in his work's critical reception) is not my primary concern here, it is important to mention the adverse climate to which he was, in part, responding. This case has been documented in

many of the essays published in the recent catalog of the Whitney Museum of American Art's retrospective of Basquiat's work. See Richard Marshall, ed., *Jean-Michel Basquiat* (New York: Whitney Museum of American Art, 1992). bell hooks offers a powerful reading of the racist slant in art journalism concerning Basquiat in her essay "Altar of Sacrifice: Remembering Basquiat," *Art in America*, June 1993, pp. 68–117. Greg Tate elegantly defended Basquiat in his important essay "Flyboy in the Buttermilk: Jean-Michel Basquiat, Nobody Loves a Genius Child," *Village Voice*, November 14, 1989, reprinted in *Flyboy in the Buttermilk: Essays on Contemporary America* (New York: Simon and Schuster, 1992). In that essay Tate produces a damning indictment of the New York art world: "No area of modern intellectual life has been more resistant to recognizing and authorizing people of color than the world of the 'serious' visual arts. To this day it remains a bastion of white supremacy, a sconce of the wealthy whose high walled barricades are matched only by Wall Street and the White House and whose exclusionary practices are enforced *24-7-365*. It is easier for a rich white man to enter the kingdom of heaven than for a Black abstract and/or conceptual artist to get a one woman show in lower Manhattan, or a feature in the pages of *Artforum, Art in America* or *The Village Voice*" (234).

2 Fred Brathwaite, "Jean-Michel Basquiat," *Interview*, October 1992, p. 112.

3 J. Laplanche and J.-B. Pontalis, *The Language of Psycho-Analysis*, trans. Donald Nicholson-Smith (New York: W. W. Norton, 1973), p. 206.

4 Louis Althusser, *Lenin and Marxism and Other Essays*, trans. Ben Brewster (New York: Monthly Review, 1971), pp. 127–187.

5 Michel Pecheux, *Language, Semantics, and Ideology* (New York: St. Martins, 1982).

6 Judith Butler, *Bodies That Matter: On the Discursive Limits of "Sex"* (New York: Routledge, 1993), p. 219. Žižek's discussion of disidentification can be found in Slavoj Žižek, *The Sublime Object of Ideology* (New York: Verso, 1991).

7 Butler, *Bodies That Matter*, p. 219.

8 One of Freud's accounts of identification can be found in *Group Psychology and the Analysis of the Ego*, trans. James Strachey (New York: W. W. Norton, 1959). In this book Freud schematizes three types of identification: the original emotional tie with an object, which is central to the theory of the Oedipus complex; identification with a substitute for a libidinal object; and a nonerotic identification with a subject who shares common characteristics and investments. The first route is clearly the road to normative heterosexual identity formation. The second notion of identification is the pathologized and regressive possibility that can account for the taking on of various queer object choices. In this mode of identification the object is not successfully transferred as it is in the Oedipal identificatory circuit. Instead, what I understand as a *queer* introjection occurs and circumvents such identifications. The final option allows for identifications that are same-sex and decidedly nonerotic, thus permitting same-sex group identifications that are not "regressive" or pathological. Throughout Freud there is a curious interlacing of desire and identification. Identification with a same-sex model is necessary for the process of desiring an opposite-sex object choice. "Desire" is then, for Freud, a term that is reserved for normative heterosexuality, and homosexual emotional and erotic connections are talked about in terms of "identification." The theory of disidentification proposed here is offered, in part, as a

substitute to this Freudian model, even though its workings also depend on certain forms of introjection, as described in Freud's second modality of identification. In what follows I make links between my understanding of disidentification and the Freudian and post-Freudian understanding of melancholia. Melancholia is a process that also depends on introjection. In my analysis this introjection is described as the "holding on to" or incorporation of or by a lost object.

9   Eve Kosofsky Sedgwick, "Queer Performativity: Henry James's *The Art of the Novel*," *GLQ* 1, no. 1 (Summer 1993): 13.

10 Michele Wallace, "Race, Gender, and Psychoanalysis in Forties Film: *Lost Boundaries, Home of the Brave,* and *The Quiet One,*" in *Black American Cinema,* ed. Manthia Diawara (New York: Routledge, 1993), p. 257.

11 Ibid., p. 264; emphasis mine.

12 Toni Morrison, "Unspeakable Things Unspoken: The Afro-American Presence in American Literature," *Michigan Quarterly Review* 28, no. 1 (Winter 1989): 14. Morrison goes on to delineate these ideas further in her study *Playing in the Dark: Whiteness and the Literary Imagination* (Cambridge: Harvard University Press, 1992).

13 Eve Kosofsky Sedgwick, "Across Gender, Across Sexuality: Willa Cather and Others," in *Displacing Homophobia: Gay Male Perspectives in Literature and Culture,* ed. Ronald R. Butters, John M. Clum, and Michael Moon (Durham: Duke University Press, 1989), p. 65.

14 Butler, *Bodies That Matter,* pp. 143–166.

15 Wayne Koestenbaum, *The Queen's Throat: Opera, Homosexuality, and the Mystery of Desire* (New York: Vintage, 1993), pp. 84–85.

16 See their essays in this volume.

17 Greg McCue and Clive Bloom, *Dark Knights: The New Comics in Context* (Boulder, Colo.: Pluto, 1993), p. 20.

18 Ibid.

19 Sander Gilman, *The Jew's Body* (New York: Routledge, 1991), p. 53.

20 A recent disidentification with the superhero form, operating on an entirely different cultural register, can be seen in the emergence of *Milestone Comics.* Milestone has rewritten Superman, for instance, in the form of Icon, an alien child who was not found by white Kansas farmers but instead by slaves on a nineteenth-century plantation in the United States. The shapeless alien took on the racial characteristics of the earth people who discovered him and "passes" as an African American human. It is interesting to note that the Milestone comic book universe is also populated with more gay, lesbian, Asian, and Latino characters than are the books of any other major U.S. comic company. For an informative journalistic account of the Milestone revolution in comics and a survey of the African American superhero, see Gary Dauphin, "To Be Young, Superpowered and Black, Interdimensional Identity Politics and Market Share: The Crisis of the Negro Superhero," *Village Voice,* May 17, 1994, pp. 31–38.

21 Warhol himself, as Moon has shown us, was not content just to "reproduce" Superman's image. He also let the paint splashes rupture the illusion of comic book perfection. Basquiat, in my estimation, follows this lead in his "homages" to childhood heroes.

22 Lucy Lippard, *Pop Art* (New York: Praeger, 1966).

23 Susan Stewart, *Crimes of Writing: Problems in the Containment of Representation* (New York: Oxford University Press, 1991), p. 207.

24 Paul Gilroy, "Whose Millennium Is This? Blackness: Pre-Modern, Post-Modern, Anti-Modern," in *Small Acts: Thoughts on the Politics of Black Cultures* (New York: Serpent's Tail, 1993), p. 164.

25 Ibid.

26 Lauren Berlant, "National Brands/National Bodies: *Imitation of Life*," in *Comparative American Identities: Race, Sex, and Nationality in the Modern Text*, ed. Hortense Spillers (New York: Routledge, 1991), p. 121.

27 Tate, *Flyboy*, p. 231.

28 Stewart, *Crimes of Writing*, p. 227.

29 Andy Warhol, *The Andy Warhol Diaries*, ed. Pat Hackett (New York: Warner Books, 1989), p. 572.

30 Ibid., p. 592.

31 Quoted by Brathwaite, "Jean-Michel Basquiat."

32 See Philip Brian Harper's "Eloquence and Epitaph: Black Nationalism and the Homophobic Impulse in Responses to the Death of Max Robinson," *Social Text* 28, no. 9.3 (1991): 68–86, for an excellent discussion on the African American reception of Robinson's life and death.

33 Laplanche and Pontalis, *Language of Psycho-Analysis*.

34 hooks, "Altar of Sacrifice," p. 71.

35 hooks rightfully explains that "in Basquiat's work, flesh on the black body is almost always falling away" (ibid.).

36 Ibid., p. 74.

37 For an interesting discussion of the "black life world," see Manthia Diawara, "*Noir* by *Noirs*: Towards a New Realism in Black Cinema," in *Shades of Noir*, ed. Joan Copjec (New York: Verso, 1993), pp. 261–279.

38 hooks, "Altar of Sacrifice," p. 74.

39 Greg Tate also points out the occlusion of black women in Basquiat's art, but he arrives at a very different understanding of this trend in the painter's work: "If you're black and historically informed there is no way you can look at Basquiat's work and not get beat up by the black male's history as property, pulverized meat, and popular entertainment. No way not to be reminded that lynchings and minstrelsy still vie in the white supremacist's imagination for the Black male body's proper place" (*Flyboy*, p. 238). I wish to assert that Tate's statement should not be seen as an attempt to deny the history of the black female body's exploitation under white supremacy. Instead, I see his statement, like Basquiat's paintings, as an explication of the specific position of black men in the dominant culture's imagination.

40 Hortense Spillers, "Mama's Baby, Papa's Maybe: An American Grammar Book," *Diacritics* (Summer 1987): 65–81.

41 Moynihan, Daniel P., "The Moynihan Report" *The Negro Family: The Case for National Action* (Washington, D.C.: U.S. Department of Labor, 1965), in *The Moynihan Report and the Politics of Controversy: A Transaction Social Science and Public Policy Report*, ed. Lee Rainwater and William L. Yancey. (Cambridge: MIT Press, 1967), pp. 47–94.

42 Spillers, "Mama's Baby," p. 80.

43 A more recent cultural text that examines the workings of mourning and melancholia from a female perspective is Toni Morrison's *Jazz,* a novel that, like this chapter's final section, is inspired by a James Van der Zee photograph. Set in Harlem in 1927, seven years after the armistice, the book concerns a door-to-door salesman who is married and fifty and who meets and completely falls in love with an eighteen-year-old girl. The affair ends with the older man, the aptly named Joe Trace, sick and mad with love, shooting the young woman, Dorcas, in a fit of passion. The tragedy becomes even more profound when Joe's wife, Violet, in a fit of blinding madness, lashes out with a knife during the girl's funeral. Mourners look on horrified as the beautiful, light-skinned girl's face is mutilated. And this is where the book begins. It goes on to tell the story of the way in which Dorcas's face, captured in a photograph on the mantelpiece, haunts Joe and Violet. The character of Violet embodies an aspect of African American female mourning. Her story is, like the Basquiat paintings discussed in this section, a meditation on the workings of mourning in African American culture. Toni Morrison, *Jazz* (New York: Alfred A. Knopf, 1992).

44 See my essay "Photographies of Mourning: Melancholia and Ambivalence in Van der Zee, Mapplethorpe, and *Looking for Langston*," in which I offer an account of the specificities of black male mourning in twentieth-century U.S. cultural production. In *Race and the Subjects of Masculinity,* ed. Michael Uebel and Harry Stecanopolis (Durham: Duke University Press, 1995).

BRIAN SELSKY

"I Dream of Genius . . ."

think the title of this paper should actually be "I Dream of Geniuses," because I am going to knead and perhaps, unfortunately, only half-bake more than one. And, also, because the shelves of my fantasy store—and likewise the walls of my kitchen—are full of the serial images that reflect an extensive personal investment in these figures. Barbara McClintock, Julia Child, Charles Mingus, Zsa Zsa Gabor, Michel Foucault, Gertrude Stein. All geniuses, for me. All part of my superhero canon, or rather my boutique—the pantheon of possible outfits.

Figure 1. Andy Warhol, *Gertrude Stein* (1980). ©1996 Andy Warhol Foundation for the Visual Arts/Ronald Feldman Fine Arts/ARS, New York.
Figure 2. Andy Warhol, *Sigmund Freud* (1980). ©1996 Andy Warhol Foundation for the Visual Arts/Ronald Feldman Fine Arts/ARS, New York.

But, as José Esteban Muñoz has so insightfully suggested, complex problematics—differing, of course, according to one's position—exist in the process of identification, especially with popularized cultural narratives. While we might want a private and exclusive relationship with our heroin(e), we are always vulnerable to *giving up* too much of ourselves and *giving in—* "signing on," as Muñoz suggested (this volume)—or perhaps selling out to fantasies of insidious intent.

Thus my relationship to the dream of genius is always at once denied, diverted, distanced. First, because the dream *about one* so easily slips into the dream *of being one*. (Here we get a kind of homology to "homosexual panic.") Just toying with the idea is to do some heavy-duty, pretentious self-fashioning, both because of an implied arrogant posturing of knowledge and because of an allegiance with an the elitist intellectual economy that monopolizes, rarefies, regulates, and empowers this position.

To stand aloof in this way is intolerable, if not downright ludicrous. Yet, a desire for distance—for being uncoupled, singular, and solitary, the outsider, perhaps—is not necessarily about elitism. The fantasy of existing apart, detached from particular standards and practices, particular economies and expectations, might be both useful and desirable. Especially if, opposed to a notion of asceticism, one could at the same time circulate observant and unobstructed within society. Think of what work you might accomplish, what havoc you might wreak.

To be designated a genius—within particular discourses—is to be given this hypothetical space, a position where one's behaviors, tendencies, and idiosyncracies would all be accommodated. The mumbling of one's talk, the stumbling of one steps, and the awkwardness of one's hair: all passed over, without much question, all in light of some presumed "inner" core of divinity. A place where timeless wisdom is produced unadulterated by popularity. Here, the content of one's closet never goes out of fashion.

Perhaps the dream is beyond pretension, moving instead toward *pretend,* opening a space of "make-believe" or, rather, a condition of making others believe, through performance, that one is not *this* or *that* but a genius, a process of managing one's identity—however peculiar—into a position of self-empowerment. Or if not empowerment, at least into a kind of cohesiveness, differently regulated. But this fantasy is, of course, symptomatically utopic and I must move on to the business at hand.

I will pick up a few threads of this fantasy within the work of the great genius of the nineteenth century, George Eliot, and then with that of the twentieth, Gertrude Stein. Perhaps I will say something about Freud, as well, because Warhol put him on the same wall as Stein—as part of his Jewish genius series. And because this essay is also and always about Warhol, who put Freud there. And about us, who, by paying for him, put him there as well.

In George Eliot's novel, *Daniel Deronda,* the marriage of Catherine Arrowpoint is, for her upper-class parents, an anxiety born of its absence and agitated by the repeated deferral of its probability. Already well within "the age" to take the plunge, and incessantly positioned before a steady stream of "suitable" mates, Catherine refuses to choose a suitor. We begin to wonder, if for only a few brief pages and with mounting excitement and pom-poms at the ready, if she really likes men at all. Ignoring this possibility—either out of ignorance or out of a sense of its irrelevance to the "duty of matrimony"—the family becomes increasingly apprehensive, more so because Catherine is an heiress, a result, as Mrs. Arrowpoint often bemoans, of her own "inability"— painfully internalized as inadequacy—to produce a son.

Thus, when Catherine suddenly confronts her parents about her decision to wed the composer/musician Herr Klesmer, a tangled set of reactions fills the ensuing uproar. The main objection comes from Mrs. Arrowpoint, who cannot fathom her daughter married "to a man who has been paid to come to the house—who is nobody knows what—a gypsy, a Jew, a mere bubble of the earth." With indignation, Catherine responds, "Never mind, momma. . . . We all know he is a genius."[1]

For the Arrowpoints, the possibility of this union exposes a set of fears on which the ordered fabric of both their daughter and their entire society founders. With the interruption of the traditional means of family transmission—the name and property passed, and thus reproduced, from a "gentleman" to his son—Mr. Arrowpoint finds *himself,* not his daughter, as the bride to be. Thus Klesmer is not denied the right to marry Catherine but rather "her fortune," her father's heredity. But Klesmer, as a Jew, spoils the possibility of an immaculate transmission, because he cannot be received as an equal partner within the homosocial exchange. It is this forced recognition of difference which is seen as perverting the repetition and reproduction of lineage.

By marrying out of caste, Catherine is seen as lowering herself, defiling the sacred responsibilities of her class duty. But by wedding a Jew, the other axes of identity which help maintain class definition reveal their ineluctable connections. As a Jew, Klesmer is otherly white, at once racialized and erased within and without white European society. Thus, reproduction between Gentile and Jew is viewed as a form of miscegenation and/or an "unnatural" comingling of character types. Likewise, as a foreigner, Klesmer is a threat to the national basis of the Arrowpoint pedigree. What happens to Catherine's body will allegorize the reproduction of England, and thus, Mr. Arrowpoint informs his daughter: "We must do as other people do. We must think of the nation and the public good."

But the anxiety around Klesmer goes beyond pure national sentiment. Systems of exchange across these borders do function, but only under markers that guarantee—or at least give the impression—of a common, homogeneous positionality. The seal of approval—the denominator—is a national flag, a standard that Klesmer's diasporic identity cannot fly. He is typed as the wandering Jew, the gypsy, the leftover of a closed system of economy. He is the usurer, the perverter of exchange, one who takes pleasure and profit from this excess, making money from money, something from nothing. He can be only ambiguous, without a solid origin: a "bubble of the earth," possessing a stereotypical "shiftiness" that taints any deal he might make with Arrowpoint.

Likewise, Klesmer is also viewed as unsuitable for the duties of managing property. Under the labels of both Jew and musician, he signifies the misogynic meanings of effeminacy and sensuality—or rather that which is bodily, consumptive, diseased, and dirty. For Arrowpoint then, Klesmer's artistic unpracticality, his inability to deal properly with worldly, masculine matters, likewise designates his impotence in dealing/copulating with his daughter.

Thus, in an attempt to assuage her parents' fears, Catherine offers counterarguments in defense of Klesmer, while also remaking him under the label of "genius." In doing this she sets up a screen—or, we might say, she runs *interference*—behind which, or through which, the Jew can be assimilated into an acceptable caste narrative.

Klesmer, himself, wants nothing of that caste, or of a Jewish identity. He stands aloof, self-fashioned, beyond words, as the musical genius. When received in this light, he is endowed if not with a phallic national or class property—something that we might call modern—then instead with a transcendent, perhaps classical, spirit whose origin cannot be questioned, understood, or remembered.

Although a diversity of European narratives deploy the concept of genius, especially in the nineteenth century, they might be said to share a common function in relation to these concerns around modern identity formation. Briefly, we might say that the concept of *genius* becomes a way of safely incorporating certain cultural performances. It "rescues" some of the excess of the economy, assigning new value to unnatural (queer) or archaic (spiritual) forms.

Eliot records the deployment of genius to mediate the precarious path of social reproduction, whereas Freud, in *Leonardo da Vinci and a Memory of His Childhood,* works to make genius cover the process of artistic production. While Freud screens off the homophobia of da Vinci's uptight biographers— those who indignantly "reject the possibility that there was a sexual relationship between him and his pupils"—he (Freud) is at the same time running his own phobic interference to shield his idol, and himself as idolater, from scandal: "We may take it as much more probable that Leonardo's affectionate relations with young men . . . did not extend to sexual activity."[2] He goes on then to rationalize this screen by explaining that the assumed fact of da Vinci's genius indicates "a man whose sexual need and activity were exceptionally reduced, as if a higher aspiration had raised him above the common animal needs of mankind."[3] Thus, for Freud, his genius was the result of the sublimation of "his sexual instinct . . . into a general urge to know."[4]

With the rise of mechanical reproductive technology, the anxieties around class and property transmission—read from Eliot—spill over to both artistic production and its reception. The endangered mythologies around originality, authenticity, and aura, within the realms of cultural production, become haunted by the nightmares of heterosexuality and white social maintenance. Thus, the Jew and the queer once again become vulnerable loci for the regulation of these fears. We can register the response to these new conditions by reading the critical reception and self-fashioning practices of two artists: Gertrude Stein and Andy Warhol.

Before considering how these two artists produce themselves in the age of mechanical reproduction, I would like to cite an anecdote of their reception. At the beginning of a lecture on Gertrude Stein, a professor told the class, "If you don't believe that Stein was a genius, there is no point in reading her work." Now what was I to make of this double-edged disclaimer? On the one hand, it was to be taken as my professor's admirable acceptance of Stein's literary worth, one that enabled her (uncommon) presence in the syllabus. On the other hand, I had to wonder, what kinds of value would we derive from this faith? And perhaps, more important, what kinds of readings were being interfered with? And further still, what were the conditions that made necessary this field order—what I will call the *prime directive*—that is, an a priori insistence in *belief before reception?*

Such leaps of faith intrigue me, because we find them performed throughout the so-called critical literary field, and we begin to notice that they aren't really leaps at all. Instead, the great chasm is the projection of the directive itself, a set of pitfalls, perhaps, that screen over other, more unmanageable snares. The illusion of danger is really no sweat at all, as the way is navigated by some familiar narratives. The anxiety, then, is avoided less by a blind jump and more by an agreement not to look down at the precarious construction that is taking us across.

In this case, the prime directive sets up a scenario for our encounter with the so-called difficult Stein. Either our incomprehension is the author's fault—and what they are really writing is pretentious nonsense—or the work's value is beyond us—beyond the popular—and is instead the precious gift of genius. Similar options are possible in response to works that seem overly simplistic: Duchamp's bicycle wheel on a stool, Cage's textually silent piece of music, and Stein's seemingly infantile repetitions: "If I told him would he like it. Would he like it if I told him. Would he like it would Napoleon would Napoleon would would he like it."[5] If we do not obey the directive for genius, then we are left with the sense that it is trash. That *anyone* could have done that! But, in considering it a work of genius, we posit its value outside itself, into the transcendent idea originating in the artist. From this point, once we have safely rooted the object of our interest under a particular aesthetic protocol, we can go on to harvest its value.

Now, in going back to the texts through this interference, we are diverted from other identity signifiers, such as sexuality and race. But in the standard discourse of genius, these are particulars—secondary social contingencies—that only detract from the artistic evaluation. Thus, through genius, Stein can be assimilated into the realm of critical worth over, and around, her queer Jewish presence.

All this suggests a critical anxiety around Stein's particular form of cultural production and self-fashioning. Wendy Steiner, in her introduction to Stein's *Lectures in America,* attributes much of this to her particular relationship to the emergent technologies of mechanical reproduction. Although others might fear the machines that made the position of the master artist quite tenuous, Steiner suggests that Stein is able to empower herself in connecting with them.[6]

But what kind of liaison is Stein making with these new technologies? And would the Napoleons of aesthetic regulation like it, at all? No, I don't think so. I don't think so, at all.

In a brilliant unpublished essay on *Tender Buttons,* Katie Kent reveals just what kind of work Stein is up to. She demonstrates how Stein subverts the normatively reproductive economies of both linguistic and sexual value through a sort of textual usury. In this way, the author is able to coin queer meaning and queer pleasure out of an interest accrued from alternative means of circulating language. In her comparison between "usury [which] produces money from money, and sodomy [which] produces sexual pleasure without sexual reproduction," we can see familiar connections that shape cultural anxieties around Jewish and queer signifiers.[7]

Stein, however, rarely, if ever, operated explicitly under these labels. Instead, she often screened herself through the sign of American—which deferred notions of ethnicity—and, likewise, under the sign of genius. Thus, our directed faith in Stein is something that she encouraged and facilitated.

Under the banner of genius she was able both to hide and to protect a set of social and artistic practices that were being perceived by the high literary world, as Mabel Dodge suggested in a letter, as "something degenerate & effete & decadent."[8] Self-promotion under that sign, however, empowered her into a position of knowledge and mastery. Her enigmatic stances made her both difficult to read and difficult *not* to read. While knowledge is what we know, we often have the sense that she knows much more than do we and that we must labor in different ways to access this information. We can hear this in Florence Blood's letter to Stein in response to her "Portrait of F. B.": "Oh! dear Miss Stein—oh! am I really like that & what—oh! what does it mean? I feel like a person who has rushed eagerly to the looking glass to see themselves with new eyes, but alas, all the familiar landmarks have been quite swept away. . . . I feel convinced you know me better than I do myself & if your knowledge is contained in these leaves do do give me the key!"[9] The production of F. B.'s portrait mirrors the way in which Stein painted herself a genius. The method of producing a masterpiece, as we will see, was homologous to the self-production of the great artist. Although I can only gloss over this methodology, perhaps we can extract at least a sense of how Stein deployed this concept.

Identity, for Stein, was a limiting position. It was the result, she felt, of an "existing" bound to context—both to the composition of one's generation (the relativity of historical time) and to the space in which one interacted. Identity was the result of difference, of how one resembled or differed from something outside the self. The clearest example, perhaps, is Stein's dictum that "I am I because my little dog know me." Because I am recognized—because in someone's memory I resemble a past image of myself and not another—I achieve identity.

But this process bound one to history, and for Stein, the genius, like and *as* a masterpiece, needed to be beyond this kind of contingency. Beyond the need for popular recognition, and relation. Beyond the need to resemble anything. Instead, she suggests that a genius might talk and listen at the same time, and thus, being one's own audience, in a way you achieved a performative status that removed you from relative historical time. In being completely present, you sublimated past and future. By talking and listening at the same time—by working both sides of stage—you achieved an existing that was not bound to cultural recognition and memory. Likewise, the masterpieces of artistic product achieved their immortality by avoiding resemblance.

Now, although Stein's method of creating portraits was not, much to Frances Blood's dismay, making these kinds of likenesses, Warhol's portraits, as with his own self-fashioning, depended on relations. Let me read a few condensed entries from the diaries:

> Had to meet the LeFraks. And they hated their portrait. She said I made her look too much like Kitty Carlisle. . . . Mr. LeFrak said why weren't Mrs. LeFraks eyes hazel in the portrait, and then he said his nose was too bulbous. So maybe if we fix those two things it'll get by. . . . John [Powers] was great, he embarrassed Mr. LeFrak into finally accepting the portraits—he told them what more do you want, and then later he told me, "I can't believe you made him look so good."[10]

Stein, perhaps, bought into and reworked a standard of artistic reception, using the label of genius as both a screen for subversive self-fashioning and a theory of art itself, whereas Warhol attempts to interfere with the receptive protocols of high art. It was a buyer's market, and the (silk)screen would be reworked to meet demand.

Like Stein, Warhol toyed with the social anxieties around reproduction. But he refused, in theory, to set himself up as master and originator. "When I look around today," he writes in his *Philosophy*, "the biggest anachronism I see is pregnancy. I just can't believe that people are still pregnant."[11] Warhol substitutes, instead, the factory system, which distributed the production of work among many people. While the art did circulate under a single trademark, the inevitable problem of transmission—as we see in Eliot—is refigured in terms of productive transmutation. In this way, the misunderstanding between the members of the Factory—most clearly between Warhol and his assistants—created an interest and valuable excess.

Thus, Warhol refused the label and position of genius because it attempts to imbue the artist as a solitary value maker—in turn, devaluing the artistic product. If Warhol's business is art, and vice versa, then the locus of evaluation must occur around the screen itself, both of the painting and of the artist's own self-fashioning.

But Warhol's brave plunge into the "stream of commerce" did not mean that he was immune from the narratives that regulated artistic reception. Certainly the diaries are full of examples depicting a jealous Warhol whose ideas have been stolen, his works forged, and his paintings of lesser market value than those of his competitors. Thus, making business into the greatest art reopened the anxieties around transaction that figured in Eliot's work. In the diaries, he describes the sale of a particular series: "The Ten Jewish Geniuses portfolio really sold, so now Ron Feldman wants to do Ten Rock Stars, by that's corny, isn't it? Or Ten Phantoms, like Santa Claus. But I think the Jewish Geniuses *only* sold because they were *Jewish,* so we should do Ten Jewish something else. Like Ten *Jewish* Rock Stars."[12] I wonder, then, who would they be, these Jewish Rock Stars? Lou Reed? As if. And Bob Dylan? Well, Warhol had already speculated on this in another diary entry: "I think they were considering Bob Dylan," he said. "But I read that he turned born-again Christian."[13] Of course, Dylan himself had already undergone a kind of plastic surgery, not the rearticulating of a well-deviated encasement of his trademark sound but the originating change of name, from Zimmerman to Dylan. But we might read this physical transformation of a stereotyped Jewish signifier in Warhol's own *Before and After III* (p. 115), which I tend to read as an imagined operation on Gertrude Stein.

We might gingerly infer from this entry, however, that what counted for Warhol in these portraits was not that they were geniuses but that they were Jewish and that a certain amount of uneasiness exists here. There is a suggestion then—following an anti-Semitic logic—that these paintings sell because Jews have money or that Jews control the art world or are the star makers of Hollywood. Perhaps, then, I might say with caution that Warhol, always anxious in his public renunciation of the genius, is here trying to recuperate an authentic connection to it. It is this screen splitting here—between Jew and genius—that reveals, perhaps, an unexamined—or uncontextualized—relationship to commercial narratives and the fantasies of popular culture.

Now, by serving up the anxieties around reproduction and scoffing off the label of genius, Warhol makes our attempts at receiving his work that much more clumsy. This has been noted to some extent by others. Elsewhere in this book, Mandy Merck discusses the rather "straight" reception of Warhol, and Sasha Torres describes the way in which Pop Art is screened through or around camp and queer culture. But even as we investigate these narratives of reception, we tend to play out and perform the very anxieties that they encode. Thus, for instance, the fear registered that only on occasion does Warhol rise above mere opportunism toward genius. Obviously, much work needs to be done in the overhaul of the ideology that narrates our critical/political way of reading. But perhaps we are already moving toward a new sense of what we mean by political, conceding that consumption—and production—is more complicated than we might have thought. And in this way we can leave room within the narratives of exchange—between the shopping and the selling—for a bit of haggling.

NOTES

1   George Eliot, *Daniel Deronda* (London: Penguin, 1986), p. 289.

2   Sigmund Freud, "Leonardo da Vinci and a Memory of His Childhood," in *The Standard Edition of the Complete Psychological Works of Sigmund Freud,* ed. James Strachey, vol. 11 (London: Hogarth, 1955), p. 73.

3   Ibid., p. 101.

4   Ibid., p. 132.

5   Gertrude Stein, *Portraits and Prayers* (New York: Random House, 1934), p. 21.

6   Wendy Steiner, introduction to *Lectures in America*, by Gertrude Stein (Boston: Beacon, 1985), p. xiv.

7   Katie Kent, " 'Excreate a No Sense': The Erotic Currency of Gertrude Stein's *Tender Buttons*." Unpublished essay, 1992.

8   Donald Gallup, ed., *The Flowers of Friendship: Letters Written to Gertrude Stein* (New York: Alfred A. Knopf, 1953), p. 96.

9   Ibid., p. 79.

10   Andy Warhol, *The Andy Warhol Diaries*, ed. Pat Hackett (New York: Warner Books, 1989), pp. 474, 477, 478.

11   Andy Warhol, *The Philosophy of Andy Warhol* (New York: Harcourt Brace Jovanovich, 1975), p. 118.

12   Warhol, *Diaries*, p. 279.

13   Ibid., p. 237.

JENNIFER DOYLE

Tricks of the Trade: Pop Art/Pop Sex

Love and sex are a business.—Andy Warhol, *The Philosophy of Andy Warhol*[1]

INTRODUCTION

■

I f we take him at his word, Andy Warhol was pretty certain that love had a price, that it was a business much like art was a business, that sex was work, and that these could be good things. He thought that "making money is art and working is art and good business is the best art" and recommended that in love affairs we follow at least one rule: "I'll pay you if you pay me."[2] But where Warhol's fans might be galvanized by his aphorisms on the business of art, love, and sex, and where a jilted superstar might find solace in his advice, "Don't worry, you're going to be very famous someday and you'll be able to buy him,"[3] readers are probably more familiar with the endless citation of Warhol's axioms by grumpy pundits who read them as the cynical expressions of the whore who embraces the very system that exploits her.

If we removed figures of sex work from the vocabulary of criticism, Warhol's critics would have no small problem on their hands. Whores, hustlers, madams, and drag queens are popular among Warhol critics as figures for Pop's perversions—for how Pop flaunts the business of art, for how Warhol wasn't really an artist because he pandered to a popular audience, and for how the dubious pleasures of Pop are extracted from the very act of "selling out." When you sell your art, you also risk selling your place in an avant-garde that imagines itself, in the words of Andreas Huyssen, as a "resistance to the seductive lure of mass culture, (and) abstention from the pleasure of trying to please a larger audience."[4]

In Warhol criticism, a rhetoric of prostitution tends to link sex and work in a way that gives the critic leverage to distinguish Warhol's work from the kind of work other people do, and to make the judgment that his art fails to provide a meaningful social critique. Moreover, in figuring Warhol's relationship to his work as a kind of prostitution, critics discredit his relationship to art by suggesting he also had a perverse relationship to sex. The use of a rhetoric of prostitution and its stigma of outlaw sex to name the artistic practices of a famous (and famously) gay man more often than not functions to signal (but only through inference) Warhol's homosexuality while also displacing the discussion of sexuality in Warhol's work onto a feminized, particularly public and abjected figure.

Critics will hint at Warhol's sexuality as being in relation to his work (by, for example, invoking Oscar Wilde as a figure with a similar understanding of celebrity)[5] and will suggest, in effect, that Warhol's work is all about sex, but they will nevertheless stubbornly refuse to make either inference explicit. The result is a kind of critical shell game that cloaks not only the libidinal investments *of* Pop but the critic's libidinal investments *in* Pop, declaring on the one hand that Pop is not about art but about sex (that it is ultimately prurient) and on the other that this sex is not about love but about money (and is therefore not a sex that counts as such).

This condensation and dismissal of issues key to his work under the rubric of prostitution is the starting point for my own approach to Warhol. After briefly indicating what these highly volatile and conflicted rhetorical gestures in Warhol criticism look like, I will turn to Warhol's work to recover his career-long struggle to take advantage of the incoherencies and contradictions in and around definitions of work in order to challenge limiting conceptions of authorship, art, and sex.

MADAM WARHOL
■

"Warhol managed the Factory not like a boss, but like a madam, if he managed it at all."—Thierry De Duve, *October*[6]

Representations of Warhol as a whore and Pop as prostitution are often concerned with the question of whether the way Warhol and other Pop artists produced art counts as a legitimate form of art making. Thierry De Duve's above comment exemplifies the way such rhetoric circles around Warhol's problematic relation to categories of art and work. In casting Warhol as a madam, he responds not just to how Warhol made his art or to how he made his art a business. Although these aspects of Warhol's art are interesting to De Duve, what distinguishes Warhol from other artists is how his work manipulated and manufactured "fantasies." In his view Warhol was like a "madam" because he was "content to base his art on the universal law of exchange" and to make "himself the go-between for the least avowable desires of his contemporaries, each with his or her own 'look,' quirks, neurosis, sexual specificity, and idiom." Ever so obliquely referencing Warhol's homosexuality, De Duve imputes the "lifestyle" of Warhol and his friends as a way of life that was "beautiful only in its coherence, that wasn't a life, and was in no way the life of the species-being . . . [which] links the individual to the destiny of the species." He then slides from a discussion of Warhol's (non-reproductive) "lifestyle" to a diagnosis of Warhol's work as embodying "the cynicism of capital interiorized even by those it causes to suffer . . . the pleasure of the prostitute."[7] From his awkwardness with the word "manage" to his characterization of Warhol as a symptom of a larger social crisis, De Duve performs his discomfort with Warhol's relation to art and work (not to mention Warhol's sexuality) using a language of prostitution.

Critics use prostitution and sexual deviance (for example, drag) as metaphors for Warhol's production of art as though the logic of that comparison were absolutely transparent. In a 1980 editorial for *Art in America,* for example, Suzi Gablik casually figures the Pop artist as a streetwalker when she criticizes Warhol for generating an atmosphere that makes "the practice of art . . . like any other career" whereby artists "lose their identity as artists" and will do anything to "make it," "even if it means hanging from the lamp posts."[8] In his 1963 editorial "The Phony Crisis in American Art" for *Artnews,* Thomas Hess invokes both drag and prostitution as metaphors for "phony" cultural production in worrying that Pop encouraged artists to "fake it" for profit. Pop was "phony" because it was motivated by money and not the "real crisis" expressed in modern painting, "which can kill or forge a man's identity." Real art is what real men produce and what produces real men. According to his argument, "phony" modes of artistic production threaten that masculinity. He thus warns his readers against allowing themselves to be seduced by Pop's production of the "phony crisis which kills (mostly with kindness)." "How long," he wonders, "will even the most talented be able to resist the equivalents of cloche hats, beaded skirts, and the shimmy?" Pop, for Hess, as the art of "phony crisis," is the dangerously seductive art of faked orgasm—an on-demand performance that "avoids the real crisis by painting it over with a trademark or a sentimentality."[9] It is the doubly fraudulent spectacle of a drag ("cloche hats and beaded skirts") imitation of the already-imputed ecstasy of Woman. According to this story, in the same way that a woman is compromised by prostitution or a man is compromised by drag, Warhol and his audiences are compromised by his success. The logic of the story is that a woman who takes money for sex or a man who dresses as a woman are degraded versions of the real thing.

When they cast Warhol as a madman, a hustler, or a whore, critics draw the pejorative energy of their rhetoric from the pathologization of prostitution in order to negotiate, among other things, the question of what art is and is not and of what it ought to do.[10] In doing so, they also partake in discourse on prostitution which, on the one hand, localizes prostitution to a "certain type of girl" belonging to a "certain part of town" and which, on the other, figures nearly every imaginable social relation of exchange as a kind of prostitution—from marriage to labor, consumption, and art-making.[11] These minoritizing and universalizing impulses operate in tandem. At times the latter will borrow from the criminalization and stigmatization of sex work as a venal practice to point up a crisis in all social relations; in turn, a minoritizing discourse converts the exigency of this crisis into the fervent policing of prostitutes to reassure us that we *do* know a whore when we see one and that we *can* tell the difference between prostitution and, say, the institution of marriage. In other words, this discourse both articulates and manages the possibility that all of us are whores—in how we address others sexually, in where we shop, in how we dress, in our professional lives, and in what we do for money, for love, and for pleasure. Any relationship involving an exchange (of looks, of money, of favors) can look like prostitution.

Insofar as it is present in pointing up the absence of a solid apparatus for making distinctions between high art and mass culture or between the art object and the commodity, Warhol's work is a magnet for this rhetoric of prostitution. When art critics mobilize this discourse to evaluate Warhol's work, they map the anxieties of prostitution onto the vicissitudes of the category of art itself. The end product is a profoundly tautological rhetoric (in the words of one California judge, "A whore is a whore is a whore")[12] that backs up the assertion "I know art when I see it" with the accusation "I know a whore when I see one."

So when Warhol the artist is outed as a fraud, it is by referencing a language of fraudulent, phony, imitation, or failed sex. In his responses to Warhol, Robert Hughes consistently reads his work as a kind of pornography, as the mediated and false representation of the "real thing." In this spirit he describes *Marilyn Monroe's Lips* (1962) as a cynical representation of "the administration of fantasy by the media, and not the enjoyment of fantasy by lovers," and characterizes Warhol as a "diligent and frigid" celebrity who surrounded himself with an entourage of characters with "unfulfilled desires and undesirable ambitions."[13] The presumption is that Warhol's work, as a kind of pornography, mistakes mediated sex for the "real thing" and that people who make or enjoy such representations of sex and pleasure are "frigid," "unfulfilled," and "undesirable."

The thematization of erection and orgasm as what Pop either can't do or as what Pop fakes begins early with Peter Selz's 1963 article "Pop Goes the Artist." Amazingly retitled "The Flaccid Art," this essay is unembarrassed in its complaints about the failure of the Pop artist to produce himself as a phallic hero, describing him as "slick, effete, and chic" and Pop as "limp art" generated by an "extraordinary relaxation of effort, which implies . . . a profound cowardice."[14] This rhetoric of complicity was itself inspired by Aline Saarinen's 1963 survey of Pop artists in which she attributes the weakness of Warhol's work to a lack of "the penetrating gaze" necessary to the production of real art and speculates on Warhol's incapacity for feeling: "I suspect he feels not love, but complacency and that he sees, not with pleasure or disgust, but with acquiescence. These are weak ways of seeing and feeling."[15] Even today reviewers reference and impute his sexual practices as they evaluate, for example, the merits of the Warhol Museum in Pittsburgh. Writing for the *Wall Street Journal,* Debora Solomon takes the following swipe: "The Warhol Museum is like a chic YMCA, turning the artist's dissolute ways and pursuit of celebrity into so much moral uplift for the community."[16] Dissolute, effete, frigid, indifferent, complacent, acquiescent—these words all work at hinting and inferring Warhol's sex and sexuality to make value judgments about his art.

Whether a whore or a hustler, the prostitute has been defined by legal and social apparatuses as a venal body, as a perversion of femininity, and as a person who has a passive relation to sex—either in the act of selecting a partner or in the performance of sex acts, or both.[17] Often it is the paradoxical *willfulness* of that passivity that is the crux of some anxious writing about prostitution—the paradox of someone whose "preferment of indolent ease to labor" and eagerness to turn a profit combine to make a job of sex. In her writing on sex work, Anne McClintock has argued that the figure of the prostitute embodies a "pathology of agency" as well as sex. While the prostitute is understood as having no agency in selecting partners and as being a pure commodity, she is also represented as "having an excess of agency, as irresponsibly trafficking in male fantasies and commodification."[18] This particular logic shapes discussion of intentionality in Warhol's work: when critics ascribe intentionality to Warhol, it is the intention to submit (or, more nearly, the intention not to resist). Thus Pop, according to one critic, wants us "to believe that it is in fact adopting a critical posture towards that to which it has actually surrendered."[19] To this effect, Dore Ashton, in a key 1963 symposium on Pop, remarked, "Far from being an art of social protest, [Pop Art] is an art of capitulation."[20] For Jean Baudrillard, one of Pop's more nuanced critics, its sense of humor is "not the smile of critical distance, but the smile of *collusion*."[21]

As often as Warhol critics leer at hustlers, whores, and drag queens, they avoid speaking about the place of sex, gender, and sexual practices in Warhol's art. Criticism animated by sex but which evacuates sex from Warhol's work makes up a substantial amount of writing on the artist, from philosophical essays to the reviews, feature stories, and obituaries on Warhol that appeared in art journals and in such publications as the *New York Times*, *Time*, and *Esquire*. In glossing the language of Pop criticism, I am suggesting that we not take the queer figures that populate it for granted. They draw out some of Pop's most interesting attitudes—its curious configuration of agency which looks both active and passive, its investment in art and sex as sites of exchange, and its use of the queerness of these sites to resist monolithic narratives about what sex and art are.

SEX WORK/POP SEX

∎

Kent: Blue Movie has recently been declared "hard-core pornography."
Warhol: It's soft-core pornography. We used a misty color. What's pornography anyway? The muscle magazines are pornography, but they're really not. They teach you

how to have good bodies. They're the fashion magazines of Forty-Second Street—that more people read. I think movies *should* appeal to prurient interests. I mean, the way things are going now—people are alienated from one another. Movies should—uh—arouse you. . . . I really do think movies *should* arouse you, should get you excited about people, should be prurient.—Interview with Warhol conducted by Leticia Kent, *Vogue*[22]

Warhol "loved porno" and "bought lots of the stuff all the time—the really dirty, exciting stuff."[23] Responding in his diary to a complaint that he missed a luncheon appointment because he was "just down at Chris's to take male porno photographs," Warhol explains that of course he was, but "it was for *work!* I mean, I'm just trying to work and make some money. . . . I mean, the porno pictures are for a *show.* They're *work.*"[24] Throughout his career as an artist, Andy Warhol was asked to defend his work against the charge of pornography. Thus he did not balk when in the above exchange Leticia Kent outed him as a pornographer; instead, he corrected her classification of *Blue Movie* as hard-core ("It's soft-core pornography. We used misty colors") and offered a case for the "social" uses of porn (it can "teach you"). Blithely ignoring the line between art and porn, Warhol contradicts the rhetoric of his critics at the very moment he agrees with them. Yes, his work is pornographic. But art "should appeal to prurient interests" because "people are alienated from one another" and porn gets you "excited about people." When asked if this approach to art as a mechanism for "arousing" people contradicts his famous declaration about wanting to be a machine, Warhol retorts: "Prurience is part of the machine. It keeps you happy. It keeps you running."[25] At nearly every level of his work, Warhol challenged and parodied the fantasy of artistic production as original, unmediated expression. Mechanization and mediation are not obstacles to being "excited about people" but the very mechanisms by which that arousal happens. These answers to the charge of pornography look to his critics like hopeless cynicism. But from another angle his refusal of the fantasy of unmediated exchange looks like an incredible optimism about what art, as mediated exchange, can do.[26]

The relationships between sex, work, and art are as important to Pop as they are problematized. Nothing in the film *Flesh* (Warhol and Paul Morrissey, 1968–69), for example, lines up "straight." The equations by which heterosexuality, marriage, love, and reproduction are derived from one another are irrelevant to *Flesh*'s hustler Joe (played by Joe Dallesandro, Pop's "working-class hero")[27] and his family. Joe hustles to make money for his wife so she can pay for her lover's abortion; he is married and supports his wife by having sex with men; his wife has a lesbian girlfriend and she (the girlfriend) is pregnant but is not having a baby because Joe is paying for the (illegal) abortion. The networks articulated around the hustler redefine and confound any received idea about what a family looks like, about what work is, and about what sex means.

Sex, art, and money are all part of the same economy in *Flesh*. *Flesh* acts out the capaciousness of the categories of art and work around the figure of the hustler. As it scripts artistic exchange as the setting for erotic, sexual exchange and frames both as kinds of economic activities, *Flesh* dramatizes some of what Warhol may have meant when he said that art "*should* appeal to prurient interests." By unpacking the hustler's relationship to "work," we also find that category unraveled.

Take, for example, one scene in which an older john (Maurice Bradell) cruises Joe Dallesandro and initiates the following exchange:

John: Do you know anything about art?
Hustler: A little. I did a little modeling.
John: Now, isn't that strange. That's exactly what I had in mind when I saw you. [Pause] How much do you think you're worth?
Hustler: One hundred dollars.
John: One hundred dollars? For that you'll have to take your clothes off.

Here, the query "Do you know anything about art?" is the perfect solicitation because of the expansiveness and ambiguousness of "art" as a term. In this exchange, "art" becomes a euphemism for sex and, more specifically, for sex that you pay for. Once they've negotiated the terms of their econo-erotic exchange, Joe goes to the john's apartment where, scantily clad, he models classical poses for his customer, who bores him with lengthy but enthusiastic musings on how "body worship is the whole thing behind all art, all music, and all love." In a double-reverse take on "artistic production," the artist is positioned as a john/consumer, who then proceeds to do most of the "work"—if what we mean by "work" is "activity"—as he philosophizes, sketches, and directs the hustler, who, in turn, poses and looks bored.

Dallesandro's affect of boredom and disinterest (an affect often attributed to Warhol himself) is what, on the street, translates into the look of availability which makes him a good hustler (see p. 63). This element of his "look" prompted Stephen Koch to theorize that "the hustler, identifying himself as the sexuality of his flesh and nothing more, proposes himself as a wholly passive and will-less being, subject exclusively to the will of others."[28] But this reading of the hustler's "look" does not address all the ways that the hustler reverses the opposition of passive and active and then turns that opposition inside out. Often it appears as if most of the energy expended in the film goes into consuming Joe Dallesandro. Yet even when it looks like he does nothing or, more to the point, when it looks as if his customers are doing all the "work"—painting, talking, or giving him a blow job—he is the one getting paid for it. David James foregrounds the hustler's demeanor as a kind of "self-presentation" so as to draw out how that very appearance of "extreme passivity" itself constitutes a kind of performance.[29] I think here Gayatri Spivak's neologism "actively passive" (which she uses to convey the work that goes into the performance of a fake orgasm) gives us some traction on the slippery slope of agency in these scenes of posing and on the complicated place of agency in Warhol's own relationship to his work.[30] In thinking of the hustler as "actively passive," we can read the hustler's affect not as a mask that hides or denies a true self (as Koch seems to argue) but as a strategic gesture, as a pose that clears the space for his work, a pose that, indeed, is his work.

The hustler's pose enables the disavowals (the hustler's "I'm not queer, I do it for the money," or the john's "I'm not queer, just ask my wife"), which anchor the positions of both participants.[31] The condition of possibility for this queer practice is its status as an economic exchange. That the hustler is getting paid for doing what he does makes it "work." And because he does it for money means that it is not "real" sex, at least not sex that might make him "queer." These disavowals are equally important to the john. Because he is paying for the sex, it similarly doesn't "count" except as something he bought.

Hustling and prostitution are practices that insist on sex not as an expression of a congenital identity but as "trade." Anything that produces money is work, and thus whatever you do for money you can disavow as work. The presence of money in any exchange renders that exchange a kind of prostitution, because each time you accept money for something that you do, you, in a sense, sell yourself. Warhol reverses the truism that all kinds of labor are forms of prostitution to suggest that there is *no* sex that is *not* work and, by extension, that sex work is not some kind of exception (and therefore sex

 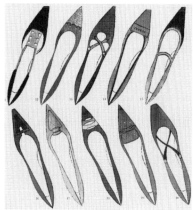

that doesn't "count") but is, instead, paradigmatic. Thus the hustler's second axiom on sex work and the work of sex: "Nobody's straight—You just do whatever you have to do." Here, Warhol's art, as it luxuriates in this exchange and its slippage, is not attacking the "heterosexual dollar" (as one early reviewer, citing Allen Ginsberg, put it) so much as it suggests that the dollar itself is a queering thing.[32]

Warhol's "Crazy Golden Slippers" (as *Life* magazine called his early shoe drawings) also luxuriate in the overlapping and excessive meanings of sex, work, and art. Whether Cinderella's pumps revised for Zsa Zsa Gabor and Truman Capote (see figure 1) or Dorothy's ruby slippers worked as *Diamond Dust Shoes* (1986), his shoe portraits wrap a rendition of the incoherencies and complexity of authorship in a visually indulgent celebration of one of femininity's most necessary accessories. By-products of his illustrations for I. Miller & Sons Shoes (see figure 2) the shoe drawings were Warhol's work, his "bread and butter."[33] Their painstaking detail imitates the work of the sewing machine—a mimetic relation he emphasized by visually likening his line drawing to the stitches produced by a sewing machine (see figure 3). They accomplish what Tina Fredricks, as the art director of *Glamour,* asked of them: "They have to look neat, have to 'sell'; you have to see every stitch, you have to really want to wear them, or be able to tell what they're like."[34] The dainty and precious detail of these drawings references machine-made fingerwork and engages a confusion of hands and machines. It also metonymically signals another kind of enterprise, the involved work of wearing high heels. Walking in a pair of heels is an acquired skill. The work embod-

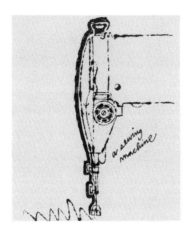

Figure 1. Andy Warhol, *Za Za Gabor* (1957).
©1996 Andy Warhol Foundation for the
Visual Arts/ARS, New York.
Figure 2. Andy Warhol, shoe illustration
from *Harper's Bazaar* (1952). ©1996 Andy
Warhol Foundation for the Visual Arts/ARS,
New York.
Figure 3. Andy Warhol, *"a sewing machine"*
(c. 1952). ©1996 Andy Warhol Foundation for
the Visual Arts/ARS, New York.

ied by the fantastic heels of *A La Recherche du Shoe Perdu* lies in walking in them. On the runway, the well-trained supermodel walks toe to heel, an awkward step, but one that makes you sway your hips and lift your knees in a runway sashay that constitutes the performance of high fashion femininity.

Remarking on the amount of energy required by this kind of performance (specifically, the work of drag), Warhol once said "being sexed is hard work." Part of the appeal of Warhol's use of the term "work" is that it can accommodate a range of activities that are generally thought of in opposition to work—even pleasure is a production, when we, like Andy, consider that "having sex is hard work." "Being sexed" is "so much work at something you don't always want to do."[35]

Behind the syntax of statements like "having sex is hard work" and "being sexed is hard work" is a complex assertion about the strangeness of "sex." The actively passive syntax of these maxims reproduces the difficulty of sorting out who we are from what we do by clouding the difference between subject and object, noun and verb. How a subject performs being sexed and having a body is a question that orients a substantial tradition in theoretical work on gender and identity, from Joan Riviere's assertion that "womanliness" is "masquerade" to Simone de Beauvoir's more widely referenced "Women are not born, they are made" and to Judith Butler's often-cited arguments: "There is no gender identity behind expressions of gender; that identity is performatively constituted by the very 'expressions' that are said to be its results," and "Gender is always a doing, though not by a subject who might be said to preexist the deed."[36] All these theorists problematize the relationship between agency and the constitution of gender identity. Butler's work, as it advises us to be wary of formulations of identity in terms of the presence or absence of will, seems especially salient for reading Warhol given the ambiguous place of agency in his work and the frequency with which his relationship to will, desire, gender, and sexuality has been pathologized by his critics. Like Warhol's superstars, who in *Esquire*'s words, are "neither born nor made," who "just happen," the Pop subject "happens" within and through its queer grammars.[37]

The ambiguity of Warhol's syntax is by no means limited to his aphorisms. The very way he made his work reconfigured agency so as to make saying how Warhol actually created or authored his art not only difficult but also in many aspects irrelevant. He deliberately tinkered with melodramas of authorship and boasted that his art-making process was so routinized that, ideally, no matter who followed the routine, the result was the production of a Warhol. "I want to be a machine" announces what David James locates as his "most characteristic authorial gesture," the "erasure of authorship."[38] Or, as James himself argues when he suggests we think of Warhol as a kind of producer, Warhol's most characteristic authorial gesture was to insist on authorship as itself an effect.

Many have argued that it is unproductive to read even accidental marks on the canvas of *Marilyn Monroe* (see figure 4), for instance, as the return of a repressed authorial presence.[39] Its overlapping and disjointed layers of color and image draw attention not to the accidents of the artist's hand but to the accidents of the layered mechanical reproduction definitive of Warhol's style (photography and silkscreening). Warhol's painted but paradoxically not painted face replaces a fantasy of unmediated self-expression with the manufacturing of the "painted woman." Making a joke of a long tradition in painting of acting out struggles with self-expression and quests for encounters with the "real" in representations of the sexualized female body, *Marilyn Monroe* enacts both a parody of the fantasy of authorship and a parody of gender identity. Like Warhol's shoes that mimic the work of wearing high heels in their worked detail, the celebrity portrait maximizes the slippage of the mechanical production of the work of art to underscore the degree to which "being sexed" is a kind of work, is something that is itself produced. The "painted woman," to borrow Butler's words, is not an artificial version of the real thing but a parody of "the very notion of an original. . . . It is a production which, in effect—that is, in its effect—postures as an imitation."

Figure 4. Andy Warhol, *Marilyn Monroe* (1962). ©1996 Andy Warhol Foundation for the Visual Arts/ARS, New York.

Marilyn Monroe is so overdetermined as "produced" as to suggest what Butler has formulated as "the imitative structure of gender itself."[40] The "painted woman" amplifies, in its effects, the authorship of art and the authorship of gender *as* effects.

Forged Images: Centerfold by Andy Warhol, a special project Warhol designed for *Artforum,* explicitly links what Pop has to say about the commodification of art and the commodification of sex (see figure 5a). In the center of the magazine on opposing pages are a dollar sign (borrowed from the 1981 *Dollar Sign* series) and Christopher Makos's photograph of Warhol in drag (in citation of Duchamp). This arrangement of drag and the dollar toys with the format of the centerfold. The centerfold spread is not an unveiling of Warhol which establishes a real, or original, identity underneath the drag. Unfolding the page yields three panels from the *Dollar Sign* series (figure 5b) for a total of three dollar signs. In short, *Forged Images* juxtaposes what Trevor Fairbrother has noted as "the things about him that most bothered most people"—Warhol's commercialism and his fagginess.[41]

His drag queerly adopts a range of gender affiliations at the same time—

Figures 5a and b. Andy
Warhol, a special project for
Artforum Forged Images (1982).
© 1996 Andy Warhol
Foundation for the Visual
Arts/ARS, New York.

femininity (the wig and makeup), mannishness (the jeans, the shirt, and the
tie), and girlishness (the pose). The utterly mundane "look" of Warhol's drag
and the refusal of the drag to disavow its drag-ness dramatize what Judith
Butler, drawing on the work of Esther Newton, has described as the principal
property of drag, that is, "not the putting on of a gender that belongs properly
to some other group, i.e. an act of *ex*propriation or *ap*propriation that assumes that gender is the rightful property of sex, that 'masculine' belongs to
'male' and 'feminine' belongs to 'female.' . . . Drag constitutes the mundane
way in which genders are appropriated, theatricalized, worn, and done; it
implies that all gendering is a kind of impersonation and approximation."[42]
Butler's words here seem especially appropriate as they resonate with the
banality of Warhol's pose and with the curiously flat-footed title of the centerfold, *Forged Images*. As if confirming her argument, the centerfold spread
unveils no "doer behind the deed" but instead offers us dollar signs—an
abstraction, the very symbol for U.S. exchange itself—as what are "behind"
or "inside" drag. The rhetorical force of the juxtaposition of drag and the
dollar is to make even more visible the status of gender as "produced" by
framing it as both "drag" and "work." In doing so, Warhol suggests an interesting homology between drag and his self-production as an artist.

The conjunction of drag and the dollar in the centerfold of an art magazine
likens both being sexed (the work of drag) and selling sex (what a centerfold
does) to art. Thus Warhol divulges the open secret of art, that it is something
that is also "done," and done for money. *Forged Images* formally recalls a porn
centerfold, playing on all the promises a centerfold offers its consumers: the
promise of seeing someone undressed, something "dirty," the promise to
appeal to your "prurient interests."

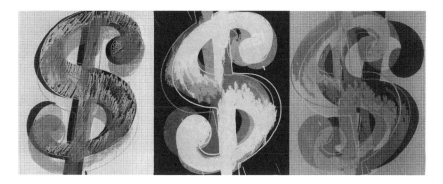

In offering dollar signs as the art world denuded (the promise of a good investment—as others have noted, the *Dollar Sign* series uncannily anticipates the art market boom and bust of the 1980s), Warhol's centerfold enacts a version of one of his most often recalled fantasies about art: "I like money on the wall. Say you were going to buy a $200,000 painting. I think you should take that money, tie it up, and hang it on the wall."[43] The irony, of course, is that he did not hang a bag of money on the wall. That would be beside the point. The *Dollar Sign* series makes visible how even when Warhol manufactures "painted" money, it has value on the art market insofar as it is "painted," as it is a "forgery." The "forgery" or painted-ness of the *Dollar Sign* series allows for the disavowal of its status as a commodity, even as the dollar sign makes that disavowal visible.

Like the drag image (or the "painted woman") that maximizes the incongruities of a "look" to expose not the imitative structure of drag but of gender, the painted dollar signs make visible art's refusal to acknowledge its status as a commodity. Thus the homology between pornography and art— where porn makes an industry out of selling representations of something that is not "supposed" to have a market (but does), what we might call Warhol's "money shots" obscenely undress the extent to which art is invested in the disavowal of its relationship to the art market. The "trick," then, is to carry off the double action of the disclaimer—to sell the pose. In this sense the pose the john solicits from the hustler—the pose that disavows the queer nature of the sexual exchange by asserting its nature as a *monetary* one—is a mirrored version of what is solicited from the artist—a pose that, in disavowing a relationship to the art market, allows the artist entry into its economy, into the pages of an art critic's magazine such as *Artforum.*

Pornography, in the oldest sense of the word, is writing about or representations of prostitution (pornográph[os]: writing about harlots). In more contemporary usage, the word "pornography" signals something as appealing to our "prurient interests" and that has no value as "art."[44] *Forged Images* works both these aspects of the word—speaking (like a child who should know better) of how sex sells art and art sells sex, of how art sells itself and of how all these things are the invisible supports of the system by which art is identified as such. Warhol's suggestion that pornographic magazines are the "fashion magazines of Forty-Second Street" turns itself inside out to recast *Artforum* as the "porno" of SoHo.

Forged Images uses the feedback generated from the rhetoric of "bad sex" that polices the art world's territories to sing an ode to the "drag" of art. This is the kind of song that an artist who makes queer art can sing. Warhol's conjunction of a portrait of himself as the artist in drag with a three dollar triptych offers us a clever pictograph: art-making can make an artist queer as a three-dollar bill.

NOTES

1   Andy Warhol, *The Philosophy of Andy Warhol* (New York: Harcourt Brace Jovanovich, 1975), pp. 92, 43.

2   Ibid.

3   Ibid., p. 51.

4   Andreas Huyssen, *After the Great Divide: Modernism, Mass Culture, Postmodernism* (Bloomington: Indiana University Press, 1986), p. 55.

5   W. F. Haug, *Critique of Commodity Aesthetics*, trans. Robert Bock (Minneapolis: University of Minnesota Press, 1986), p. 85.

6   Thierry De Duve, "Andy Warhol; or, the Machine Perfected," trans. Rosalind Krauss, *October* 48 (Spring 1989): 3–14.

7   Ibid., pp. 3–14, 3–6.

8   Suzi Gablik, "The Art Job, or, How the Avant-Garde Sold Out," *Art in America* (April 1980): 9–13, 9.

9   Thomas B. Hess, "The Phony Crisis in American Art," *Artnews* 62, Summer 1963, pp. 24–28.

10 For writing about the stigma of prostitution, see, for example, Frédérique Delacoste and Priscilla Alexander's collection of writings by women in the sex industry, *Sex Work* (Pittsburgh: Cleis Press, 1987), and *Social Text* 37 (Winter 1993) for a special section on women and the sex trade edited by Anne McClintock.

11   Here I am borrowing Eve Kosofsky Sedgwick's useful formulation of universalizing and minoritizing discourses on sexuality and identity which she develops in *Epistemology of the Closet* (Berkeley: University of California Press, 1990), pp. 82–90.

12   Anne McClintock, "Screwing the System: Sex Work, Race, and the Law," in *Feminism and Postmodernism*, a special issue of *boundary 2* (Summer 1992), ed. Margaret Ferguson and Jennifer Wicke (Durham: Duke University Press, 1992), p. 76.

13   Robert Hughes, "The Best and Worst of Warhol," *Time*, February 13, 1989, pp. 94–95, 95; and Hughes, "The Rise of Andy Warhol," *New York Review of Books*, February 18, 1982, pp. 6, 7.

14   Peter Selz, "The Flaccid Art," in *Pop Art: The Critical Dialogue*, ed. Carol Anne Mahusen (Ann Arbor: UMI Research Press, 1989), pp. 77–82, originally published as "Pop Goes the Artist," *Partisan Review* (Summer 1963).

15   Aline B. Saarinen, "Explosion of Pop Art," *Vogue*, April, 1963, 86–87, 134, 136, 142, 134.

16   Deborah Soloman, "Pittsburgh's Warhol Museum: Pop Art . . . in a Grimly Rehabbed, Final 'Factory,'" *Wall Street Journal*, May 18, 1994, A12.

17   This is a gloss of a definition of prostitution written by Henri Turot in 1904 and cited by T. J. Clark in his study of Manet's painting *Olympia*, "Olympia's Choice," in *The Painting of Modern Life* (Princeton: Princeton University Press, 1984), p. 281 n.

18   Anne McClintock, "Sex Workers and Sex Work: An Introduction," *Social Text* 37 (Winter 1993): 1–10, 7. The phrase "pathology of agency" belongs to Mark Seltzer as he uses it in "Serial Killers (1)" in *Differences: A Journal of Feminist Cultural Studies* 5, no. 1 (1993): 92–127.

19   Jeremy Gilbert-Rolfe, "Popular Imagery," in *Theories of Contemporary Art,* ed. Richard Hertz (Englewood Cliffs, N.J.: Prentice Hall, 1985), pp. 129–130. Cited by David James in his suggestive article "The Unsecret Life: A Warhol Advertisement," in *October* 56 (Spring 1991).

20   Peter Selz, ed., "A Symposium on Pop Art," a special supplement to *Arts Magazine,* April 1963, pp. 36–45.

21   Jean Baudrillard, *Revenge of the Crystal: Selected Writings on the Modern Object and Its Destiny, 1968–1983,* ed. and trans. Paul Foss and Julian Pefanis (Sydney, Australia: Pluto Press, 1990), p. 87.

22   Leticia Kent, "Andy Warhol, Movieman: 'It's Hard to Be Your Own Script.'" *Vogue,* March 1970, p. 204.

23   Andy Warhol and Pat Hackett, *POPism: The Warhol Sixties* (New York: Harcourt Brace Jovanovich, 1980), p. 294. As virtually any account of the Factory life will tell you, Warhol had a significant place in the every life and imaginary of the sex industry in New York. Kathy Acker illustrates this nicely when she recalls that while working at FUN CITY, "One of the lines in our sex-shows was that we were waiting to be discovered by Andy Warhol. We weren't entirely joking, we were hoping." Acker remembers the Factory as welcoming those the art world and hippie culture disparaged: "Whores, pimps, working girls of all sorts, drug dealers, transsexuals and transvestites—the general population of forty-second street." Kathy Acker, "Blue Valentine," in *Andy Warhol: Film Factory,* ed. Michael O'Pray (London: British Film Institute, 1989), pp. 62–64.

24   Andy Warhol, *The Andy Warhol Diaries,* ed. Pat Hackett (New York: Warner Books, 1989), p. 799.

25   Ibid.

26   I am drawing from Michael Moon's discussion of reading poetry and pornography in "Rereading Whitman under Pressure of AIDS," in *The Continuing Presence of Walt Whitman: The Life after the Life,* ed. Robert K. Martin (Iowa City: University of Iowa Press, 1992), pp. 53–66.

27   Callie Angel, *The Films of Andy Warhol: Part 2* (New York: Whitney Museum of American Art, 1994).

28   Stephen Koch, *Stargazer: Andy Warhol's World and His Films* (New York: Praeger, 1973), pp. 124–133. I owe David James, "Andy Warhol: The Producer as Author," in his book *Allegories of Cinema* (Princeton: Princeton University Press, 1989), pp. 77–79, for bringing these passages to my attention.

29   James, *Allegories of Cinema,* pp. 67, 77–79.

30   I am borrowing the phrase "actively passive" from Spivak in the spirit in which Craig Owens cites her in his essay "Posing." Spivak coins the term in when suggesting that feminist criticism: "produce useful and scrupulously *fake* readings in place of the actively-passive fake orgasm." Gayatri Spivak, "Displacement and the Discourse of Woman," in *Displacement: Derrida and After,* ed. Mark Krupnik (Bloomington: Indiana University Press, 1983), p. 186. Owens uses the phrase in his insightful reading of feminist appropriations of the pose in the visual arts; see "Posing," in *Beyond Recognition: Representation, Power, and Culture,* ed. Scott Bryson, Barbara Kruger, Lynne Tillman, and Jane Weinstock (Berkeley: University of California Press, 1992), pp. 201–217, 214.

31   Michael Moon has recently read these disavowals as kinds of cross-dressing. By dressing each other up as "not really queer," the hustler and his client in a sense fetishize sexuality itself, so that "both men 'never feel straighter' than when they are having sex with each other." The tenuous hold that this script has on "being straight" accrues a kind of erotic value as it manages to clear the space for an exchange between men that is already prohibited, under any condition. Michael Moon, "Outlaw Sex and the 'Search for America': Representing Male Prostitution and Perverse Desire in Sixties Film (*My Hustler* and *Midnight Cowboy*)," *Quarterly Review of Film and Video* 15, no. 1 (1993): 27–40, 31.

32   Philip Leider, "Saint Andy," review of the Pop exhibition "The Arena of Love," *Artforum,* February 1965, pp. 26–28, 28.

33   Peter Palazo, art director for I. Miller, cited by Donna M. De Salvo, "Learning the Ropes: Some Notes about the Early Work of Andy Warhol," in *"Success is a job in New York": The Early Art and Business of Andy Warhol* (Pittsburgh: Carnegie Museum of Art, 1989), p. 12.

34   Tina Fredricks, cited by De Salvo, "Learning the Ropes," p. 4.

35   Warhol, *Philosophy.*

36   Roughly, Riviere's passing remark has been taken to mean that women do not adopt a mask of womanliness as such; rather, womanliness or the psychological position of women is defined by, or is constituted as, masquerade. Joan Riviere, "Womanliness as Masquerade," in *Formations of Fantasy,* ed. Victor Burgin, James Donald, and Cora Kaplan (New York: Routledge, Chapman and Hall, 1986), pp. 35–44. Beauvoir argued that "woman" is a social and not a natural construct. Simone de Beauvoir, *The Second Sex,* trans. E. M. Parshley (New York: Vintage, 1973). Butler's citation of Nietzsche describes gender identity as a never-ending citation of prior "expressions" and not the externalization of an interior,

prior, and congenital condition. Judith Butler, *Gender Trouble* (New York: Routledge, 1990), pp. 24–25.

37 Elenore Lester, "The Final Decline and Total Collapse of the American Avant-Garde," including a photo album by Andy Warhol, *Esquire*, May 1969, pp. 143–149, 144.

38 James, *Allegories of Cinema*, p. 64.

39 Benjamin Buchloh puts this well when he remarks that, given the shaky status of authorship in Warhol's work, critics who try to read it by the codes of painterly expression generally succeed only in embarrassing themselves. "Andy Warhol's One Dimensional Art: 1956–1966" in *Andy Warhol: A Retrospective,* ed. Kynaston McShine (New York: Museum of Modern Art, 1989), pp. 39–61, 50.

40 Butler, *Gender Trouble*, pp. 137, 138.

41 Trevor Fairbrother, "Tomorrow's Man," in *"Success is a job in New York,"* p. 73.

42 Judith Butler, "Imitation and Gender Insubordination," in *Inside/Out: Lesbian Theories, Gay Theories,* ed. Diana Fuss (New York: Routledge, 1991), p. 21.

43 Warhol, *Philosophy,* pp. 133–134.

44 See, for example, Linda Williams's discussion of legal approaches to classifying works as pornography in *Hard Core: Power, Pleasure, and the "Frenzy of the Visible"* (Berkeley: University of California Press, 1989), pp. 85–91.

MARCIE FRANK

Popping Off Warhol: From the Gutter
to the Underground and Beyond

n June 3, 1968, in the middle of the afternoon, Valerie Solanas shot and critically wounded Andy Warhol. Three hours later, she surrendered to a traffic cop in Times Square, saying, "He had too much control over my life." While Solanas was being booked at the police station, reporters asked her about her motivations. She answered, "Read my manifesto and it will tell you what I am."[1] Solanas again offered her manifesto as an explanation for her assault when she submitted it at her trial as part of her defense.[2] Maurice Girodias of Olympia Press capitalized on the connection between Solanas's crime and her writing when he published *The SCUM Manifesto* later in 1968, where SCUM stands for the Society for Cutting Up Men. Girodias was not the only one to exploit Solanas's insistent presentation of her manifesto as the theory and her attempt on Warhol's life as the practice.

On June 14, 1968, the *New York Times* reported that two representatives of NOW, the National Organization of Women, appeared in State Supreme Court to claim Solanas as a "heroine of the revitalized feminist movement." Ti-Grace Atkinson and Florynce Kennedy, both of whom would resign from NOW that October, met the press and characterized Solanas as "one of the most important spokeswomen of the feminist movement."[3] The fact that Solanas's crime came with a cultural analysis gave her symbolic value to Atkinson, in particular, who repeatedly compared Solanas to Jean Genet. But Solanas refused Atkinson's attempt to dress her up in the intellectual fashions of existentialism. Dismissing Atkinson's transatlantic comparison when she was asked about it later that afternoon, Solanas said, "Genet just reports, despite what Sartre and De Beauvoir, two over-rated windbags, say about the existential implications of his work. I, on the other hand, am a social propagandist." Deflating the prestige of Atkinson's analogy—Sartre and de Beauvoir are "over-rated windbags"—and distinguishing herself from Genet, the "journalist," Solanas intervened in Atkinson's attempt to recuperate her as a feminist heroine, insisting on a different kind of connection between her writing and her crime when she called herself a "social propagandist."

Solanas was not on the scene to intervene in another, later feminist attempt to recuperate her: if, in 1968, Atkinson wanted to turn Solanas into Genet, in 1979, independent scholar, Meaghan Morris, tried to turn her into Foucault. In the winsomely titled "The Pirate's Fiancee: Feminists and Philosophers, or maybe tonight it'll happen," Morris used Solanas to mediate her opposition of theory to feminist activism.[4] I propose to begin with a description of Morris's misappropriation of Solanas, because it is through Solanas that Morris presents contradictory versions of the relation of theory to activism and various places for the academy in this relation. Morris's contradictions represent an important transition in the history of feminism. I then move to a reading *The SCUM Manifesto,* a task Morris incapacitates herself from performing because of her misappropriation of Solanas, and end by looking at Andy Warhol's reactions to the shooting that, together with his comments about his practice of recycling, constitute another misappropriation of Solanas, one that has repercussions for our understandings of the relations between high and low culture. By specifying the relation between the underground scene of the Factory and the gutter, the site of scum, I invite speculation about the relations between the underground, the high culture to which Warhol now belongs, and the academy.

Between 1979 and the mid-eighties, it seemed a matter of some urgency to describe, define, advocate, or circumscribe the possible relations between (mainly French) theory and "the women's movement." Morris's proposal of the usefulness of Foucault to feminists seems prescient, considering that in the intervening years, the role of theory has been settled as both necessary and important and Foucault's status has become canonical, particularly in recent work in gender studies and queer theory.

For Morris, however, Foucault's work is available to feminists because it "is not the work of a ladies' man"; furthermore, "any feminists drawn in to sending love letters to Foucault would be in no danger of reciprocation" ("Pirate's Fiancee," 26). Morris represents the relation of feminist activists to theorists as a dangerous flirtation; from her perspective, all theorists are men and the only safe theorist is a gay theorist. Moreover, her recommendation of "wanking" (that is, jerking off) as the only other alternative to being "thoroughly screwed" by theorists firmly precludes both sexual and intellectual interaction among women.[5] For Morris, Foucault's theories can resolve or dissolve the problematic relation of feminist activism to theory and to the academy.[6] But Morris supplements Foucault with Valerie Solanas, whom she treats paradoxically, both quoting her repeatedly and suppressing her authorship. The sites of her citations suggest that Morris aims to produce Solanas as Foucault's female counterpart.

"The Pirate's Fiancee" begins with a disavowal: "This isn't a theoretical text; though that is not because I wish to avoid being caught at commentary, or to tick down my allegiance automatically to a politics (which I do support) of the provisional and definitely uncertain" (21). Morris disavows the theoretical nature of her own text, but her essay, with its complicated wordplay, clearly inhabits the academic feminist discourse it claims to distrust. In addition, although Morris notes that ongoing feminist work on the project of a theory of the subject and the project of a feminine writing "probably impassion[s] remarkably few women," she uses these projects to pose the question of the place of theory in the women's movement. Strangely, she dismisses the very question she poses, calling it a "ridiculous political question."[7] The contradictions of Morris's text sustain her goal: to present herself as the intermediary between the university and the street who therefore has the authority to recommend Foucault. Her performance is effected by means of her textual treatment of Solanas. Solanas is her proof that her text is not theoretical; paradoxically, Solanas functions in her text as a methodological framework that makes coherent Morris's "atheoretical" use of theory.

Morris's use of Solanas to present herself as a feminist theorist with activist credentials is most evident in her choice of textual frame. She both begins and ends her essay with unattributed citations from *The SCUM Manifesto*. She also quotes liberally from *The SCUM Manifesto* at key transitional moments in her essay.[8] Although one of the citations is accompanied by a footnote in which one might expect to find mention of Solanas, the note instead acknowledges Andre Frankovits's "relaxed assistance in ordering this text" ("Pirate's Fiancee," 41). Morris's unattributed uses of *The SCUM Manifesto* are the more remarkable because she does refer twice to Solanas by name. The first reference is brief and beside the point here.[9] The second one is more extended and worth examining. At the conclusion of her essay, she describes Solanas as "a woman who wrote most certainly in order to become something else than a great writer," a woman, moreover, who "reminds us from a place far beyond the construction sites of 'theory' or the dressings-up of analytical practice . . . [that] there are lots of other things to do" (40). Although, like Atkinson, Morris dresses Solanas up in French male garb, her appeal nevertheless rests on the claim that she returns us to naked activism.

Morris's final citation of Solanas occurs at the end of her essay, after she evokes what she calls "the dinosaurs of the late 60's." However, if a look at late 1960s feminists would revise the perhaps too easy contrast Morris has drawn between *Speculum of the Other Woman* and *The Woman's Room* by contextualizing the state of feminism in 1979, she backs off: such "savagely ingenuous texts," such "genuinely disastrous texts" as Ti-Grace Atkinson's *Amazon Odyssey* and Monique Wittig's *Les Guérillères* are "impossible to mention . . . without incurring suspicion of nostalgia, saccharine celebration, necrophilia, romantic anachronism, belief in the timeless subversive integrity of texts irreducibly outside truth" ("Pirate's Fiancee," 40). Now that it is possible to read Atkinson and Wittig without incurring the dangers that Morris outlines, this task would offer one way to resituate academic feminism in relation to its 1960s roots.

Morris ends her essay with the opening paragraph of the still-unidentified manifesto: "Life in this society being, at best, an utter bore and no aspect of society being at all relevant to women, there remains to civic-minded, responsible, thrill-seeking females only to overthrow the government, eliminate the money system, institute complete automation, and destroy the male sex" (40). These, presumably, are the things that remain to be done, according to Morris, though she supplies no progress report, that is, no mention of Solanas's attempt to destroy Warhol.

The result of Morris's idiosyncratic "citational" style is that if you don't happen to recognize that the epigraph to her essay and other citations are from the *SCUM Manifesto* and if you don't know that Solanas wrote it, "The Pirate's Fiancee" provides no way of putting the two together. Solanas is never credited with writing the manifesto; nor is that text ever identified. Morris's suppressions of Solanas's authorship and her crime allow her to align herself with Solanas "outside" the academy and to call for action that, in Morris's case, anyway, stops short of active destruction. Morris's production of Solanas as the female and feminist Foucault is, perhaps, facilitated by

Solanas's own treatment of gender in *The SCUM Manifesto,* the text Morris has disabled herself from reading. I would like to turn now to that task.

An amazing piece of writing, *The SCUM Manifesto* deserves attention less as an explanation for why Solanas shot Warhol than as an angry, urgent cry for the reevaluation of gender identity.[10] A complicated line of reasoning underpins Solanas's call for the elimination of the male sex, and her appeal to immediate violent action ultimately rests on her description of how gender roles work and on the connections she draws between gender, economics, culture, and politics.

Solanas argues that the male sex, because of its nature, has come close to ruining the world. Her inimitable prose describes men this way:

> Completely egocentric, unable to relate, empathize or identify, and filled with a vast, pervasive, diffuse sexuality, the male is physically passive. He hates his passivity, so he projects it onto women, defines the male as active, then sets out to prove that he is ("prove he's a Man"). His main means of attempting to prove it is screwing (Big Man with a Big Dick tearing off a Big Piece). Since he's attempting to prove an error, he must "prove" it again and again. Screwing, then, is a desperate, compulsive attempt to prove he's not passive, not a woman; but he *is* passive and *does* want to be a woman. (*Manifesto,* 33–34)

Solanas's pithy conclusion, "Women don't have penis envy; men have pussy envy" (35), follows from her elaboration of the projective mechanism by which men give women all male traits—for example, vanity, frivolity, triviality, and weakness—while retaining for themselves all the traits of women, such as emotional strength and independence, forcefulness and dynamism.

Yet the reversal in which men come to recognize their true nature as feminine (that is, passive, trivial, and so forth) and women realize their reality as "truly female" (exhibiting the characteristics traditionally associated with heroic men), cannot be fully effective because Solanas locates "true nature" at the level of genital organization. This is evident in her description of sex as the sublimation of the male desire to be female. She gets to her pronouncement that "sex is sublimation" by a chain of reasoning in which the feminized man first becomes a transvestite and then a transsexual: "When the male accepts his passivity, defines himself as a woman, and becomes a transvestite he loses his desire to screw (or to do anything else, for that matter; he fulfills himself as a drag queen) and gets his cock chopped off.

He then achieves a continuous diffuse sexual feeling from 'Being a woman.' Screwing is, for a man, a defense against his desire to be female. Sex is itself a sublimation" (*Manifesto*, 35). If it looks like sex is here a question of gender attributes, Solanas once again asserts the primacy of the genital in the slippage from the transvestite to the transsexual.

Those of us who come to feminism through theory probably associate the attack on the specularity of gender with the work of French feminist Luce Irigaray.[11] Although Irigaray succeeds in distancing herself from the biological more efficaciously than Solanas, it is interesting to note that in 1969, Ti-Grace Atkinson, who credited her inaugural use of the term "radical feminism" to Solanas's example, moved away from Solanas's biologism when she offered the following qualification to Solanas's goal, to eliminate men: "Sex-roles—both male and female—must be destroyed, not the individuals who happen to possess either a penis or vagina or both or neither."[12] (Atkinson's reservation did not prevent her from recommending *The SCUM Manifesto*, along with her own essays and de Beauvoir's *The Second Sex*, to an audience of college students whom she introduced to feminism in 1969.)[13]

Just as some of the limits of Irigaray's political effectiveness are reached in her treatment of "homosexuality," so Solanas's projective mechanism gets bogged down in her treatment of "the fag" or "faggot." According to Solanas, faggots "by their shimmering, flaming example encourage other men to de-man themselves, thereby make themselves relatively inoffensive" (*Manifesto*, 74). Moreover, fags are recuperable as members of the Men's Auxiliary of SCUM, those "men who are working diligently to eliminate themselves" (74). For Solanas, fags are at their most honest in drag. Fags admit their femininity because they don the trappings Solanas believes the real females will divest themselves of, if they haven't already.

However, unlike Irigaray, who takes as her point of departure the "nonexistence" of woman, Solanas argues that it is not woman that doesn't exist but man who shouldn't: "Maleness is a deficiency disease"; the male Y chromosome is an incomplete female X chromosome, and men are incomplete women—they are, as she puts it, "walking abortions" (*Manifesto*, 31–32). Thus men should be eliminated.

Although Solanas characterizes the specularity of gender differences, she treats them as authentic. And although, for her, the gender categories, male and female, are "real," her text proliferates their possibilities. For Solanas, there are male females, female females, female males, and male males. For example, Solanas argues that since men have contempt for themselves and all who love them, they functionally prevent love or friendship. Women, however, have the capacity for love and friendship, but Solanas can establish this capacity only by means of a redistributive logic:

> Men have contempt for themselves, for all other men and for all women who respect and pander to them; the insecure, approval seeking, pandering male females have contempt for themselves and for all women like them; the self-confident swinging, thrill-seeking female females have contempt for men and for the pandering male females. . . . Love can't exist between two males, between a male and a female or between two females [when] one or both, is a mindless, insecure pandering male. [L]ove can exist only between two secure, free-wheeling, independent, groovy female females. (*Manifesto*, 56–57)

In other words, all males and some females, most prominent among whom are those Solanas calls "Daddy's girls," are females, whom Solanas calls "male females"; those Solanas calls female females are their counterparts, who are disallowed by society. Female females, however, retain the characteristics traditionally associated with males, characteristics that, in Solanas's account, the male females have abdicated.

According to Solanas, men are females and women are males. Despite her mobilization of several intermediary types that would seem to expand the gender binary beyond the basic opposition, her fundamental chiasmic logic both returns us to the binary and voids the system of any stable meaning. The multiplication of possible gender identities aims at demystification, but at times Solanas's contradictory text moves the category of gender back toward the biological and at times it explodes the category of gender right off the map. The repetition of the terms "male" and "female" in all possible combinations reinscribes the binary at the same time as it spins out endless possible recombinations that render almost incomprehensible any foundation for gender identity at all.

Whereas Solanas's rethinking of gender roles is somewhat problematic, stuck as it is at the level of anatomy, it is the intersection of this project with her program to overthrow society through the elimination of the male sex that attracted revolutionary feminists such as Ti-Grace Atkinson and Meaghan Morris to *The SCUM Manifesto*. Solanas outlines what SCUM wants: "What will liberate women from male control is the total elimination of the money-work system, not the attainment of economic equality with men within it" (*Manifesto,* 38). Further on, she notes:

> If a large majority of women were SCUM, they could acquire complete control over this country within a few weeks by simply withdrawing from the labor force, thereby paralyzing the entire nation. . . . Women [could] declare themselves off the money system, stop buying, just loot and simply refuse to obey all laws they don't care to obey. . . . If all women simply left all men, refused to have anything to do with any of them, ever, all men, the government and the national economy would collapse completely. (70–71)

Automation and destruction of the money system are essential to SCUM's goals, and Solanas advocates criminality rather than civil disobedience, which she sees as a search for power within the system that exhibits pointless confidence in existent legal structures. Moreover, Solanas promises that the overthrow will be easy since men will actually like following women around because they "want Mama in charge."

Interestingly, this observation prompts Solanas to relocate the conflict between men and women once again. Although she has redescribed the conflict between men and women as a conflict between male females and groovy, freewheeling female females, she ultimately portrays the real battle as a conflict between SCUM and Daddy's girls.

> The conflict, therefore, is not between females and males, but between SCUM—dominant, secure, self-confident, nasty, violent, selfish, independent, proud, thrill-seeking, free-wheeling arrogant females, who consider themselves fit to rule the universe, . . . and nice, passive, accepting, "cultivated," polite, dignified, subdued, dependent, scared, mindless, insecure, approval-seeking Daddy's Girls . . . who want to continue to wallow in the sewer that is, at least, familiar. (71–72)

In a sense, this displacement anticipates the factionalizing of feminism in the seventies that might be seen as having derailed the then imminent revolution. But Solanas herself recognizes the pitfalls of fighting among women, which she aims to forestall, declaring: "But SCUM is too impatient to hope and wait for the debrain-washing of millions of assholes. . . . Why should the swinging females continue to plod dismally along with the dull male ones? Why should the fates of the groovy and the creepy be intertwined? Why should the active and imaginative consult the passive and dull on social policy? Why should the independent be confined to the sewer along with the dependent who need Daddy to cling to?" (73). Solanas thus advocates "systematically fucking up the system, selectively destroying property and murder" (73). The conclusions to which Solanas comes in her writing, in conjunction with her crime and her appropriation, are salient to the history of American academic feminism. In 1968, Solanas's writing and her example prompted feminist theorist-activist Ti-Grace Atkinson to describe a form of radical feminism, to investigate the Amazon legend to do so, and to express the necessary relations between lesbianism and feminism. The overlaps between Atkinson and Monique Wittig, her better-known French contemporary, suggest Solanas's importance as a representative of the elements shared by what have looked to many like divergent traditions: the empirically oriented, civil rights–based American feminist activism and the linguistically oriented poststructuralist French materialist feminism.[14]

Solanas's politics and her materialist cultural analysis might be best understood by looking more closely at the material of SCUM. Perhaps the most tantalizing aspect of Solanas's tract is the way she founds SCUM: although she was probably its only member, Solanas's manifesto aims to establish a group, the Society for Cutting Up Men, that would consist of the scum of society, the women in the gutter who are "those females least embedded in male 'culture' " (*Manifesto,* 61). She continues:

> Unhampered by propriety, niceness, discretion, public opinion, "morals," the "respect" of assholes, always funky, dirty, lowdown, SCUM gets around . . . and around . . . and around . . . they've seen the whole show— every bit of it—the fucking scene, the sucking scene, the dick scene, the dike scene—they've covered the whole waterfront, been under every dock and pier—the peter pier, the pussy pier. . . . you've got to go through a lot of sex to get to anti-sex, and SCUM's been through it all, and they're ready for a new show; they want to crawl out from under the dock, move, take off, sink out. But SCUM doesn't yet prevail; SCUM's still in the gutter of our "society," which, if it's not deflected from its present course and if the Bomb doesn't drop on it, will hump itself to death. (62)

In this passage, Solanas identifies sexuality as the major, apocalyptic preoccupation of "society"; the urgent need to deflect society from its present course also emerges clearly. Indeed, Meaghan Morris quotes the last part of this passage to illustrate or counterpoint Foucault's insight that questions of sexuality are inseparable from questions of power and knowledge. But equally important to Solanas's reasoning is her perception that women are in the sewer. The gutter perspective permits a cultural analysis that identifies the creation of such categories as art and culture among the other ruses of masculinity which are meant to keep women there, including war, death, the suburbs, the family, and higher education. Solanas's revaluation of the sewer as the site of SCUM follows the same logic as her revaluation of the values society allocates to males and females. The acronym, SCUM, is no accident. It condenses the goal of her program and the power of her cultural analysis: men need to be cut up, and only a revolutionary group located in the place below cultural production, the gutter, can eliminate them. The location of SCUM in the gutter is crucial to its strategic efficacy.

Solanas's embrace of scum in her founding of SCUM resuscitates the dirty, the lowdown, and the marginalized, elements that are retained in her writing even though she uses them to project a stance from beyond. "You've got to go through a lot of sex to get to anti-sex," says Solanas, but clearly having "been through it all" is important. The dick and dike scenes, the peter and pussy piers that Solanas evokes lend revisionary power to her allusion to the popular song "I Cover the Waterfront," for example.[15] Clichés from popular culture and the hard-boiled lingo of film noir sprinkle the endless and staggering lists that permeate the *Manifesto*. For example, Solanas's list of men whom SCUM will eliminate includes "rapists, politicians and all who are in their service; lousy singers and musicians; Chairmen of Boards, Breadwinners; landlords; owners of greasy spoons and restaurants that play Musak; 'Great Artists'; cheap pikers; cops; tycoons; scientists working on death and destruction programs or for private industry; liars and phoneys; . . . stock brokers; double-dealers; flim-flam artists; litter bugs; plagiarizers et al." (*Manifesto*, 75–76). Her regurgitation of the familiar and the idiomatic operates as a kind of sewage system appropriate to the resuscitation of SCUM. Solanas's sewage system stands in an interesting relation to the sanitary kind of recycling that Andy Warhol imagines in *The Philosophy of Andy Warhol*: "I think about people eating and going to the bathroom all the time, and I wonder why they don't have a tube up their behind that takes all the stuff out and recycles it back into their mouth, regenerating it, and then they'd never have to think about buying food or eating it. And they wouldn't even have to see it—it wouldn't even be dirty. If they wanted to they could artificially color it on the way back in. Pink."[16] Like Solanas, Warhol imagines the ways automation would obviate the money system: his recycling system would make buying food unnecessary. But when Warhol describes his interest in more detail, recycling emerges as a form of work: "I always like to work on leftovers, doing the leftover things. Things that were discarded, that everybody knew were no good, I always thought had a great potential to be funny. It was like recycling work" (93). Moreover, Warhol explicitly links the work of recycling with business.

> I'm not saying that popular taste is bad so that what's left over from popular taste is good: I'm saying that what's left over is probably bad, but if you can take it and make it good, or at least interesting, then you're not wasting as much as you would otherwise. You're recycling work, and you're recycling people, and you're running your business as a by-product of other businesses. Of *directly competitive businesses,* as a matter of fact. So that's a very economical procedure. It's also the funniest operating procedure because, as I said, leftovers are inherently funny.[17] (93; emphasis mine)

Whereas Warhol is obsessed with avoiding waste by using it for business purposes, Solanas celebrates the dirt and scum of the gutter as the site from which to overthrow business.

In 1975, Warhol understands Solanas's assault as itself a recyclable phenomenon: "I always worry that when nutty people do something, they'll do the same thing again a few years later without even remembering that they've done it before. . . . I was shot in 1968, so that was the 1968 version. But then I have to think, 'Will someone want to do a 1970s remake of shooting me?' So that's another kind of fan" (*Philosophy of Andy Warhol,* 84). It probably caused Warhol some anxiety that Solanas was incarcerated for only two years. Apparently, when she was released in late 1970, she did try to contact the Factory a number of times before fading into obscurity.[18] Casting Solanas's assault as a sort of hommage is itself an instance of the kind of recycling Warhol performed often in his career: an act of self-promotion which is also extremely suggestive about the many kinds of relations fans have to what they both admire and resent, Warhol's explanation is also an act of appropriation. From this point of view, it is instructive to contrast Solanas's gutter to Warhol's underground, which he preferred to think of as velvet.

As panhandler, writer, hanger-on of the Warhol scene, and would-be assassin of Warhol, Solanas's dramatic profile links the inception of radical feminism to other aspects of late 1960s cultural production. Moreover, the appropriations by Atkinson and Morris of her text and example as a set of street credentials and her recycling by Warhol reveal some ways in which madness, sewage, and violence remain unintegrated and perhaps unintegratable into the spheres of academic feminism and high art.

NOTES

I would like to acknowledge Bruce Russell and Rick Trembles, who kindly made their textual resources available to me, as well as the valuable editorial assistance of Michael Moon, Kevin Pask, Jill Frank, and Adam Frank.

1 Paul Krassner tells this anecdote in his afterword to Maurice Girodias's publication of Valerie Solanas, *The SCUM Manifesto* (New York: Olympia Press, 1968), p. 105.

2 Glenn S., "Valerie Solanas: Cultural Terrorist," in *Nooks 'n Crannies* (Toronto: Self-published fanzine, 1991), pp. 20–23.

3 Atkinson and Kennedy moved for a writ of habeas corpus on the grounds that Solanas was being improperly detained in the psychiatric ward of Elmhurst City Hospital in Queens. *New York Times,* June 14, 1968, p. 52.

4 Meaghan Morris's "The Pirate's Fiancee: Feminists and Philosophers, or, maybe tonight it'll happen," in *Feminism and Foucault: Reflections on Resistance,* ed. Irene Diamond and Lee Quinby (Boston: Northeastern University Press, 1988), pp. 21–32. Morris discusses her title, which she takes from the film *La fiancee du pirate,* directed by Nelly Kaplan, toward the end of her essay, pp. 39–40.

5 Morris recommends Foucault as follows: "In fact, the nicest thing about Foucault (in this respect, at least) is that not only do the offers of a philosopher to self-destruct appear to be positively serious on this occasion, but that any feminists drawn in to sending love letters to Foucault would be in no danger of reciprocation. Foucault's work is not the work of a ladies' man: and (confounding the received opinions of the advocates of plain speech, straight sex) some recent flirtations between feminists and other more susceptible thinkers would seem to suggest that there are far worse fates than wanking (like being thoroughly screwed)." See "The Pirate's Fiancee," p. 26.

6 Ibid., p. 23.

7 According to Morris, the projects of a theory of the subject and feminine writing "do pose fairly acutely, even if only in passing, an ever-discreditable and ridiculous political question—the (shaky and shifting) place within the women's movement, and beside it, of academics and intellectuals, or 'theorists,' in British-inspired terminology." Ibid., p. 25.

8 Morris poses her first unattributed citation of Solanas alongside a synopsis of Foucault; this placement establishes the relevance to feminism of his perception that questions of sexuality are inseparable from questions of power and knowledge. She next cites Solanas's text

to make the transition from her investigation of the project of the theory of the subject to the project of "feminine writing."

9 Morris's first reference to Solanas by name occurs midway through her essay, when she offers, parenthetically, to rewrite one of Solanas's observations to make it applicable to the question, hot in 1979, of whether "woman" exists. Having referred to Monique Plaza's argument with Irigaray's proposition that "woman" does not exist, and Mark Cousin's statement that from a Marxist standpoint, the patriarchal mode of production does not exist, Morris remarks "(at times it seems as though Valerie Solanas's observation, 'the ultimate male insight is that life is absurd,' only needs a little rephrasing in the days of the profound examination of the nonexistence of women)" ("The Pirate's Fiancee," p. 24). It remains unclear to me how precisely this rephrasing would go: "the ultimate male? marxist? female? insight is that woman is absurd"?

10 In an interview with Maurice Girodias that he records in the preface to his publication of *The SCUM Manifesto,* Ti-Grace Atkinson suggests that part of Solanas's motivation for shooting Warhol was her perception that Girodias and Warhol were in cahoots to gain control of her writing without appropriate economic remuneration. Solanas's statement when she was arrested, "He had too much control over my life," certainly indicates that she believed some such scenario. It is impossible at this point, however, to reconstruct what actually happened.

11 Luce Irigaray, *Speculum of the Other Woman,* trans. Gillian C. Gill (Ithaca: Cornell University Press, 1986).

12 Atkinson introduces the term "radical feminism" in *Amazon Odyssey* (New York: Links Books, 1974), p. 25. She elaborates her critique of Solanas's biologism as follows: "Some people say that men are naturally, or biologically aggressive. But this leaves us at an impasse. If the values of society are power-oriented, there is no chance that men would agree to be medicated into a humane state. The other alternative that has been suggested is to eliminate men as biologically incapable of humane relationships and therefore a menace to society. I can sympathize with the frustration and rage that leads to this suggestion, but the proposal to eliminate men, as I understand it, assumes that men constitute a kind of social disease, and that by 'men' is meant those individuals with certain typical genital characteristics" (54–55).

13 Ti-Grace Atkinson's address at Juniata College, Huntingdon, Pennsylvania, in June 1969 is included in *Amazon Odyssey,* p. 30.

14 See the editors' introduction to Elaine Marks and Isabelle de Courtivron, eds., *New French Feminisms: An Anthology* (New York: Schocken, 1981).

15 Inspired by the 1933 movie of the same name that featured Claudette Colbert and Ben Lym, "I Cover the Waterfront" was written in 1933 by Johnny Green and Edward Heyman and made famous in 1942 by Billie Holiday. Solanas's description of how SCUM covers the waterfront injects grit into the sentimental scene evoked by the melancholy love song. The fact that the movie took its title from an autobiography of a Pacific Coast waterfront beat reporter is, perhaps, relevant to Solanas's self-description as a "social propagandist."

16 Interestingly, Warhol then goes on to say that he got the idea from thinking that bees shit honey. Andy Warhol, *The Philosophy of Andy Warhol* (New York: Harcourt Brace Jovanovich, 1975), p. 146.

17 Warhol's example of the humorous and recyclable is an imagined outtake from an Esther Williams movie in which the girl who fails to jump off the swing becomes the star of her own recycled film.

18 According to the only source of information I have been able to find about Solanas after she was released from prison, Glenn S.'s "Valerie Solanas," Solanas was found dead on April 25, 1988 (by the landlord), in a rented motel room. "Cause of death: pneumonia" (p. 23).

MANDY MERCK
Figuring Out Andy Warhol

The resemblance of my title to D. A. Miller's monograph *Bringing Out Roland Barthes* is as fortunate as it was, originally, fortuitous. Miller's essay is perhaps best known for suffering the very extrusion of the homosexual hermeneutic which it regrets in Barthes's criticism. Commissioned as an introduction to the University of California Press's translation of *Incidents,* the posthumously published memoirs of the critic's cruising days in Morocco, *Bringing Out Roland Barthes* was ultimately brought out, but not bound with, its ostensible subject, at the insistence of the Barthes estate. Having now read this semidetached preface (literally tied to its text in an apparently unironic gesture of fetishistic disavowal), I am happy for Miller to introduce *my* remarks, since they, too, constitute an inquiry into the relation between a body of work and the practice of gay sexuality.

Nevertheless, the writing of Roland Barthes may seem a rather perverse place to start. Doesn't Miller himself acknowledge that "however intimately Barthes's writing proved its connection with gay sexuality, the link was so discreet,"[1] whereas Richard Dyer salutes Warhol as perhaps "the most famous openly gay artist who ever lived"?[2] Then again, Miller describes Barthes's "most invidiously written texts" as "phobically sacrific[ing] homosexuality-as-signified" while "happily cultivat[ing] homosexuality-as-signifier" (28), yet we know that the postmodernity of which Warhol is so celebrated an avatar has put an end to all such binary nonsense, indeed to semiotics itself: "The era of signs is rapidly fading. We have already entered the age of the figural," writes D. N. Rodowick in an essay whose epigraph concludes "Campbell, Campbell, Campbell, Campbell."[3]

So why bring up Miller's Barthes? Because, quite simply, Barthes's criticism is not the only one that might be accused of sacrificing to what Miller calls the "deity of general theory as fixed as ever in its white-male-heterosexual orientation" (28). Whether you endorse this Straight White Male characterization of Theory (and I'm not sure I do), the reproach is difficult to ignore on this occasion. For out as Warhol may have been, gay as *My Hustler, Lonesome Cowboys, Blow Job* may seem, his assumption to the postmodern pantheon has been a surprisingly straight ascent, if only in its stern detachment from any form of commentary that could be construed as remotely sexy.[4]

Thus, in typical terms, David James describes "the withdrawal of sensuality" from Warhol's early Pop paintings,[5] the lack of a "personal inflection" in his prints (60), the "draining" of "presence from his images of media personalities" (61), and their "flattening of fleshly or psychic depth" (61). And when he arrives at the films, this ascription of superficiality is matched by an appropriately abstract, almost taxonomic, rendition of their ostensible subjects: "marginal subcultures," "sexual deviants," "irregular sexual practices" (67).

So widespread is this account that it styles frankly gay criticism as much as its Straight White Male counterpart. The gay British critic Emmanuel Cooper's study of homosexuality and Western art tells the familiar tale of Warhol's "avoidance of 'content' in his graphic work" or of "any mysterious meaning of classical interpretation of his work."[6] This opens Cooper to the familiar problems of explaining the flagrantly homosexual imagery in Warhol's films, a difficulty resolved in equally familiar fashion by eliding signification with affect. Thus *Blow Job* is said to make the audience "a dispassionate voyeur, led to assume all but being given little explicit information." And this is followed by a description of Warhol himself, in his "life and friendships," avoiding "direct communication and the expression of feelings" (268).

Most surprising for a gay critic, Cooper assigns this antihermeneutical commitment to the figure of the drag queen, recycling in the process the oldest Holly Woodlawn line in the book. Replying to Geraldo's quizzing on his ABC show in 1976 "What are you? Are you a woman trapped in a man's body? Are you heterosexual? Are you homosexual? A transvestite? A transsexual?" Woodlawn answered, "But darling, what difference does it make as long as you look fabulous?" (268). Now Camille Paglia may dig out the same anecdote in defense of her disaffection with identity politics,[7] but it isn't difficult to demonstrate that drag does make a difference and that this difference is quite legible in Warhol's work.

Before offering such a reading, I want to turn back to an aesthetic precursor of Warhol, one whose representations of a very similar milieu were also recuperated, this time to modernism and *its* repudiation of "systems of significance."[8] The poet Frank O'Hara was no great friend of Warhol (like the onetime lovers Jasper Johns and Robert Rauschenberg, he loathed his notoriously "swish" demeanor), but he shared Warhol's involvement in the New York art world and its large homosexual constituency. A curator at the Museum of Modern Art and author of an influential study of Jackson Pollock, O'Hara (who once signed a letter "yours in action art") drew knowing comparisons between his poetry and the aesthetics of abstract expressionism: "Perhaps the obscurity comes in here, in the relationship between the surface and the meaning, but I like it that way since the one is the other (you have to use words) and I hope the poem to *be* the subject, not just about it."[9] Critics who took O'Hara at his word (and by the early 1970s, some years after his death and the posthumous publication of his collected poems, there were many) were nevertheless stuck with what Helen Vendler called "the sex poems": "We may regret the equableness and charm of our guide and wish him occasionally more Apollonian or more Dionysian (the sex poems aren't very good, though they try hard and are brave in their homosexual details), but there's no point wishing O'Hara other than he was" (20).

I am indebted for this review of O'Hara's criticism to Bruce Boone, whose pioneering study of 1979 (in the very first issue of *Social Text*)[10] set out to reconsider the poet's successive canonizations as a modernist, refusing "ideologies, causes and systems of significance" (Vendler, 9), and then as an early deconstructionist—presence "stripped of . . . ontological vestments, . . . without depth [and] underlying significance."[11]

Boone traces this "programmatic misinterpretation by euphemism" ("Gay Language," 72) to the understandings of camp represented by Susan Sontag's famous "Notes on 'Camp,'" in which the affection with which camp is said to behold human failings somehow sets it against any kind of engagement and, of course (after thirty years we should see this coming), *Against Interpretation.*[12] This might explain how critics could miss the patent elegy of O'Hara's famous "Lana Turner Has Collapsed," but how devoid are these lines of "significance"?

> Then too, the other day I was walking through a train
> with my suitcase and I overheard someone say "speaking of faggots"
> now isn't life difficult enough without that
> and why am I always carrying something
> well it was a shitty looking person anyway
> better a faggot than a farthead
> or as fathers have often said to friends of mine
> "better dead than a dope" "if I thought you were queer
> I'd kill you." (441–442)

It may be, as Boone concludes, that the "dominant group" (66) just don't get it ("it" being the flitty parataxis that here calls the speaker's manhood into question). Or, as I think more likely, since gay critics schooled in a certain tradition produce similar readings of Warhol, questions of sexuality—or, more precisely, questions of homosexuality—may simply not register in the discourses of chance, process, form, materials, distance, and disciplinary critique which articulated postwar criticism and then stimulated, and in a sense shrouded, the experiments of both the poet and the painter. Although this aesthetic would eventually spawn a second (left) and third (feminist) avant-garde, enlarging in the process to include both the aesthetic object and the class or gendered subject, it still clings to Warhol in something very like its original form.

What then of postmodernism's attempts to claim Warhol for its own concerns—the erosion of designation, dissolution of categories, loss of subjective coherence? One of the most influential investigations of these features, in contradistinction to those of high modernism, is Fredric Jameson's reading of Warhol's *Diamond Dust Shoes*. This 1980 series is of sufficient importance to Jameson's *Postmodernism* to provide both the volume's cover image (in color) and a central object of comparison (another painting by the same title in black and white). Jameson reads this second *Diamond Dust Shoes* (see figure 1) against one of Van Gogh's many shoe paintings, the 1887 *Pair of Boots*, which hangs in the Baltimore Museum of Art. One image is said to offer a place for the viewer, an initial content susceptible of painterly transformation, and a consequently hermeneutical project "in the sense in which the work in its inert, objectal form is taken as a clue or a sympton for

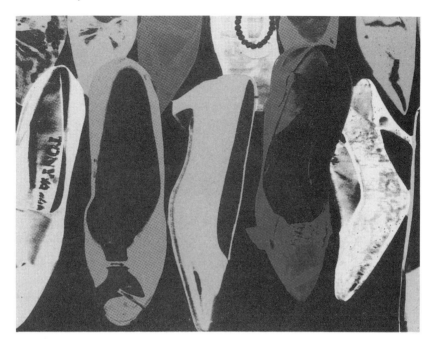

Figure 1. Andy Warhol, *Diamond Dust Shoes* (1980). ©1996 Andy Warhol
Foundation for the Visual Arts/ARS, New York.

some vaster reading which replaces it as its ultimate truth."[13] The other
image, Jameson argues, refuses "even a minimal place for the viewer" (8), as
well as any putative connection between its ostensible content and a social or
symbolic context. The first is said to accomplish a utopian transformation of
its "drab peasant object world" (7) through the vivid color of oil paints, the
second, to strip away any possible gloss from its potentially glamorous subject by reducing it to the ghostly black and white of a photographic negative.

In offering some footnotes to this very suggestive reading, I want to seize
on three important opportunities that it presents. The first is Jameson's Ben-
jaminian conviction that the extensive reproduction of the Van Gogh *Boots*
will reduce the painting to wallpaper unless its "initial situation" is reconstructed, "somehow mentally restored." And that "situation" (defined as both
content and raw material) is immediately identified with the hard life of the
peasantry: "the whole object world of agricultural misery" (7).

How does Jameson infer this world? In part, his subsequent remarks
suggest, through recalling other paintings by the artist, "backbreaking peas-

ant toil" (see, for example, *Women Picking Green Sprouts in the Snow*, 1890) and faces "worn down to skulls" (7), such as the 1885 *Potato Eaters*. But there is also a famous precedent for Jameson's description in Heidegger's discussion of "a well-known painting by Van Gogh" in *The Origin of the Work of Art*. Ironically, this account of a "pictorial representation" of "a pair of peasant shoes" begins by denying them any discernible context. "From Van Gogh's painting," Heidegger complains, "we cannot even tell where the shoes stand." The painting offers neither background nor ground of any kind— "not even clods of soil from the field or the field-path sticking to them." "And yet," in a remarkable turnabout, Heidegger suddenly takes off from a description of the "worn insides" and "rugged heaviness" of the shoes into an unabashed evocation of an exhausted peasant woman trudging across a windswept field on a winter's evening in an atmosphere charged with want, fear, and impending mortality.[14]

Heidegger's setting of this scene, which Jameson again describes as a "recreation" of a "whole missing object world" (8), takes us to his second point, the *work* of art. The philosopher's definition of art as "the setting-into-work of truth" (71), illustrated by a work of art said to be about work ("the toilsome tread of the worker," 33–34), is appropriated to Jameson's account of the shared materiality of agriculture and oil painting. But if this materiality participates in some "equipmental being" (34), the utility that Heidegger perceives in the Van Gogh boots, Warhol's shoes are deemed quite useless.

In the third of his observations, Jameson pronounces *Diamond Dust Shoes* mute ("I am tempted to say that it does not really speak to us at all"), ineffectual ("Nothing in this painting organizes even a minimal place for the viewer"), and lifeless ("a random collection of dead objects"). The accusation becomes one of fetishism, "in both the Freudian and Marxist senses," the latter alleging the shoes' commodified indifference to mere use value, the former consigning them to a perversion explicitly contrasted with Van Gogh's "heterosexual pair" (8). The citation for this final observation is Derrida's own commentary on Van Gogh in *The Truth in Painting*.[15]

Taking these three points in order, I want to ask whether Warhol's painting would necessarily resist the hermeneutical treatment that Heidegger and Jameson give Van Gogh's. Those who seek, for example, an "initial situation" for *Diamond Dust Shoes* will find a number of accounts. Bob Colacello maintains that the series began as an advertising assignment for the designer Halston:

Victor Hugo sent down a big box of various styles to be photographed for the ad campaign of Halston's shoe licensee, Garolini. Ronnie turned the box upside down and dumped the shoes out. Andy liked the way they looked spilled all over the floor. So he took a few Polaroids and had Ronnie take a lot more. The diamond-dust idea was stolen from Rupert Smith, who had been using the industrial-grade ground-up stones on some prints of his own. He was foolish enough to tell Andy where to buy it and foolish enough to be surprised when it turned up as Andy's art. "Oh, it fell on my painting and stuck," said Andy.

Warhol himself noted in his diary entry for July 24, 1980, "I'm doing shoes because I'm going back to my roots."[17] But which roots? The elegant shoe illustrations of his 1950s commercial art? Or the serigraph style of the 1960s? By 1979, when Warhol was commissioned to redo his best-known Pop paintings for the *Reversals* and *Retrospectives* series that accompanied his autobiography, *POPism,* his reconsideration of the latter movement was underway, culminating in the stripped-down post-Pop of another set of shoes, the black-and-white ads for the *Pumas* ("$24.99 pr.") and—shades of Van Gogh—*Work Boots* of the mid-1980s.

But if this return to footwear could allude to the graphic styles of two earlier eras, the jeweled appliqué of *Diamond Dust Shoes* was also very eighties, the 1980s of the deficit-funded Reagan budget (subject of a painted Warhol calculation c. 83–84), the infamous 1981 *Dollar Sign* series, and, most surprising, perhaps, the 1980 portrait of the German artist who would attend the *Dollar Sign* opening, the *Diamond Dust Joseph Beuys.* This diamanté tribute to the Marxist who employed "poor" materials and autographed deutsche marks with "Creativity = Capital," like Beuys' own portraits of Warhol from the same year, reflected their mutual interest in the exchange value of the artwork—and of the artist. (Warhol also did a diamond dust Georgia O'Keefe in 1980.) But while he agrees that Warhol's Coca Cola and Campbell's containers "explicitly foreground" this commodity fetishism, Jameson deems his shoes merely to *be* fetishes, stranded stand-ins for some unretrievable significance: "There is therefore in Warhol no way to complete the hermeneutic gesture and restore to these oddments that whole larger lived context of the dance hall or the ball, the world of jetset fashion or glamour magazines" (8–9).

Yet when we turn to another Warhol biography, not coincidentally titled

Loner at the Ball, we learn that in 1980 Warhol asked his assistant Rupert Smith (Rupert Smith of the diamond dust) to buy large quantities of shoes in the Jewish wholesale district where he lived. "They often had sidewalk sales," Smith recalled, "and one time I bought two thousand pairs of shoes for Andy; they were all really odd, either four quadruple A, petite little Cinderella feet, or they were Drag Queen shoes, size 13 quadruple D like Divine boats!"[18] (That's Divine with a big, indeed, quadruple D—the John Waters star.)

Now, if Jameson will allow Heidegger the "delirious dramaturgy"[19] of his reconstitution of the peasant scene, ("the loneliness of the field-path as evening falls . . . the silent call of the earth, its quiet gift of ripening grain" (*Postmodernism,* 34), I should be permitted to summon up the tackiness of a sidewalk display in the garment district, where outsized remnants of some previous year's fashions stand racked for wholesale, party pumps with bows and slingbacks, one shoe from each pair. Yet this remaindered footwear is also precious, dusted with diamonds, a jeweled allusion to Dorothy's ruby slippers and through their color and magical powers to Moira Shearer's *Red Shoes* and always, of course, to the glass four quads of that other "loner at the ball," another pair that get separated in the course of the story, leaving behind a lost lure for a pursuing prince or for Proustian remembrance. (Decades before *Diamond Dust Shoes,* Warhol moved from fashion illustration to fantasy with a series of jeweled shoes, drawings dressed with lace and gold leaf, ladies' shoes dedicated to the likes of Truman Capote and, yes, Judy Garland. One such print, the title page of a portfolio dated 1955, is headed "A la Recherche du Shoe *Perdu.*")[20]

Who would wear such shoes? Cinderella and the Drag Queen, Rupert Smith tells us, sizes four and thirteen, the ingenue and the ugly stepsister, femininity and masculinity, brought together by work. Of which, two venerable citations:

> I'm fascinated by boys who spend their lives trying to be complete girls, because they have to work so hard—double time, getting rid of all the tell-tale male signs and drawing in all the female signs. . . . It's very hard work. You can't take that away from them. It's hard work to look like the complete opposite of what nature made you and then to be an imitation of what was only a fantasy woman in the first place.

> When she takes off her shoes late in the evening, in deep but healthy fatigue, and reaches out for them again in the still dim dawn, or passes

them by on the day of rest, she knows all this without noticing or reflecting. The equipmental quality of the equipment consists indeed in its usefulness.

The first passage is from *The Philosophy of Andy Warhol.*[21] The second is from the philosophy of Martin Heidegger, the section of *The Origin of the Work of Art* which discusses Van Gogh's shoes (p. 34).

Heidegger's conviction that the wearer of these shoes is a peasant woman may be even more perverse than my assumption that Warhol's would be worn by a drag queen. As Derrida points out in his review of the dispute between the philosopher and the art historian Meyer Schapiro (who thought the shoes in the picture were Van Gogh's own), there is no way to ascertain the gender of their wearer or even, for that matter, whether Van Gogh's various paintings on the subject portray *pairs* of shoes at all (although Derrida does think the Baltimore image may be "perhaps a pair," 287). Resisting the temptation to restore the *Old Laced Shoes* in another Van Gogh painting to some unified bipedal subject, Derrida muses on the "strange, worrying, perhaps threatening and slightly diabolical" possibility of two *right* or two *left* shoes (265). And in a comparison of the earthy utility of Van Gogh's flats to the fetishist's single stiletto, he observes: "It is perhaps in order to exclude the question of a certain uselessness, or of a so-called perverse usage, that Heidegger and Schapiro denied themselves the slightest doubt as to the parity or pairedness of these two shoes" (333).

And what is the "perverse usage" to which the *Diamond Dust Shoes* will be put? Not the traditional purpose of the fetish proper, substitute for the woman's missing penis, but rather the dick's disguise, the equipment that some boys employ in the hard work of "trying to be complete girls." In this respect, as Derrida points out after Freud's observations on the bisexuality of dream images, the shoe is an ideal transitional object: "Could it be that, like a glove turned inside out, the shoe sometimes has the convex 'form' of the foot (penis), and sometimes the concave form enveloping the foot (vagina)?" (267).

Of course, the transvestite has often been named the central figure of Warhol's work, from Stephen Koch's 1973 positing of his drag queens as "the pivot of a conundrum about being and appearing"[22] to Jean Baudrillard's "Transpolitics, Transsexuality, Transaesthetics," in which he proposes War-

hol himself, "like Michael Jackson," as a postaesthetic "mutant": "an andro-
gyne of the new generation, a sort of mystical prosthesis or artificial machine
which delivered us from sex and aesthetics, thanks to its perfection."[23] True
to form, this deliverance is attributed to indifference—indifference not only
to aesthetic valuation (e.g., Warhol's famous declaration that "all art works
are beautiful") but to sex, as designation and as affect, "an indifferentiation
of sexual poles and an indifference to *jouissance,* that is to say, to sex as pleasure and joy" (19). Something like this is also suggested in Jameson's reading
of *Diamond Dust Shoes,* whose reversed-out photo negative is seen as a
"deathly" apparition, an intimation, indeed, of the "waning of affect in postmodern culture" (9–10).

I want to conclude these remarks with this specter, the same ghost that
Derrida claims to haunt Van Gogh's shoes, those foot-shaped supports of
some invisible wearer, explicit personifications, whose worn leather (unlike
wooden clogs) displays "*face-on . . .* individual traits, wrinkles" (370). Finally,
there's the painting's representation of the shoes, the "ghosting" that all pictures perform in doubling their subject.

In her reading of the 1963 horror film *The Haunting,* Patricia White describes a representational strategy that renders homosexuality as a haunting
invisibility, a "process whereby the apparition of lesbian desire is deferred
to manifestations of supernatural phenomena."[24] Diana Fuss takes up this
theme in her introduction to the collection in which White's essay appears,
noting its authors' "preoccupation with the figure of the homosexual as
specter and phantom, as spirit and revenant, as abject and undead."[25] The
ghost that haunts heterosexuality is its uncanny double, the illicit desire
necessary to define legitimacy. The liminality of this figure, as Fuss and
others have observed, reflects its ambiguity as a term of exclusion which
nonetheless confers interiority. If the term functions as a "negative image" for
the straight world, it is nevertheless not nothing, no more than a photographic negative is nothing. In a subsequent study, Terry Castle has invoked Freud's "On Negation" to argue that the homosexual phantom gains
entry to representation by virtue of its deniability: its ghostly appearance
allows the culture both to register and to refuse its existence.[26]

If we turn this "spectral analysis"[27] to shoes whose magic purpose may
be travesty, we find, as Teresa de Lauretis describes the butch-femme role-
playing in *She Must Be Seeing Things,* that they show "the uncanny distance,

like an effect of ghosting, between desire (heterosexually represented as it is) and the representation; and because the representation doesn't fit the actors who perform it, it only points to their investment in a fantasy."[28]

This doubling (of desire and its representation, girl and boy, straight and gay) is uncanny precisely because it refuses Baudrillard's transcendence. Drag fascinates in its simultaneous display of contradictory sexual meanings, not in their resolution or dispersal. It no more transcends gender than Michael Jackson's surgically altered appearance transcends race. Instead, we might describe cross-dressing, with Severo Sarduy, as "the coexistence, in a single body, of masculine and feminine signifiers: the tension, the repulsion, the antagonism which is created between them."[29]

In an analysis that exerts a powerful influence on Marjorie Garber's *Vested Interests*, Sarduy defines drag as "probably the best metaphor for what writing really is": sheer inscription, the mask without the face.[30] The opacity that renders it impossible to identify a true gender beneath the makeup and the mustache may also be discerned in Warhol's painting. Despite its "glacéd X-ray elegance" (in Jameson's evocative phrase, 9), it fails, unlike the shoe shop machines that irradiated American feet in the 1950s, to reveal the bare bones of the matter. We see only the shoes, glowing eerily in the dark. If, as Jameson argues, that "depthlessness" suggests a "mutation" in an object world "contaminated" by its contact with advertising, it does not divest it of meaning. Shoes are, after all, clothing, and clothing in art, as Derrida insists, is more than the fig leaf of form, draped over some material body. The irridescence of another man's clothes, for example, may alert the wary male spectator to the hazards of homosexual contamination.

By what I take to be coincidence, Baudrillard has christened the latest stage in the "microphysics of simulacra," that of the image in infinite series, as "the irradiated stage of value" (15). Here, too, the consequence of this "chain reaction" is disease, "a sort of epidemic of value, a general metastasis of value" (16). Baudrillard diagnoses this epidemic as the "diffraction" of meaning: "We cannot read ['works of art'] any longer; we can only decode them according to more and more contradictory criteria" (11). Yet, despite the centrifugal rhetoric ("physics," "particle," "acceleration," "trajectory"), his discourse turns inward, cohering in the all too legible figure of the drag queen. Transvestite or transsexual, this exquisite artifact is named the spirit of our age, since s/he fulfills the body's postmodern destiny: "to become a prosthesis" (20).

Shoes are clothing at its most prosthetic, not only reinforcing the feet but retaining their form, "ghost-limbs" in Derrida's description (266). They stand without us, but the pathos of their erection makes us want to fill them all the more. Thus our desire to restore Van Gogh's *Boots*, and indeed Warhol's *Shoes,* to some original owner. If this is impossible in any case—art being, as Heidegger finally concludes, "by nature an origin" (78)—it is doubly so in drag. The transvestite explicitly resists such restitution, defying its opposition of appearance to reality, phantom to flesh. How can you, s/he asks with withering contempt, even try to identify the original of an imitation of what was only a fantasy in the first place? (And as for the original of a *representation* of an imitation of what was only a fantasy . . .)

Like the drag queen, the copy without an original has become emblematic both for queer theory and for postmodernism. That isn't altogether surprising, since the first is closely related to the second, and both come equipped with a genealogy of contamination, mutation, and pathology. But neither is it a matter of indifference. Despite Baudrillard's best hopes for "the triumph of a medley of all erotic simulacra," this "topsy turvy" age is not yet upon us (20). The "epidemic" he writes of has not been a proliferation of competing (and therefore mutually nullifying) values but one of "signification"—the homophobic signification still hegemonically constructing AIDS.[31] (Witness Baudrillard's own embarrassing elision of drag, mutation, and disease.)

This is not to deny that *Diamond Dust Shoes* (silkscreen of a photographic negative of a commercial display) radiates seriality and simulation. The resemblance of these dozen shoes to one another (and to previous generations of the image) emphasizes an internal correspondence that abstracts the figure from the ground.[32] The consequential self-referentiality is indisputable, but not in a way that resists interpretation. On the contrary, the circuitry of reference, the simulacral shadows, disclose a very vivid specter, still waiting to be laid by postmodernity. In outing this figure, in ascribing significance to simulation, I offer you no deliverance, either from aesthetics or from sex.

NOTES

■

1   D. A. Miller, *Bringing Out Roland Barthes* (Berkeley: University of California Press, 1992), p. 6. Further page citations will be given in the text.

2   Richard Dyer, *Now You See It: Studies on Lesbian and Gay Film* (London: Routledge, 1990), p. 149.

3   D. N. Rodowick, "Reading the Figural," *Camera Obscura* 24 (1990): 10–15. The epigraph is from Michel Foucault, *This Is Not a Pipe* (Berkeley: University of California Press, 1983), p. 54.

4   Here, two incipient departures from this tradition should be saluted. In *The Optical Unconscious* (Cambridge: MIT Press, 1993), pp. 276–277, Rosalind Krauss acknowledges Warhol's urinary emulation of Jackson Pollock in his *Piss* and *Oxidation* paintings as golden showers, a "homosexual decoding of the drip technique" motivated by "the erotics of aggressive rivalry." And in *The Cinematic Body* (Minneapolis: University of Minnesota Press, 1993), p. 237, Steven Shaviro argues that Warhol's films, "by taking 'deviance' for granted—which, among other things, was a way of articulating a gay style in those pre-Stonewall days . . . drown the postmodern technologies of power in a sea of limitless approbation, in the perverse excesses of their own exercise."

5   David E. James, *Allegories of Cinema: American Film in the Sixties* (Princeton: Princeton University Press, 1989), p. 59. Further page citations will be given in the text.

6   Emmanuel Cooper, *The Sexual Perspective* (London: Routledge & Kegan Paul, 1986), p. 267. Further page citations will be given in the text.

7   Camille Paglia, "The M.I.T. Lecture," in *Sex, Art, and American Culture* (London: Viking, 1992), p. 277.

8   Helen Vendler, "The Virtues of the Alterable," *Parnassus* (Fall–Winter 1972): 9. Further page citations will be given in the text.

9   Frank O'Hara, *The Collected Poems of Frank O'Hara*, ed. Donald Allen (New York: Knopf, 1971), p. 497. Further page citations will be given in the text.

10 Bruce Boone, "Gay Language as Political Praxis: The Poetry of Frank O'Hara," *Social Text* 1 (Winter 1979): 70.

11 Charles Altieri, "The Significance of Frank O'Hara," *Iowa Review* 4 (Winter 1973): 90–104.

12 Susan Sontag, "Notes on 'Camp,'" in *Against Interpretation and Other Essays* (New York: Farrar, Straus and Giroux, 1966), pp. 291–292. In "Raiding the Icebox," in *Andy Warhol: Film Factory*, ed. Michael O'Pray (London: British Film Institute, 1989), Peter Wollen attempts to resolve the supposed opposition between Warhol's "minimalist aesthetic" and his "own voyeurism and love of sexual gossip" by the "literalism" of his early films, their "insistence on missing nothing, suppressing nothing" (25). Wollen also notes that the "Campbell" which Foucault repeats so mantrically at the end of *This Is Not a Pipe* can be deconstructed as "camp" and "belle" (27).

13 Fredric Jameson, *Postmodernism, or, The Cultural Logic of Late Capitalism* (Durham: Duke University Press, 1991), p. 8. Further page citations will be given in the text.

14 Martin Heidegger, "The Origin of the Work of Art," trans. Albert Hofstadter, in *Poetry, Language, Thought* (New York: Harper and Row, 1975), pp. 32–34. Further page citations will be given in the text.

15 Jacques Derrida, *The Truth in Painting*, trans. Geoff Bennington and Ian McLeod (Chicago: University of Chicago Press, 1987), pp. 255–382. Further page citations will be given in the text.

16 Bob Colacello, *Holy Terror: Andy Warhol Close Up* (New York: Harper Collins, 1990), p. 443.

17   Andy Warhol, *The Andy Warhol Diaries*, ed. Pat Hackett (New York: Warner Books, 1989), p. 306.

18   Fred Lawrence Guiles, *Loner at the Ball: The Life of Andy Warhol* (London: Black Swan, 1990), p. 354.

19   The phrase is Derrida's, who points out in *Truth in Painting*, pp. 272–273, that "the pathos of the 'call of the earth' . . . was not foreign" to the Nazi ideology of the 1930s.

20   Jesse Kornbluth, *Pre-Pop Warhol* (New York: Panache Press at Random House, 1988), p. 49.

21   Andy Warhol, *The Philosophy of Andy Warhol* (New York: Harcourt Brace Jovanovich, 1975), p. 54.

22   Stephen Koch, *Stargazer: Andy Warhol's World and His Films* (New York: Praeger, 1973), p. 122.

23   Jean Baudrillard, "Transpolitics, Transsexuality, Transaesthetics," in *Jean Baudrillard: The Disappearance of Art and Politics*, ed. William Stearns and William Chaloupka (New York: St. Martin's, 1992), p. 19. Further page citations will be given in the text.

24   Patricia White, "Female Spectator, Lesbian Specter: *The Haunting*," in *Inside/Out: Lesbian Theories, Gay Theories*, ed. Diana Fuss (New York: Routledge, 1991), p. 157. See also Tania Modleski, *Feminism without Women* (New York: Routledge, 1991), pp. 131–134, for a related reading of the aptly titled *Ghost.*

25   Diana Fuss, "Inside/Out," in *Inside/Out*, ed. Fuss, p. 3.

26   Terry Castle, *The Apparitional Lesbian* (New York: Columbia University Press, 1993), pp. 60–62.

27   Derrida, *Truth in Painting*, p. 373.

28   Teresa de Lauretis, "Film and the Visible," in *How Do I Look?* ed. Bad Object Choices (Seattle: Bay Press, 1991), p. 251.

29   Severo Sarduy, "Writing/Transvestism," *Review* 9 (Fall 1973): 33.

30   Severo Sarduy, ibid., cited in Marjorie Garber, *Vested Interests: Cross-Dressing and Cultural Anxiety* (New York: Routledge, 1992), p. 150. Sarduy's argument is also crucial to the "Warhol's Bodies" chapter of Steven Shaviro's *Cinematic Body*, pp. 227–229.

31   Paula Treichler, "AIDS, Homophobia, and Biomedical Discourse: An Epidemic of Signification," *Cultural Studies* 1, no. 3 (October 1987): 263–305.

32   "[F]igure rather than ground, figure as ground, and as the calling into question of the possibility of ground"; see Garber, *Vested Interests*, p. 150.

SASHA TORRES
The Caped Crusader of Camp:
Pop, Camp, and the *Batman* Television Series

n this essay, I explore the mutually appropriative relations between
"high" and "mass" culture in the sixties, through a reading of the deployment of the terms "Pop" and "camp" in the popular press reception
of the *Batman* television series. I take queerness to be the most important point of intersection in the cultural nexus I describe here; it energizes
not only the series but also the extensive public debates about the meanings
of the series and of Pop and camp.

To understand the density of these debates, it is crucial to recall the moment, in 1954, when Batman and Robin were "outed" by New York psychia-
trist Fredric Wertham. Wertham claimed, in a book called *Seduction of the
Innocent,* that the Batman comics depicted a gay relationship or, in his words,
represented "a wish-dream of homosexuals living together."[1] In "I Want to Be
a Sex Maniac," a chapter analyzing the effects of comics on the psychosexual
development of children, Wertham asserts that "only someone ignorant of
the fundamentals of psychiatry and of the psychopathology of sex can fail to
realize a subtle atmosphere of homoeroticism which pervades the adventures of the mature 'Batman' and his young friend 'Robin.' "[2]

As I argue at greater length elsewhere, Wertham's account has had consistently organizing effects on Batman representation ever since the mid-fifties,
because he managed, in his bumbling, homophobic way, to voice Batman
narrative's open secret: that the elements of Batman representation that invite speculation about Batman's sexuality are so deeply structuring of that
representation that they can't be excised.[3] The presence of Robin is the most
obvious but also the most expendable of these elements. More crucial in

continually reintroducing these questions of homo-hetero definition with respect to Batman are two foundational elements of all narratives about him: the originary and traumatic replacement of Bruce Wayne's heterosexual nuclear family with a series of all-male parenting relations, and the homologous relation between having a secret identity as a crime fighter and having a secret identity as a closeted homosexual.

Batman emerges in response to a familial tragedy that significantly disrupts both gender and sexual identity for Bruce Wayne; indeed, the Batman origin story, which has been reproduced obsessively throughout Batman's history, is most centrally about the status of gender and sexuality within these narratives.[4] Batman is born, we are told, the night young Bruce Wayne's parents are mugged. The thief wants Martha Wayne's necklace; her husband tries to intervene and is shot and killed. Martha Wayne calls for the police and is also shot. Bruce vows to bring their killer to justice and to fight "all criminals." Obviously, this is a story about the relative efficacy of the men within it: the mugger, Dr. Wayne, Bruce. Martha Wayne serves merely as the excuse for urban class warfare and male violence—both the violence of the mugger and the violent stupidity of her rich husband, who could presumably have afforded another necklace and kept them both alive. That this story is only about masculine agency is confirmed by the self-evidentness with which it presents Bruce Wayne's choice to become a vigilante crime fighter as a solution to the loss of his parents. For Bruce to have adopted a more private solution would have meant that he had missed the point of the story.

Because the insistent repetition of the origin story in Batman representation continually reinscribes the connection between Bruce Wayne's personal loss and his public career, it's important to specify what exactly gets lost in this scene. Crucially, this moment marks a shift, for Bruce, out of a heterosexual nuclear family in which traditional gender arrangements still obtain, to a male parenting configuration in which he is raised by Alfred, his butler. Bruce/Batman's crime fighting is motivated, therefore, not only by the child's anger at and fear of separation from his parents but also by nostalgia for the conventional versions of gender and sexuality that the nuclear family is supposed to install—and for the conventional version of heterosexual masculinity to which Bruce might have otherwise had relatively unproblematic access. Instead, given that this moment inaugurates Bruce/Batman's participation in a series of all-male families—not only Alfred with Bruce but also Bruce with his ward, Dick Grayson, and Batman with Robin—Bruce's masculinity and heterosexuality are inescapably compromised: in a culture that sees the nuclear family as the proper route to normative gender and sexual identity, Batman representation's insistence on these alternative familial configurations raises real questions about the possibility of straight masculinity for its characters.

Further, in its persistent play with secret identities, Batman narrative instantiates the structure Eve Kosofsky Sedgwick identifies, in the titular essay of *Epistemology of the Closet,* as "the distinctively indicative relation of homosexuality to wider mappings of secrecy and disclosure."[5] Indeed, since Bruce and Batman both encode a cultural stereotype of the male homosexual— Bruce is a fairy, and Batman is a secretive, hypermasculine character who spends a lot of time prowling city streets at night—the Bruce/Batman dyad is *itself* a figure for a gay couple, in which the ontological impossibility of their ever being in the same place at the same time recapitulates in extreme form the logic of the closet.[6] Even Mark Cotta Vaz, who wrote the DC-endorsed history of Batman for the fiftieth anniversary of the character, is forced to admit, in the chapter "The Loves of Batman," that Batman has often "inhibited the flowering of love" in Bruce Wayne's "romantic entanglements."[7] Batman performs such inhibition because he is the man to whom Bruce Wayne has a secret connection and because this connection fully structures Bruce's public and private lives.[8]

When Wertham opened the door to Batman's closet, the Batman industry panicked, going so far, in the early sixties, as to kill off Alfred the butler (to quash speculation about three adult men living together in Bruce Wayne's mansion) and to add Batwoman and Batgirl as appropriate heterosexual love interests for Batman and Robin. Given its post-Wertham timing, then, the *Batman* series, with its self-conscious appropriations of Pop and camp, has been read, by Batman fans and producers, as a major setback in the project of Batman's redemptive heterosexualization.[9]

In the rest of this essay I take up the oscillation of rumor and recuperation that the problem of Batman's sexual identity continually produces and ask what it has to do with the industrial practice that produces the television series and with the show's reception in the popular press. In particular, I will consider the ways in which "camp" and "Pop," as categories of taste and as codes for—rumors of—queerness, are deployed both by the series and by the larger cultural discourse that the series generated. And since the definitional

elusiveness of camp and Pop produces contortions and elisions in the popular discourses not unlike those evident in the academic debates about these
categories, I will revisit some of the latter as well.

II
■

On January 13, 1966, the *New York Times* ran an article covering some of the
local hoopla surrounding the premiere of the *Batman* television show. The
article, written by Val Adams and entitled "Discotheque Frug Party Heralds
Batman's Film and TV Premiere," makes clear how hard ABC, *Batman*'s network, was working to position the series to cash in on the capital—cultural
and otherwise—that Pop was so successfully attracting.[10] As Adams's lead
puts it, "An attempt to establish a Batman society whose primary function
would be to work for a high Nielsen rating was begun here last night by the
American Broadcasting Company." The "attempt" consisted of cocktails and
dancing at Harlow's and a bus ride to the York Theater to see the world premiere of *Batman,* commercials and all. Jackie Kennedy was invited but didn't
come. Harold Prince, Tammy Grimes, and Burgess Meredith did, though.
And, despite the fact that *Batman* owes more, visually, to Lichtenstein, "Andy
Warhol, the pop artist, was there." When the company reached the York, they
found "Batman drawings and stickers that said 'authentic pop art,'" but as
one observer remarked, "The real pop art are the people who are attending
this party."

  The *Times* leaves open the question of whether the Pop mavens at ABC
might have understood "authentic pop art" ironically. The article's own
stance, however, is clear with regard to *Batman*'s mass-cultural appropriation of Pop, a high-cultural style that appropriates mass culture. In noting
that "there was no applause when the world premiere of 'Batman' ended,"
whereas "guests in the theater cheered" at a cornflakes commercial, Adams
situates Pop's apparent celebration of consumer culture and ABC's crass pursuit of ratings on the same bat-continuum.[11] Awash in the fluidity Pop en-
courages among distinctions like art/commodity, art/television, and authen-
ticity/copy, Adams casts about for that category of taste pressed into service
by intellectuals or TV critics with high-cultural aspirations to solidify such
distinctions: camp. How else to read camp's cameo appearance here—" 'Bat-

man' has been around since the 1930's, but now ABC is out to make him the caped crusader of high camp"—than as the life preserver clutched by a drowning arbiter of mass culture discernment?

I allude to Andrew Ross's "Uses of Camp," in which he argues that "camp was . . . a defense against the decease of the traditional panoply of tastemaking powers which Pop's egalitarian mandate had threatened."[12] Contending that "for intellectuals, the espousal of Pop represented a direct affront to those who governed the boundaries of taste," because "Pop arose out of problematizing the question of *taste* itself," Ross situates camp as an elitist solution to the problems posed by Pop.[13] He further suggests that, by claiming to "discover" the American landscape of the everyday that Pop celebrated and by salvaging the artifacts of the throwaway culture Pop refigures and always itself risks becoming, "camp intellectuals" in the sixties tried to manage "Pop's commitment to the new and the everyday, to throwaway disposability, to images with an immediate impact but no transcendent sustaining power."[14]

In their discussion of the contemporary press garnered by *Batman*, Lynn Spigel and Henry Jenkins follow Ross's lead by situating camp as a reception strategy that allowed television critics and other arbiters of mass taste to manage Pop's disquieting self-alignment with precisely those elements of television which they had always disdained most.[15] Arguing that influential critics such as Jack Gould of the *New York Times* valued the "intimacy, immediacy and presence" of realist, live, Golden-Age drama, Spigel and Jenkins read Pop as rejecting these values in favor of "cartoonish characters, cheap industrial tools, gimmicky special effects, a flattened-out and exaggerated sense of color, repetitious imagery, and factory-like production."[16] For Spigel and Jenkins, Pop thus endorses precisely those elements of "television's dominant practice" with which sixties critics were most uncomfortable.[17] Even worse, they suggest:

> *Batman* precipitated a questioning of critical hierarchies because it self-consciously placed itself within the Pop art scene. While shows like *Bewitched, Mr. Ed* and *My Favorite Martian* stretched the limits of tv's realist aesthetic, *Batman* laughed in the face of realism, making it difficult for critics to dismiss the program as one more example of tv's puerile content. *Batman* presented these critics with the particularly chilling possibility that this childish text was really the ultimate in art circle chic.[18]

Figure 1. Video still, Batman (1966).

In Spigel and Jenkins's account, then, camp allowed critics another way to approach *Batman*. Referring to Newton Minow's 1961 influential assessment of U.S. television as a "vast wasteland," they contend that "the camp sensibility" afforded viewers "who had previously displayed disdain for mass culture" a comfortable distance from the show's comic book materials, because it reworked the aesthetics of Popism in a way more in line with the firmly entrenched " 'wasteland' critique."[19]

But if Ross, Spigel, and Jenkins read camp as a solution to the crisis of taste which Pop inaugurates, another *New York Times* article from January 1966 suggests that, given the history of Batman representation, "camp" raises as many problems for the makers of the series as it might solve. The article, an interview with *Batman* cast and crew by Judy Stone called "Caped Crusader of Camp," quotes series producer William Dozier as saying: "In Hollywood they're calling me the 'King of Camp.' I hate the word 'Camp.' It sounds so faggy and funsies."[20] Stone uses the problem of "camp," with its attendant (for Dozier, at least) associations with homosexuality, as the central organizing principle of this article, polling writers, producers, and actors for their reaction to reminders of the Caped Crusader's outing by Wertham. With the

exception of Lorenzo Semple, a writer for the series, who charmingly remarks that "on a very sophisticated level, [the show] is *highly* immoral,
because crime seems to be fun" (emphasis in original), most of those involved with the production blanch. But Ward, for example, responds testily
that "Batman and Robin represent the wish-dream to do good, to be a morally
good person. I don't think it's wrong to go out and catch crooks." And Dozier
replies "severely" that "I never saw anything like that in the comic book.
There will be no doubt on TV that Batman and Robin like girls, even though
they may be too busy fighting crime to have much time for them."

Dozier combats potentially contaminating insinuations about Batman's
sexual identity, insinuations for which camp serves as the most discursively
present code, by redefining the problem of the series as a problem of taste.
And, in a structure precisely the opposite of that suggested by Ross, Spigel,
and Jenkins, the solution to *this* problem is "Pop." For Dozier, the show's
appropriation of Pop is both a marketing mechanism and a way to circum-
vent Batman's associations with low culture and children's entertainment. As
a marketing mechanism, Pop allows *Batman* to bridge the gap between children and adult viewers or, in the words of the *Times*, "to transform the comic
into the number one TV choice of everyone from the milk to the martini set."
As Stone puts it, Dozier "decided to apply the pop art technique of the
exaggerated cliché, laying it on to the point where it becomes amusing to
adults." Simultaneously, Dozier is able to align Pop's *cachet* high cultural
with his high-concept programming *coup* and thus explain away the apparent disparity between his past work, as a producer of "quality television" like
Playhouse 90, Studio One, and *You Are There,* and his current endeavor. As
Stone informs us, Dozier "was stupefied when ABC asked him to develop the
program." Stupefied, presumably, because of the distance between the high
seriousness of Golden-Age drama and this bit of kiddie fluff, *Batman.* Thus,
as a synecdoche for adult, even avant-garde taste, "Pop" performs multiple
functions here: it allows Dozier to define, and thus promote, his crossover
programming strategy; it grants him distance from his ephemeral material;
and it diverts, if only momentarily, the course of Judy Stone and her readers
toward the dangerous territory of "camp."[21]

The first lesson to be learned from Stone's article is that Pop and camp bear
multiple relations to each other in the public discourse of the period and that
any account of camp's "management" of Pop is insufficient to describe the
richness and multiplicity of these relations. As Dozier's rhetorical two-step

suggests, each was potentially unsettling, and under the right conditions, each had the capacity to assuage some of what was troubling about the other. But in several other 1966 discussions of *Batman,* the two terms appear to be so closely linked as to be almost synonymous with each other. Shana Alexander (remember her?), for example, included "High Camp and Low Camp, pop art and op art" as part of a long list of reasons she wouldn't ordinarily watch *Batman.*[22] Robert Terwilliger, an Episcopalian minister whose reading of Batman as a "messianic" figure received enough attention to be written up in the *New York Times* twice, said in his well-covered sermon that camp, "this elusive, undefinable 'in' term, signifies a new 'Pop' aestheticism."[23] In *Life,* Tom Prideux suggested that "Pop art and the cult of camp have turned Superman and Batman into members of the intellectual community."[24] *Time* called camp "a sort of tongue-in-cheek philosophy of pop culture" and hinted that "there is . . . every expectation that grown men will be showing up at Andy Warhol's next party dressed like the Batman."[25] And in Jack Gould's review of the series, camp and Pop collapse into each other completely: "The point about 'Batman,' of course, is that the show has been construed as a belated extension of the phenomenon of pop art to the television medium. And contrary to the mournful misgivings of some who felt this act was a ghastly affront to culture, it could be an unseen blessing of major proportions." A "blessing" because what Gould calls "non-events in the arts"—which I take to be a reference to Pop and particularly to Warhol, who is mentioned in this article's lead—have succeeded because they have been "shielded against overexposure." Surrounded by enormous publicity, Batman will perform a service because, as Gould puts it, "the only way to eradicate a non-event is to let it wear everybody out." But his next sentences make clear that for Gould, camp is of a piece with Pop, not an antidote to it: "The secret answer to camp is exhaustion, not protest. 'Batman' promises to be a real help."[26]

Warhol keeps showing up in this discourse, not only because commentators may have been familiar with his own forays into Batman representation—particularly in the 1964 film *Batman Dracula,* on which he collaborated with Jack Smith and which mined the homoerotic resources of these legends, featuring walk-ons in aluminum foil–covered jockstraps—but also because the popular press knew in 1966 what is elided by the determination of later commentators to situate Pop and camp in opposition: that Warhol's work, an important engine of Pop's development, was during this period as deeply informed by the styles and sensibilities of camp practice as it was by the

Figure 2. Video still, Batman (1966).

acuity of his reading of commodity culture. His work thoroughly articulated this relation by this point. Think, for example, of the collation of glamour, power, and death to be found in the early *Marilyns* (1962) and in *Sixteen Jackies* (1964). Or think of his refiguration of the pin-up boy at about the same time (for example *Troy Donahue* in 1962). The imbrications of Pop and camp, of which Warhol's work during the early- to mid-sixties reminds us, brings me to the second lesson to be learned from Stone's article, a lesson having to do more specifically with camp.

Dozier's phobic defense against the *word* "camp," let alone the attendant chain of associations that suggests itself so easily even to the readers of the *New York Times,* should remind us that the failure—or refusal—to really theorize the queer valences of camp's history, to understand the thorough-going and persistent connection, in the everyday "uses" of the term, between camp and gay subcultural tastes, performances, and persons, is a very basic conceptual failure: it is the failure to account for the complexities of the interface between subcultural style and its more "mainstream" appropria-tions. More specifically it is the failure—or refusal—to ask fairly obvious historical questions about the role of gay taste not only in the important political and artistic moments of the sixties counterculture, like Pop, but also in the mass-cultural popularizations and cannibalizations of those moments, like *Batman*. And this failure—or refusal—is rendered all the more perplexing—or suspicious—by camp's unrelenting presence as the key modifier in accounts of the *Batman* series, since Batman representation, in the wake of Wertham's scandalous accusations, has been organized not only by the generic obsessions that are the superhero's stock in trade—the promise of technology, the limits of masculine agency, the role of the vigilante in the ideology of law and order—but also by the difficulties of managing the question of homo-hetero definition that Batman continually begs.

This failure is, of course, as old as Susan Sontag's "Notes on 'Camp,'" with its bland assurance that

> even though homosexuals have been its vanguard, Camp taste is *much more than* homosexual taste. Obviously, its metaphor of life as theater is peculiarly suited as a justification and projection of a certain aspect of the situation of homosexuals. (The Camp insistence on not being "serious," on playing, also connects with the homosexual's desire to remain youthful.) *Yet one feels that if homosexuals hadn't more or less invented Camp, someone else would.*[27]

D. A. Miller has characterized this moment as "that unblinking embrace of counterfactuality" that allows Sontag to imagine that she herself might have invented camp, and indeed, Miller is perfectly right to remind us, in his reading of this passage, of the opening of Sontag's essay, in which she "justified her phobic de-homosexualization of Camp as the necessary condition for any intelligent discourse on the subject."[28] In Sontag's by-now-infamous formulation:

> I am strongly drawn to Camp, and almost as strongly offended by it. That is why I want to talk about it, and why I can. For no one who wholeheartedly shares in a given sensibility can analyze it; he can only, whatever his intention, exhibit it. To name a sensibility, to draw its contours and to recount its history, requires a deep sympathy modified by revulsion.[29]

Though I certainly share *Miller*'s revulsion, I am less interested in Sontag's reinscription of herself as camp's inventor than I am in what that reinscription prevents her from theorizing. That is, I am less concerned with why she might make recourse to the counterfactual than in what the effects of that recourse might be. It seems to me that Sontag's de-gaying of camp itself *performs* what it most crucially fails to *explain*. Even as she enacts the straight appropriation of camp with her assertion that "Camp taste is much more than homosexual taste," she renders invisible the most interesting and elusive thing about camp: its placement at the borderlines of gay and non-gay taste. In this regard, it becomes possible to read Sontag's refusal of the essay form—a form that might require her actually to argue her assertions—in favor of "jottings," as another way in which this writing anticipates, formally, the seemingly-haphazard processes of non-gay appropriations of camp, processes this essay inaugurates and makes possible, even as it tries to make them theoretically irrelevant.[30]

Though Ross makes more conceptual room than Sontag does for gay camp as part of the range of "uses" to which camp was put in the sixties, he, too, fails to chart the articulations of gay uses with those of others. As I have suggested, Ross is most interested, in this essay, in situating camp's effectivity for intellectuals challenged by Pop's assault on categories of taste. But in his discussion of gay camp, Ross admits that "unlike the histories of Pop and camp which I have discussed, the gay camp fascination with Hollywood had much less to do with transformations of taste. In its pre-Stonewall heyday . . . [i]t was part of a survivalist culture which found, in certain fantasmatic elements of film culture, a way of imaginatively communicating its common conquest of everyday oppression."[31] The question Ross entertains, in his final section on Warhol, but declines, finally, to answer is what difference these two "uses of camp" might have made for each other.[32]

This problem of how to understand camp's placement at the intersections of gay and non-gay style during the period of *Batman*'s production is solved no more satisfyingly, alas, by Andy Medhurst's explicitly gay-affirmative reading of Batman, "Batman, Deviance, and Camp."[33] Medhurst, in "offer[ing] a gay reading of the whole Bat-business," usefully traces the history of attempts by the producers of Batman narrative to close down the questions about Batman's sexuality that have been opened up by readers such as Wertham. But his attention to the definitional constraints imposed by the larger homophobic markets in which Batman narrative circulates stops short when he discusses the TV series. Medhurst claims that the televisual *Batman*, produced during what he calls "the decade in which camp swished out of the ghetto and up into the scarcely prepared mainstream," was an example of what Sontag would call "deliberate camp": according to Medhurst, it "employed the codes of camp in an unusually public and heavily signalled way."[34] By camp, Medhurst clearly means gay camp. Alongside the show's parodic hyperseriousness, that is, Medhurst discerns more or less explicit, if "joking," reference to Batman and Robin's "relationship":

> The Batman/Robin relationship is never referred to directly; more fun can be had by presenting it "straight," in other words, screamingly camp. Wertham's reading of the Dubious Duo had been so extensively aired as to pass into the general consciousness, it was part of the fabric of Batman, and the makers of the TV series proceeded accordingly.[35]

As evidence for this claim, Medhurst offers canny readings of several episodes, including one guest-starring Tallulah Bankhead as the Black Widow. As Medhurst puts it:

> Best of all, and Bankhead isn't even in this scene but the thrill of having her involved clearly spurred the writer to new heights of camp, Batman has to sing a song to break free of the Black Widow's spell. Does he choose to sing "God Bless America?" Nothing so rugged. He clutches a flower to his Bat chest and sings Gilbert and Sullivan's "I'm Just Little Buttercup."[36]

Now, however convincing one finds Medhurst's account of this particular episode, it still begs the larger question of what the producers of the series might have been up to when they broadcast this show—and others—to what Medhurst himself calls "the scarcely prepared mainstream." It is telling that Medhurst goes right from a direct assertion of the producers' camp intentions to the texts of the program itself, rather than, say, to any of the many statements those producers made to the press during the series' run. Many of those statements gleefully use the term "camp," but none of them, except for the Judy Stone interview I've quoted, situates camp's gay associations in relation to Batman's post-Wertham history.

But I do find Medhurst's readings convincing, and so the question—the same question I've been asking about camp's interstitial status, now posed in a more specific form—becomes, Why would the makers of the *Batman* series risk self-consciously deploying the codes and icons of gay camp in the context of their massively popular network TV show? The answer, I think, lies in all those other, "straight" responses to the show, which talk about the show as camp but which have in mind definitions of the term very different from Medhurst's, definitions that have little to do with gay subcultures. In the public discourses generated by *Batman,* camp is defined variously as "nostalgic";[37] as that which brings forth "accumulations of debris from the recent past . . . to be admired, reproduced and treasured";[38] as "tongue in cheek";[39] as "involv[ing] a wry sophistication";[40] as "a sneering fake enthusiasm for whatever is pretentious and not quite successful": as "contempt set in code";[41] and, most often, as that which "decrees that anything that is really bad must be awfully good."[42]

Even if we entertain the characterization of camp as "so bad it's good" as a denseley encoded (and widely and unself-consciously circulated) reference to gay identifications and practices, the range of connotative associations *Batman* discourse generated about camp—from "faggy and funsies" to "nostalgic" to "contempt set in code"—is still sufficiently wide as to suggest that it was precisely the term's ambiguity that made it attractive to the show's producers. "Camp" was a way for them both to shut down and to open up Batman's gayness, a way for them both to dispense with Batman's history and to realize its potential in an unprecedented way. Camp was paradoxically useful in effacing popular memory of Wertham's reading of Batman because, in the wake of Sontag's account, it was going through the same de-gaying that Batman was, saddled—as he was in the early sixties—with the tiresome Batwoman and Batgirl. Camp thus serves as a perfectly condensed marker for the simultaneous admission and denial of Batman's queerness. But, of course, the makers of the series were also unable to purge camp of its connotative associations with gay culture. And there is some evidence to suggest that they didn't want to: Adam West (who played Batman) quips in the Stone article that "with the number of homosexuals in this country, if we get that audience, fine. Just add 'em to the Nielsen ratings." It would be a mistake, I think, to discount this joke, because I suspect that *Batman* succeeded quite well in garnering a gay audience and because West's off-the-cowl remark is on to something crucial about Batman and about sixties television: in voicing this "hypothetical" appeal to a gay audience, West, I suggest, demonstrates an almost uncanny connection to the mass-cultural zeitgeist and actually manages to identify the *Batman* series with what was most pleasurable about both.

A lot of the pleasure Batman offers his consumers—gay and straight, male and female—comes precisely from his sexual undecidability. Arguably, Batman narrative's oblique articulation of questions about gender and sexuality has at least contributed to—if not constituted—the character's enduring appeal. As evidence in favor of this hypothesis, I submit Dick Giordano's recollections of his childhood encounters with the early Batman. Giordano, vice president of DC Comics (the division of Warner Communications that publishes Batman comics) and a former editor and illustrator of Batman stories, describes these encounters in the introduction to *The Greatest Batman Stories Ever Told:*

> There were many . . . elements that added to the appeal of the character—his alter ego Bruce Wayne being rich and pretending to be an ineffectual playboy was part of the fun. I felt like an "insider" when I saw Bruce acting silly at a party because I knew he was The Batman and before long he would put aside his foppish ways, don cape and cowl and bring the bad guys to justice, returning to the role of useless playboy before the story ended.[43]

Giordano suggests that the "fun" of reading Batman comics lay in charting Bruce Wayne/Batman's dichotomous, contradictory relation to heterosexual masculinity; his description of Bruce—"foppish," "ineffectual," "useless"—evokes both femininity and effeminacy, while Batman represents pure masculine effectivity, "bringing the bad guys to justice." The pleasure Giordano depicts in this passage seems to come not only from identifying these differing relations to hegemonic masculinity and sexuality but also, and perhaps more important, from seeing them coexist in the same person. Bruce/Batman, as Giordano describes him, enables a fantasy of being at once passive and active, silly and serious, leisured and hardworking, feminine and masculine, gay and straight—with the latter term always comfortingly available to recuperate the former.

And a lot of the pleasure sixties television offers its consumers—gay and straight, male and female—comes from its covert critiques of life in the suburban nuclear family. This was, after all, the moment in which television gave us the anti-familial grousing of Samantha Stevens's mother, Endora, and the grim and pathetic attempts at suburban assimilation by poor old Herman Munster.[44] And it wasn't unprecedented for such critiques to be aligned with gay-coded characters. *Batman* actually aired opposite *Lost in Space*, which, as you surely recall, featured the unrelentingly savage commentary of "Dr.

Smith," forced to spend his foreseeable future marooned on another planet with a nice nuclear family that might, under other circumstances, have lived out their days quite happily next door to Ward and June Cleaver.[45] I like to imagine that it might have been difficult, in those days before the VCR, for some viewers, those who belonged to the community whose idiom *Lost in Space* and *Batman* borrowed, to choose between them.

The *Batman* series understood these simple truths about the enduring appeal of its source material and the emergent pleasures of its medium. The circulation of camp's gay meanings allowed its producers to mine the resources of both, and its straight flow allowed them to cash in—almost—without risk.

NOTES

∎

I am grateful to Siobhan Burns for research assistance and to Michèle Barale, Judith Frank, Annelise Orleck, Eve Kosofsky Sedgwick, and the editors of this volume for their comments on earlier drafts of this essay.

1   Fredric Wertham, *Seduction of the Innocent* (New York: Rinehart, 1954), 190. Wertham's larger agenda was to link comics to juvenile delinquency; his book participated in growing national hysteria about comics' effects on their readers, hysteria which prompted Senate hearings and industry self-censorship (in the form of the "Comics Code Authority") and which prefigured the Dodd committee's congressional hearings in the early sixties on the relation between television and juvenile delinquency. Wertham's rantings, in other words, lassoed Batman representation for the first time, but not the last, into the arena in which the meanings and functions of childhood, and especially of children's sexuality, are contested. On the comics scare, see James Gilbert, *A Cycle of Outrage: America's Reaction to the Juvenile Delinquent in the 1950s* (New York: Oxford University Press, 1986); and Jed Rasula, "Nietzsche in the Nursery: Naive Classics and Surrogate Parents in Postwar American Cultural Debates," *Representations* 29 (Winter 1990): 50–77. These concerns about Batman's effects on children were revived and widely circulated in strikingly similar form in relation to the television series. See, for example, Eda LeShan, "At War with Batman," *New York Times Magazine,* May 15, 1966, p. 112. She writes, "If camp involves a wry sophistication, an adult grasp of subtleties in language and point of view, does it matter that children watching this program take it absolutely literally?" LeShan's claims that viewing *Batman* produced particularly violent play in children she observed, because the children were unable to distinguish between "real" and "camp" violence, serves as a cover, I think, for other fears about *Batman's* possible production of queer children. LeShan is more deeply worried, I think, that children might *understand* camp than she is that they might not. For responses to LeShan's article, see "Letters," *New York Times Magazine,* May 29, 1966, and June 5, 1966.

2   Ibid.

3   Sasha Torres, "Television, Homosexuality, and the History of Batman," unpublished essay.

4   The origin story was first disseminated in November 1939 in *Detective #33*. More recent versions appear in Tim Burton's 1989 film, *Batman,* and in the following, all published by DC Comics: *The Dark Night Returns,* story and pencils by Frank Miller, inks by Klaus Janson and Frank Miller, colors by Lynn Varley (1986); *Batman: Year One,* written by Frank Miller, illustrated by David Mazzucchelli, colored by Richmond Lewis (1988): *Arkham Asylum,* written by Grant Morrison, illustrated by Dave McKean (1989); and *Gotham by Gaslight,* written by Brian Augustyn, pencils by Michael Mignola, inks by P. Craig Russell, coloring by David Hornung (1989).

5   Eve Kosofsky Sedgwick, *Epistemology of the Closet* (Berkeley: University of California Press, 1990), p. 71.

6   I owe this formulation to Jeff Nunokawa.

7   Mark Cotta Vaz, *Tales of the Dark Knight* (New York: Ballantine, 1989), p. 125.

8   Most of the other comic book superheroes also lead secret double lives; if we assume, with Sedgwick, that closetedness of any kind always contains within it at least an allusion to problems of homo/hetero definition, then Superman, the Green Hornet, and others might also be read along the lines I read Batman here. But I think that Batman narrative is particularly available to such reading (that is, perhaps more so that the others), both because of the persistence of the Robin function and because of the determining effects that Wertham's account of Batman had on subsequent visions of the character.

9   See Vaz, *Tales of the Dark Knight,* for one version of how this narrative tends to go. In "Television, Homosexuality, and the History of Batman," I read at length the two major interpretations of Batman produced in the eighties—Frank Miller's 1986 graphic novel, *The Dark Knight Returns,* and Tim Burton's 1989 film, *Batman*—arguing that the hostility to television manifest in both these texts simultaneously inscribes and displaces a more specific animosity, that toward the *Batman* series and its queering of the Caped Crusader. The violent remasculinization of Batman that takes place in both these representations is thus also a violently homophobic attempt to de-gay the character.

10 Val Adams, "Discotheque Frug Party Heralds Batman's Film and TV Premiere," *New York Times,* January 13, 1966, p. 79. Andrew J. Edelstein notes that the Batman industry's efforts to appropriate Pop might be discerned in the comics as well as in the television series: "In the mid-'60s *Batman* comic book, one panel said 'At the Gotham City Museum, Bruce Wayne, millionaire sportsman and playboy, and young ward Dick Grayson attend a sensational "Pop Art" show.'" *The Pop Sixties* (New York: World Almanac Publications, 1985), p. 188.

11 Adams here anticipates Christin J. Mamiya's argument that "the [Pop Art] movement not only appropriated the images and strategies from consumer culture but also was itself absorbed into the established institutional matrix, thereby rendering it ineffective as a critique and neutralizing any potential for bringing about significant change." Mamiya, *Pop Art and Consumer Culture: American Super Market* (Austin: University of Texas Press, 1992), p. 4.

12 Andrew Ross, "Uses of Camp," in *No Respect: Intellectuals and Popular Culture* (New York: Routledge, 1989), p. 152.

13 Ibid., p. 149.

14 Ibid.

15 Lynn Spigel and Henry Jenkins, "Same Bat Channel, Different Bat Times: Mass Culture and Popular Memory," in *The Many Lives of the Batman: Critical Approaches to a Superhero and His Media,* ed. Roberta E. Pearson and William Uricchio (New York: Routledge, 1991), pp. 117–146.

16 Ibid., pp. 121 and 122.

17 Ibid., p. 122.

18 Ibid., p. 123.

19 Ibid., p. 124. Newton Minow, FCC chairman under Kennedy, gave the "vast wasteland" speech to the National Association of Broadcasters in 1961. As Spigel and Jenkins remind us, "Minow's reform plans centered around the aesthetic hierarchies of the Golden Age critics, calling for more reality-based, educational programs, and fewer game shows, sitcoms, and westerns" (122). See also William Boddy, *Fifties Television: The Industry and Its Critics* (Champaign: University of Illinois Press, 1990).

20 Judy Stone, "The Caped Crusader of Camp," *New York Times,* January 9, 1966, sec. 2, p. 15.

21 If Pop served for Dozier at this point in *Batman's* publicity cycle as the counter to the series' childishness, it is important to recognize that precisely this role was later filled by camp. This is, camp came to serve as the crucial mechanism by which the show's dual address to children and adults was both assured and managed: formulations like "To the kids it's real, to the adults it's camp" were repeated so often in the popular press that they became a kind of public interpretive mantra. To chart the development of this explanatory tic, see, for example, the following: "Holy Flypaper," *Time,* January 28, 1966, p. 61; Shana Alexander, "Don't Change a Hair for Me, Batman," *Life,* February 4, 1966, p. 21; Paul E. Cuneo, "Of Many Things," *America,* May 7, 1966, p. 635; LeShan, "At War with Batman," p. 112; Howard Thompson, "TV Heroes Stay Long," *New York Times,* August 25, 1966, p. 42; M. Conrad Hyers, "Batman and the Comic Profanation of the Sacred," *Christian Century,* October 18, 1967, p. 1322; and "Holy Cancellation," *Newsweek,* February 5, 1968, p. 84.

22 Alexander, "Don't Change a Hair," p. 21.

23 Robert E. Terwilliger, "The Theology of Batman," *Catholic World,* November 1966, p. 127.

24 Tom Prideux, "The Whole Country Goes Superman," *Life,* March 11, 1966, p. 23.

25 "Holy Flypaper," p. 61.

26 Jack Gould, "Too Good to Be Camp," *New York Times,* January 23, 1966, sec. 2, p. 17.

27 Susan Sontag, "Notes on 'Camp,'" in *Against Interpretation and Other Essays* (New York: Farrar, Straus and Giroux, 1966), p. 262; emphases mine.

28 D. A. Miller, "Sontag's Urbanity," *October* 49 (Summer 1989): 93.

29 Sontag, "Notes on 'Camp,'" p. 278.

30 Sontag writes: "To snare a sensibility in words, especially one that is alive and powerful, one must be tentative and nimble. The form of jottings, rather than an essay (with its claim to a linear, consecutive argument) seemed more appropriate for getting down something of this particular *fugitive* sensibility" (ibid.; emphasis mine).

31 Ross, "Uses of Camp," 157.

32 This question is begged as well by Philip Core's suggestion that "camp was a prison for an illegal minority; now it is a holiday for consenting adults." What happened, exactly, to

make that insouciant semicolon possible? Core, *Camp: The Lie That Tells Its Truth* (New York: Delilah, 1984), p. 7.

33   Andy Medhurst, "Batman, Deviance, and Camp," in *Many Lives of the Batman,* ed. Pearson and Urrichio, pp. 149–163.

34   Sontag, "Notes on 'Camp,' " p. 283; ibid., p. 155.

35   Medhurst, "Batman, Deviance, and Camp," pp. 156–157.

36   Ibid., p. 158.

37   Terwilliger, "Theology of Batman," p. 127.

38   Cuneo, "Of Many Things," p. 635.

39   Goodman Ace, "The Second Caesarian," *Saturday Review,* February 12, 1966, p. 8.

40   LeShan, "At War with Batman," p. 112.

41   John Skow, "Has TV—Gasp!—Gone Batty?" *Saturday Evening Post,* May 7, 1966, p. 12.

42   "Holy Flypaper," p. 61.

43   Dick Giordano, *The Greatest Batman Stories Ever Told* (New York: DC Comics, 1988), p. 9.

44   See Lynn Spigel, "From Domestic Space to Outer Space: The 1960s Fantastic Family Sit-com," in *Close Encounters: Film, Feminism, and Science Fiction,* ed. Constance Penley et al. (Minneapolis: University of Minnesota Press, 1991), pp. 205–235. Spigel argues that "fantastic family sit-coms," like *Bewitched, I Dream of Jeannie,* and *The Munsters,* voiced, with other popular media of the period, widespread disillusionment with the suburban ideal that had been promoted by earlier sitcoms such as *Leave It to Beaver* and *The Donna Reed Show. Batman,* which aired from 1966 to 1968, appeared just as the suburban family sitcoms disappeared. The fantastic family subgenre, which had begun to gain ground in the early part of the decade, was well on its way to being the hegemonic sitcom form by 1966.

45   I am indebted here to Jeff Nunokawa's discussion of Dr. Smith in "The Sun Always Shines on TV: Television Culture and the Resistance to Patriarchy in Margaret Atwood's *The Handmaid's Tale,*" paper presented at the Modern Language Association Conference, Washington, D.C., 1989.

BIBLIOGRAPHY

Ace, Goodman. "The Second Caesarian." *Saturday Review,* February 12, 1966.

Acker, Kathy. "Blue Valentine." In *Andy Warhol: Film Factory.* Ed. Michael O'Pray. London: British Film Institute, 1989.

Adams, Val. "Discotheque Frug Party Heralds Batman's Film and TV Premiere." *New York Times,* January 13, 1966.

Alexander, Shana. "Don't Change a Hair for Me, Batman." *Life,* February 4, 1966.

Althusser, Louis. *Lenin and Marxism and Other Essays.* Trans. Ben Brewster. New York: Monthly Review, 1971.

Altieri, Charles. "The Significance of Frank O'Hara." *Iowa Review* 4 (Winter 1973).

Anfam, David. "Handy Andy." *Art History* 14, no. 2 (June 1991): 270–273.

Angel, Callie. *The Films of Andy Warhol: Part 2.* New York: Whitney Museum of American Art, 1994.

Arendt, Hannah. *The Human Condition.* Chicago: University of Chicago Press, 1958.

Arthur, Paul. "Routines of Emancipation: Alternative Cinema in the Ideology and Politics of the Sixties." In *To Free the Cinema: Jonas Mekas and the New York Underground.* Ed. David E. James. Princeton: Princeton University Press, 1992.

Atkinson, Ti-Grace. *Amazon Odyssey.* New York: Links Books, 1974.

Atwell, Lee. "Homosexual Themes in the Cinema." *Tangents* (Los Angeles), March 1966.

Bangs, Lester. *Psychotic Reactions and Carburetor Dung.* New York: Vintage, 1988.

Baudrillard, Jean. *Simulations.* New York: Semiotext(e), 1983.

———. *Revenge of the Crystal: Selected Writings on the Modern Object and Its Destiny, 1968–1983.* Ed. and trans. Paul Foss and Julian Pefanis. Sydney, Australia: Pluto Press, 1990.

———. "Transpolitics, Transsexuality, Transaesthetics." In *Jean Baudrillard: The Disappearance of Art and Politics.* Ed. William Stearns and William Chaloupka. New York: St. Martin's, 1992.

Benjamin, Walter. *Illuminations.* New York: Schocken, 1969.

———. *Charles Baudelaire: A Lyric Poet in the Era of High Capitalism.* Trans. Harry Zohn. London: NLB, 1973.

———. "A Short History of Photography." In *One Way Street and Other Writings.* With an introduction by Susan Sontag. Trans. Edmund Jephcott and Kingsley Shorter. London: NLB, 1979.

Berger, John. *Ways of Seeing*. London: BBC and Penguin Books, 1972.

Bergler, Edmund. "Homosexuality and the Kinsey Report." In *The Homosexuals: As Seen by Themselves and Thirty Authorities*. Ed. A. M. Krich. New York: Citadel, 1958.

Berlant, Lauren. "National Brands/National Bodies: *Imitation of Life*." In *Comparative American Identities: Race, Sex, and Nationality in the Modern Text*. Ed. Hortense Spillers. New York: Routledge, 1991. Reprinted in *The Phantom Public Sphere*. Ed. Bruce Robbins. Minneapolis: University of Minnesota Press, 1993.

Berubé, Allan. *Coming Out under Fire: The History of Gay Men and Women in World War Two*. New York: Free Press, 1990.

Blitz, September 1989.

Bockris, Victor. *The Life and Death of Andy Warhol*. New York: Bantam, 1989.

Boone, Bruce. "Gay Language as Political Praxis: The Poetry of Frank O'Hara." *Social Text* 1 (Winter 1979).

Bourdon, David. "Andy Warhol and the Society Icon." In *Art in America*, January/February 1975.

———. *Warhol*. New York: Harry N. Abrams, 1989.

Brasell, R. Bruce. "*My Hustler*: Gay Spectatorship as Cruising." *Wide Angle* 14, no. 2 (April 1992).

Brathwaite, Fred. "Jean-Michel Basquiat." *Interview*, October 1992.

Brilliant, Richard. *Portraiture*. Cambridge: Harvard University Press, 1991.

Brooks, Peter. *The Melodramatic Imagination: Balzac, Henry James, Melodrama, and the Mode of Excess*. New Haven: Yale University Press, 1976.

Bruce, Bryan, and Gloria Berlin. "The Superstar Story." *Cineaction!* (Toronto), 1986.

Buchloh, Benjamin. "The Andy Warhol Line." In *The Work of Andy Warhol*. Ed. Gary Garrels. Seattle: Bay Press, 1989.

———. "Andy Warhol's One-Dimensional Art: 1956–1966." In *Andy Warhol: A Retrospective*. Ed. Kynaston McShine. New York: Museum of Modern Art, 1989.

Burger, Peter. *Theory of the Avant-Garde*. Minneapolis: University of Minnesota Press, 1984.

Butler, Judith. *Gender Trouble*. New York: Routledge, 1990.

———. "Imitation and Gender Insubordination." In *Inside/Out: Lesbian Theories, Gay Theories*. Ed. Diana Fuss. New York: Routledge, 1991.

———. *Bodies That Matter: On the Discursive Limits of "Sex."* New York: Routledge, 1993.

Castle, Terry. *The Apparitional Lesbian*. New York: Columbia University Press, 1993.

Clark, T. J. *The Painting of Modern Life*. Princeton: Princeton University Press, 1984.

Colacello, Bob. *Holy Terror: Andy Warhol Close Up*. New York: HarperCollins, 1990.

Cooper, Emmanuel. *The Sexual Perspective*. London: Routledge & Kegan Paul, 1986.

Core, Philip. *Camp: The Lie That Tells Its Truth*. New York: Delilah, 1984.

Vaz, Mark Cotta. *Tales of the Dark Knight*. New York: Ballantine, 1989.

Cox, Meg. "Warhol Is Dead, but He Still Puts on a Profitable Show." *Wall Street Journal*, April 18, 1988.

Crimp, Douglas. "Mourning and Militancy." *October* 51 (Winter 1989).

———. "Portraits of People with AIDS." *Cultural Studies*. Ed. Lawrence Grossberg, Cary Nelson, and Paula Treichler. New York: Routledge, 1992.

Crimp, Douglas, ed. *AIDS: Cultural Analysis, Cultural Activism.* Cambridge: MIT Press, 1988.

Crimp, Douglas, with Adam Rolston. *AIDS Demo Graphics.* Seattle: Bay Press, 1990.

Crowe, Thomas. "Saturday Disasters: Trace and Reference in Early Warhol." *Art in America,* May 1987.

Cuneo, Paul E. "Of Many Things." *America,* May 7, 1966.

Dauphin, Gary. "To Be Young, Superpowered and Black, Interdimensional Identity Politics and Market Share: The Crisis of the Negro Superhero." *Village Voice,* May 17, 1994.

de Beauvoir, Simone. *The Second Sex.* Trans. E. M. Parshley. New York: Vintage, 1973.

De Duve, Thierry. "Andy Warhol; or, the Machine Perfected." Trans. Rosalind Krauss. *October* 48 (Spring 1989).

de Lauretis, Teresa. "Film and the Visible." In *How Do I Look?* Ed. Bad Object Choices. Seattle: Bay Press, 1991.

de Man, Paul. "Autobiography as De-facement." In *The Rhetoric of Romanticism.* New York: Columbia University Press, 1984.

———. "Hypogram and Inscription." In *The Resistance to Theory.* Minneapolis: University of Minnesota Press, 1986.

D'Emilio, John. *Sexual Politics, Sexual Communities: The Making of a Homosexual Minority in the United States, 1940–1970.* Chicago: University of Chicago Press, 1983.

Derrida, Jacques. *The Truth in Painting.* Trans. Geoff Bennington and Ian McLeod. Chicago: University of Chicago Press, 1987.

———. *Memoires for Paul de Man.* New York: Columbia University Press, 1988.

De Salvo, Donna M. "Learning the Ropes: Some Notes about the Early Work of Andy Warhol." In *"Success is a job in New York": The Early Art and Business of Andy Warhol.* Pittsburgh: Carnegie Museum of Art, 1989.

Dyer, Richard. *Heavenly Bodies: Film Stars and Society.* London: British Film Institute/Macmillan, 1987.

———. *Now You See It: Studies on Lesbian and Gay Film.* London: Routledge, 1990.

Edelstein, Andrew J. *The Pop Sixties.* New York: World Almanac Publications, 1985.

Eliot, George. *Daniel Deronda.* London: Penguin, 1986.

Ellis, Albert, and Albert Abarbanel. *The Encyclopedia of Sexual Behavior.* New York: Hawthorn, 1961.

Fairbrother, Trevor. "Tomorrow's Man." In *"Success is a job in New York": The Early Art and Business of Andy Warhol.* New York: Carnegie Museum of Art, 1989.

Ferenczi, Sándor. "Confusion of Tongues between Adults and the Child" (1933). Reprinted in Ferenczi, *Final Contributions to the Problems and Methods of Psychoanalysis.* Ed. Michael Balint. New York: Brunner/Mazel, 1980.

Film-Makers' Cooperative Catalogue No. 7. New York: Film-Makers' Cooperative, 1989.

Finch, Mark. "RIO LIMPO: *Lonesome Cowboys* and Gay Cinema." In *Andy Warhol Film Factory.* Ed. O'Pray.

Flanagan, Bill. "White Light White Heat: Lou Reed and John Cale Remember Andy Warhol." *Musician* 126 April 1989.

Foucault, Michel. "The Discourse on Language," in *The Archaeology of Knowledge.* Trans. A. M. Sheridan Smith. New York: Pantheon, 1972.

——. *This Is Not a Pipe*. Berkeley: University of California Press, 1983.

Fraser, Nancy. "Rethinking the Public Sphere: A Contribution to the Critique of Actually Existing Democracy." In *The Phantom Public Sphere*. Ed. Robbins.

Freud, Sigmund. "Mourning and Melancholia" (1917). In *General Psychological Theory*. Ed. Philip Rieff. New York: Collier Books, 1963.

——. "Leonardo da Vinci and a Memory of His Childhood." In *The Standard Edition of the Complete Psychological Works of Sigmund Freud*. Ed. James Strachey. Vol. 11. London: Hogarth, 1955.

——. *Group Psychology and the Analysis of the Ego*. Trans. James Strachey. New York: Norton, 1959.

——. *The Ego and the Id*. New York: Norton, 1960.

Gablik, Suzi. "The Art Job, or, How the Avant-Garde Sold Out." *Art in America*, April 1980.

Gadamer, Hans-Georg. *Truth and Method*. New York: Crossroad, 1986.

Gallup, Donald, ed. *The Flowers of Friendship: Letters Written to Gertrude Stein*. New York: Alfred A. Knopf, 1953.

Garber, Marjorie. *Vested Interests: Cross-Dressing and Cultural Anxiety*. New York: Routledge, 1992.

Garrels, Gary, ed. *The Work of Andy Warhol*. Seattle: Bay Press, 1989.

Gelmis, Joseph. *The Film Director as Superstar*. Garden City, N.Y.: Doubleday, 1970.

Gidal, Peter. "Warhol." *Films and Filming* 17, no. 8 (May 1971).

Gilbert, James. *A Cycle of Outrage: America's Reaction to the Juvenile Delinquent in the 1950s*. New York: Oxford University Press, 1986.

Gilbert-Rolfe, Jeremy. "Popular Imagery." In *Theories of Contemporary Art*. Ed. Richard Hertz. Englewood Cliffs, N.J.: Prentice Hall, 1985.

Gilman, Sander. *The Jew's Body*. New York: Routledge, 1991.

Gilroy, Paul. "Whose Millennium Is This? Blackness: Pre-Modern, Post-Modern, Anti-Modern." In *Small Acts: Thoughts on the Politics of Black Cultures*. New York: Serpent's Tail, 1993.

Giordano, Dick. *The Greatest Batman Stories Ever Told*. New York: DC Comics, 1988.

Giorno, John. *You Got to Burn to Shine*. New York: High Risk Books, 1994.

Grafton, Sue. *"H" is for Homicide*. New York: Fawcett Crest, 1992.

Grover, Jan Zita. "Keywords." In *AIDS: Cultural Analysis, Cultural Activism*. Ed. Douglas Crimp. Cambridge: MIT Press, 1988.

Guiles, Fred Lawrence. *Loner at the Ball: The Life of Andy Warhol*. London: Black Swan, 1990.

Habermas, Jürgen. *The Structural Transformation of the Public Sphere*. Cambridge: MIT Press, 1991.

Hansen, Miriam. "Early Cinema, Late Cinema: Permutations of the Public Sphere." In *Screen* 34, no. 3 (Autumn 1993).

——. Foreword to *The Public Sphere and Experience*, by Oskar Negt and Alexander Kluge. Minneapolis: University of Minnesota Press, 1993.

Hardy, Robin. "Andy Warhol Goes Straight: How the Life of an Artist Who Liked the 'Swish' Is Being Whitewashed." *Advocate*, December 5, 1989.

Harron, Mary. "The Lost History of the Velvet Underground." *New Musical Express* (London), April 25, 1981.

Haug, W. F. *Critique of Commodity Aesthetics*. Trans. Robert Bock. Minneapolis: University of Minnesota Press, 1986.

Heidegger, Martin. "The Origin of the Work of Art." In *Poetry, Language, Thought*. Trans. Albert Hofstadter. New York: Harper & Row, 1975.

Hess, Thomas B. "The Phony Crisis in American Art." *Artnews* 62, Summer 1963.

Hinchman, Lewis P., and Sandra K. Hinchman, eds. *Hannah Arendt: Critical Essays*. Albany: State University of New York Press, 1994.

hooks, bell. "Altar of Sacrifice: Remembering Basquiat." *Art in America*, June 1993.

Hughes, Robert. "The Rise of Andy Warhol." *New York Review of Books*, February 18, 1982.

———. "A Caterer of Repetition and Glut: Andy Warhol, 1928–1987." *Time*, March 9, 1987.

———. "The Best and Worst of Warhol." *Time*, February 13, 1989.

Huyssen, Andreas. *After the Great Divide: Modernism, Mass Culture, Postmodernism*. Bloomington: Indiana University Press, 1986.

Hyers, M. Conrad. "Batman and the Comic Profanation of the Sacred." *Christian Century*, October 18, 1967.

James, David E. "Andy Warhol: The Producer as Author." In *Allegories of Cinema: American Film in the Sixties*. Princeton: Princeton University Press, 1989.

———. "The Unsecret Life: A Warhol Advertisement." *October* 56 (Spring 1991).

———. "Film Diary/Diary Film: Practice and Product in *Walden*." In *To Free the Cinema: Jonas Mekas and the New York Underground*. Ed. David E. James. Princeton: Princeton University Press, 1992.

Jameson, Fredric. *Postmodernism, or, The Cultural Logic of Late Capitalism*. Durham: Duke University Press, 1991.

———. "On Negt and Kluge." In *Phantom Public Sphere*. Ed. Robbins.

Josephson, Mary. "Warhol: The Medium as Cultural Artifact." *Art in America*, May/June 1971.

Kateb, George. *Hannah Arendt, Politics, Conscience, Evil*. Totowa, N.J.: Rowman and Allanheld, 1983.

Kent, Leticia. "Andy Warhol, Movieman: 'It's Hard to Be Your Own Script.'" *Vogue*, March 1970.

Koch, Stephen. *Stargazer: Andy Warhol's World and His Films*. New York: Praeger, 1973.

Koestenbaum, Wayne. *The Queen's Throat: Opera, Homosexuality, and the Mystery of Desire*. New York: Vintage, 1993.

Kornbluth, Jesse. *Pre-Pop Warhol*. New York: Panache Press/Random House, 1988.

Kramer, Marcia. *Andy Warhol et al.: The FBI File on Andy Warhol*. New York: UnSub Press, 1988.

Krauss, Rosalind. *The Optical Unconscious*. Cambridge: MIT Press, 1993.

Kris, Ernst, and Otto Kurz. *Legend, Myth, and Magic in the Image of the Artist*. 1934. Reprint, New Haven: Yale University Press, 1979.

Kurtz, Bruce D., ed. *Haring, Warhol, Disney*. Munich: Prestel Verlag, 1992.

Lacan, Jacques. *Feminine Sexuality*. Ed. Juliet Mitchell and Jacqueline Rose. New York: W. W. Norton, 1985.

Laplanche, Jean and Pontalis, J.-B. *The Language of Psycho-Analysis*. Trans. Donald Nicholson-Smith. New York: W. W. Norton, 1973.

Leider, Philip. "Saint Andy." Review of the Pop exhibition "The Arena of Love," *Art Forum*, February 1965.

LeShan, Eda. "At War with Batman." *New York Times Magazine,* May 15, 1966.

Lester, Elenore. "The Final Decline and Total Collapse of the American Avant-Garde." *Esquire,* May 1969.

Lippard, Lucy. *Pop Art.* New York: Praeger, 1966.

Livingstone, Marco. "Do It Yourself: Notes on Warhol's Techniques." *Andy Warhol: A Retrospective.* Ed. Kynaston McShine. New York: The Museum of Modern Art, 1989.

Lukacher, Ned. *Primal Scenes: Literature, Philosophy, Psychoanalysis.* Ithaca: Cornell University Press, 1986.

Mamiya, Christin J. *Pop Art and Consumer Culture: American Super Market.* Austin: University of Texas Press, 1992.

Marks, Elaine, and Isabelle de Courtivron. Introduction to *New French Feminism: An Anthology.* New York: Schocken, 1981.

Marshall, Richard, ed. *Jean-Michel Basquiat.* New York: Whitney Museum of American Art, 1992.

Marx, Karl. *Economic and Philosophical Manuscripts of 1844.* Trans. Martin Milligan. New York: International Publishers, 1964.

———. *Capital.* Vol. 1. Trans. Ben Fowkes. New York: Penguin/New Left Review, 1976.

McClintock, Anne. "Screwing the System: Sex Work, Race, and the Law." In *Feminism and Postmodernism,* a special issue of *boundary 2.* Ed. Margaret Ferguson and Jennifer Wicke. Durham: Duke University Press, Summer 1992.

———. "Sex Workers and Sex Work: An Introduction." *Social Text* 37 (Winter 1993).

McCue, Greg, and Clive Bloom. *Dark Knights: The New Comics in Context.* Boulder, Colo.: Pluto Press, 1993.

McShine, Kynaston, ed. *Andy Warhol: A Retrospective,* with essays by Kynaston McShine, Robert Rosenblum, Benjamin H. D. Buchloh, and Marco Livingstone. New York: Museum of Modern Art, 1989.

Medhurst, Andy. "Batman, Deviance, and Camp." *The Many Lives of the Batman: Critical Approaches to a Superhero and His Media.* Ed. Roberta E. Pearson and William Uricchio. New York: Routledge, 1991.

Mekas, Jonas. *Movie Journal: The Rise of the New American Cinema, 1959–1971.* New York: Collier, 1972.

Meyer, Richard. "Warhol's Clones," *Yale Journal of Criticism* 7, no. 1 (Spring 1994).

Miller, D. A. *The Novel and the Police.* Berkeley: University of California Press, 1988.

———. "Sontag's Urbanity." *October* 49 (Summer 1989).

———. *Bringing Out Roland Barthes.* Berkeley: University of California Press, 1992.

Moon, Michael. "Rereading Whitman under Pressure of AIDS." In *The Continuing Presence of Walt Whitman: The Life after the Life.* Ed. Robert K. Martin. Iowa City: University of Iowa Press, 1992.

———. "Outlaw Sex and the 'Search for America': Representing Male Prostitution and Perverse Desire in Sixties Film (*My Hustler* and *Midnight Cowboy*)," *Quarterly Review of Film and Video* 15, no. 1 (1993).

Morphet, Richard. "Andy Warhol." *Warhol.* London: Tate Gallery, 1971.

Morris, Meaghan. "The Pirate's Fiancee: Feminists and Philosophers, or Maybe Tonight It'll

Happen." In *Feminism and Foucault: Reflections on Resistance*. Ed. Irene Diamond and Lee Quinby. Boston: Northeastern University Press, 1988.

Morrison, Toni. "Unspeakable Things Unspoken: The Afro-American Presence in American Literature." *Michigan Quarterly Review* 28, no. 1 (Winter 1989).

——. *Playing in the Dark: Whiteness and the Literary Imagination*. Cambridge: Harvard University Press, 1992.

Negt, Oskar, and Alexander Kluge. *The Public Sphere and Experience*. Trans. Peter Lbanyi, Jamie Daniel, and Assenka Oksiloff. Minneapolis: University of Minnesota Press, 1993.

Nunokawa, Jeffrey. "The Sun Always Shines on TV: Television Culture and the Resistance to Patriarchy in Margaret Atwood's *The Handmaid's Tale*." Paper presented at the Modern Language Association Conference, Washington, D.C., 1989.

O'Farrell, Mary Ann. "Dickens's Scar: Rosa Dartle and *David Copperfield*." Unpublished Manuscript.

O'Hara, Frank. *The Collected Poems of Frank O'Hara*. Ed. Donald Allen. New York: Knopf, 1971.

O'Pray, Michael, ed. *Andy Warhol Film Factory*. London: British Film Institute, 1989.

Owens, Craig. "Posing." In *Beyond Recognition: Representation, Power, and Culture*. Eds. Scott Bryson, Barbara Kruger, Lynne Tillman, and Jane Weinstock. Berkeley: University of California Press, 1992.

Paglia, Camille. "The M.I.T. Lecture." In *Sex, Art, and American Culture*. London: Viking, 1992.

Parker, Andrew. "Unthinking Sex: Marx, Engels and the Scene of Writing." In *Fear of a Queer Planet: Queer Politics and Social Theory*. Ed. Michael Warner. Minneapolis: University of Minnesota Press, 1993.

Patton, Cindy. *Inventing AIDS*. New York: Routledge, 1990.

Pecheux, Michel. *Language, Semantics, and Ideology*. New York: St. Martins, 1982.

Prideux, Tom. "The Whole Country Goes Superman." *Life,* March 11, 1966.

Rasula, Jed. "Nietzsche in the Nursery: Naive Classics and Surrogate Parents in Postwar American Cultural Debates." *Representations* 29 (Winter 1990).

Ridgeway, James. *Blood in the Face*. New York: Thunder's Mouth, 1990.

Riviere, Joan. "Womanliness as Masquerade." *Formations of Fantasy*. Ed. Victor Burgin, James Donald, and Cora Kaplan. New York: Routledge, Chapman and Hall, 1986.

Robbins, Bruce, ed. *The Phantom Public Sphere*. Minneapolis: University of Minnesota Press, 1993.

Rodowick, D. N. "Reading the Figural." *Camera Obscura* 24 (1990).

Ross, Andrew. "Uses of Camp." In *No Respect: Intellectuals and Popular Culture*. New York: Routledge, 1989.

Ross, Jay [Jay Rosenthal]. "Gay Moviegoers Have Their Say." *Los Angeles Advocate,* January 1969.

Rousseau, Jean Jacques. *The Confessions of Jean Jacques Rousseau*. New York: Modern Library/ Random House, 1975.

Rubin, David. "Andy Warhol." Review of the *Torso* series. *Arts Magazine,* December 1978.

S., Glenn. "Valerie Solanas: Cultural Terrorist." In *Nooks 'n Crannies*. Toronto: Self-published fanzine, 1991.

Saarinen, Aline B. "Explosion of Pop Art." *Vogue,* April 1963.

Sarduy, Severo. "Writing/Transvestism." *Review* 9 (Fall 1973).

Sedgwick, Eve Kosofsky. *Epistemology of the Closet*. Berkeley: University of California Press, 1990.

———. "Queer Performativity: Henry James's *The Art of the Novel*." *GLQ* 1, no. 1 (Summer 1993).

———. *Tendencies*. Durham: Duke University Press, 1993.

Seltzer, Mark. "Serial Killers (1)." *Differences: A Journal of Feminist Cultural Studies* 5, no. 1 (1993).

Selz, Peter. "The Flaccid Art." In *Pop Art: The Critical Dialogue*. Ed. Carol Anne Mahusen. Ann Arbor: UMI Research Press, 1989.

Shaviro, Steven. *The Cinematic Body*. Minneapolis: University of Minnesota Press, 1993.

Silver, Kenneth E. "Modes of Disclosure: The Construction of Gay Identity and the Rise of Pop Art." In *Hand-Painted Pop: American Art in Transition, 1955–62*. Ed. Russell Ferguson. Los Angeles: Museum of Contemporary Art, 1992.

Skow, John. "Has TV—Gasp!—Gone Batty?" *Saturday Evening Post,* May 7, 1966.

Solanas, Valerie. *The SCUM Manifesto*. Afterword by Paul Krassner. New York: Olympia Press, 1968.

Soloman, Deborah. "Pittsburgh's Warhol Museum: Pop Art . . . in a Grimly Rehabbed, Final 'Factory.'" *Wall Street Journal,* May 18, 1994.

Sontag, Susan. "Notes on 'Camp.'" In *Against Interpretation and Other Essays*. New York: Farrar, Straus and Giroux, 1966.

Spigel, Lynn. "From Domestic Space to Outer Space: The 1960s Fantastic Family Sit-com." In *Close Encounters: Film, Feminism, and Science Fiction*. Ed. Constance Penley et al. Minneapolis: University of Minnesota Press, 1991.

Spigel, Lynn, and Henry Jenkins. "Same Bat Channel, Different Bat Times: Mass Culture and Popular Memory." In *The Many Lives of the Batman: Critical Approaches to a Superhero and His Media*. Ed. Roberta E. Pearson and William Uricchio. New York: Routledge, 1991.

Spivak, Gayatri. "Displacement and the Discourse of Woman." In *Displacement: Derrida and After*. Ed. Mark Krupnik. Bloomington: Indiana University Press, 1983.

Stein, Gertrude. *Portraits and Prayers*. New York: Random House, 1934.

———. *Lectures in America*. Boston: Beacon, 1985.

———. "What Are Master-pieces and Why There Are So Few of Them." Reprinted in *The Gender of Modernism*. Ed. Bonnie Kime Scott. Bloomington: Indiana University Press, 1990.

Stewart, Susan. *Crimes of Writing: Problems in the Containment of Representation*. New York: Oxford University Press, 1991.

Stone, Judy. "The Caped Crusader of Camp." *New York Times,* January 9, 1966.

Tate, Greg. "Flyboy in the Buttermilk: Jean-Michel Basquiat, Nobody Loves a Genius Child." *Village Voice,* November 14, 1989. Reprinted in *Flyboy in the Buttermilk: Essays on Contemporary America*. New York: Simon and Schuster, 1992.

Terwilliger, Robert E. "The Theology of Batman." *Catholic World,* November 1966.

Thompson, Dave. *Beyond the Velvet Underground*. London: Omnibus, 1989.

Thompson, Howard. "TV Heroes Stay Long." *New York Times,* August 25, 1966.

Timmons, Stuart. *The Trouble with Harry Hay*. Boston: Alyson, 1990.

Tomkins, Silvan. *Affect, Imagery, Consciousness*. 4 vols. New York: Springer, 1962–92; vol. 3, 1991.

Treichler, Paula. "AIDS, Homophobia, and Biomedical Discourse: An Epidemic of Signification." *Cultural Studies* 1, no. 3 (October 1987).

Tropiano, Stephen. "Joe Dallesandro—A 'Him' to the Gaze: *Flesh, Heat,* and *Trash.*" *Spectator* (University of Southern California) 10, no. 1 (Fall 1989).

Tyler, Parker. *Underground Film: A Critical History.* New York: Grove, 1969.

———. *Screening the Sexes: Homosexuality in the Movies.* New York: Holt, Rinehart and Winston, 1972.

Ultra Violet. *Famous for Fifteen Minutes: My Years with Andy Warhol.* New York: Avon, 1988.

Vaz, Mark Cotta. *Tales of the Dark Night.* New York: Ballantine, 1989.

Vendler, Helen. "The Virtues of the Alterable." *Parnassus* (Fall–Winter 1972).

Villa, Dana. *Arendt and Heidegger: The Fate of the Political.* Princeton: Princeton University Press, 1995.

Wallace, Michele. "Race, Gender, and Psychoanalysis in Forties Film: *Lost Boundaries, Home of the Brave,* and *The Quiet One.*" In *Black American Cinema.* Ed. Manthia Diawara. New York: Routledge, 1993.

Warhol, Andy. *The Philosophy of Andy Warhol: From A to B and Back Again.* New York: Harcourt Brace Jovanovich, 1975.

———. *The Andy Warhol Diaries.* Ed. Pat Hackett. New York: Warner Books, 1989.

Warhol, Andy, and Pat Hackett. *POPism: The Warhol Sixties.* New York: Harcourt Brace Jovanovich, 1980.

Warner, Michael. Introduction to *Fear of a Queer Planet: Queer Politics and Social Theory,* ed. Michael Warner. Minneapolis: University of Minnesota, 1993.

———. "The Mass Public and the Mass Subject." In *The Phantom Public Sphere.* Ed. Bruce Robbins. Minneapolis: University of Minnesota Press, 1993.

Wassenaar, Michael. "Strong to the Finich: Machines, Metaphor, and Popeye the Sailor," *Velvet Light Trap* 24 (Fall 1989).

Watney, Simon. *Policing Desire: Pornography, AIDS and the Media.* Minneapolis: University of Minnesota Press, 1987.

———. "The Spectacle of AIDS." In *AIDS: Cultural Analysis, Cultural Activism,* ed. Douglas Crimp. Cambridge: MIT Press, 1988.

———. "The Warhol Effect." In *The Work of Andy Warhol.* Ed. Gary Garrels. Seattle: Bay Press, 1989.

———. "Read My Lips: AIDS, Art, and Activism." In *Read My Lips: New York AIDS Polemics.* Glasgow: Tramway Gallery, 1992.

———. "In Purgatory: The Work of Felix Gonzalez-Torres." *Parkett* 39 (1994).

Waugh, Thomas. "Hard to Imagine: Gay Erotic Cinema in the Postwar Era." *Cineaction!* (Toronto), October 1987.

———. *Hard to Imagine: Gay Male Eroticism in Photography and Film from the Beginnings to Stonewall.* New York: Columbia University Press, 1996.

Weaver, Neal. "The Warhol Phenomenon: Trying to Understand It." *After Dark,* January 1969.

Wertham, Fredric. *Seduction of the Innocent.* New York: Rinehart Press, 1954.

White, Patricia. "Female Spectator, Lesbian Specter: *The Haunting.*" In *Inside/Out: Lesbian Theories, Gay Theories.* Ed. Diana Fuss. New York: Routledge, 1991.

Wilde, Oscar. *The Picture of Dorian Gray.* London: Penguin, 1985.

Williams, Linda. *Hard Core: Power, Pleasure, and "the Frenzy of the Visible."* Berkeley: University of California Press, 1989.

Willis, Ellen. *Beginning to See the Light.* Hanover, N.H.: Wesleyan University Press, 1992.

Wilson, Colin. *The Outsider.* London: Pan Books, 1956.

Wittig, Monique. "The Straight Mind." In *"The Straight Mind" and Other Essays.* Boston: Beacon, 1992.

Wojnarowicz, David. *Close to the Knives: A Memoir of Disintegration.* New York: Vintage, 1991.

Wollen, Peter. "Raiding the Icebox." In *Andy Warhol: Film Factory.* Ed. Michael O'Pray. London: British Film Institute, 1989.

Žižek, Slavoj. *The Sublime Object of Ideology.* New York: Verso, 1991.

CONTRIBUTORS

Jennifer Doyle is a Ph.D. candidate in the Program in Literature at Duke University. She is writing a dissertation on the modern preoccupation with prostitution in literature, art, and social theory.

Jonathan Flatley is a Ph.D. candidate in the Program in Literature at Duke University. His dissertation is titled "Modernism and Melancholia: Toward a Theory of Anti-Depressive Poetics."

Marcie Frank is Assistant Professor of English at Concordia University in Montreal, where she teaches eighteenth-century English literature. She has also published essays on John Dryden, David Cronenberg, Susan Sontag, and Julie Doucet and Rick Trembles. She is completing a book-length study of Restoration and eighteenth-century literary criticism.

David E. James teaches in the Division of Critical Studies in the School of Cinema at University of Southern California.

Mandy Merck teaches media studies at the University of Sussex. She has edited the film studies journal *Screen*, and was senior producer for the British television series "Out on Tuesday." She is author of *Perversions: Deviant Readings*, a collection of essays on the problems of representing sexuality in popular culture, art, and film.

Michael Moon is Associate Professor of English at Duke University. He is author of *Disseminating Whitman: Revision and Corporeality in Leaves of Grass*, and associate editor of *American Literature*.

José Esteban Muñoz is Assistant Professor of Performance Studies at New York University. He is coeditor of *Politics in Motion: Culture, Music, Dance in Latin/a America* (forthcoming from Duke) and is currently completing a manuscript titled *Disidentification*.

Eve Kosofsky Sedgwick is the Newman Ivy White Professor of English at Duke University. Her works include *Between Men, Epistemology of the Closet, Tendencies*, and *Fat Art, Thin Art*.

Brian Selsky is a Ph.D. candidate in the Program in Literature at Duke University.

Sasha Torres is the Richard and Edna Soloman Assistant Professor at Brown University, where she teaches television, film, and cultural theory in the Department of Culture and Media. In addition to serving as an editor of *Camera Obscura* she is currently finishing an anthology on television and race, titled *Living Color*, and is working on a manuscript tentatively titled *National Television: on U.S. Television's Production of National Subjectivity since 1968*.

Simon Watney is author of *Policing Desire: Pornography, AIDS and the Media* and *Practices of Freedom: Selected Writings on HIV/AIDS*. He is Director of the Red Hot AIDS Charitable Trust in London, England.

Tom Waugh teaches film studies at Concordia University as well as lesbian and gay studies in an interdisciplinary course on AIDS. His books are *Show Us Life: Toward a History and Aesthetics of a Committed Documentary* and *Hard to Imagine: Gay Male Eroticism in Photography and Film from the Beginnings to Stonewall*.

INDEX

Library of Congress Cataloging-in-Publication Data
Pop out: Queer Warhol / edited by Jennifer Doyle,
Jonathan Flatley, and José Esteban Muñoz.
p.   cm. — (Series Q)
Includes bibliographical references and index.
ISBN 0-8223-1732-X (cloth : alk. paper). — ISBN 0-8223-1741-9
(pbk. : alk. paper)
1. Warhol, Andy, 1928–1987—Criticism and interpretation.
2. Warhol, Andy, 1928–1987—Sexual behavior. 3. Gay artists in
popular culture—United States. I. Doyle, Jennifer. II. Flatley,
Jonathan. III. Muñoz, José Esteban. IV. Series.
NX512.W37P66 1996
700'.92—dc20   95-35410 CIP

grape pen 564